The London That Was Rome

by the same author

Novels

Weep for Lycidas
Spring in Tartarus
All the Trees Were Green
Vernal Equinox
What Are We Waiting For?
Battered Caravanserai
So Linked Together

Treadmill
There's Glory for You!
Long Vacation
Things Less Noble
The Dividing Stone
The Brain
A Hansom to St James's

The 'Rowcester' Novels

Higher Things
The House in Fishergate

Sinecure
The Darkened Room

Biography

Gambler's Glory (*John Law of Lauriston*)
Count Cagliostro
They Would Be King (*Lambert Simnel, Theodore of Corsica, Bernadotte, Henry Christophe*)
Prince of Hokum (*Peter Cheyney*)
Charles Dickens: A Sentimental Journey in Search of an Unvarnished Portrait
Rosa (*Rosa Lewis, of The Cavendish Hotel*)
Lord of London (*2nd Duke of Westminster*)

Travel Commentary

Dawn Express
Reported Safe Arrival: The Journal of a Voyage to Port 'X'

Historical

Airborne at Kitty Hawk
The Story of Christmas
The History of the Hat
London by Gaslight
London Growing: The Development of a Metropolis
Mulberry: The Return in Triumph

Topographical

In the Footsteps of Sherlock Holmes
London Beneath the Pavement

Advertising

Technical and Industrial Publicity

Philately

A New Approach to Stamp-collecting (*with Douglas B. Armstrong*)

Cuisine

Beer Cookery

Short Stories

Transit of Venus
Exploits of the Chevalier Dupin

The London That Was Rome

The Imperial City Recreated by the New Archaeology

THE RE-MAPPING OF LONDINIUM AUGUSTA
CAPITAL OF THE PROVINCE OF MAXIMA CAESARIENSIS
CHIEF OF THE FOUR PROVINCES OF BRITAIN

by Michael Harrison

LONDON
GEORGE ALLEN & UNWIN LTD
RUSKIN HOUSE   MUSEUM STREET

ISBN 0 04 913011 0

Printed in Great Britain
in 11pt Baskerville type
by Alden & Mowbray, Oxford

TO COLIN COOTE

A lover both of Rome and of London, Rome's
westernmost major achievement

It was in the columns of the *Daily Telegraph,* under
Sir Colin Coote's editorship, that the theory on
which this book is based was first published to the
world. It is in grateful acknowledgment of
Sir Colin's timely help in making my theory
known that I dedicate this book to him

Contents

Acknowledgments

As with any book based on much research, this book of mine owes an incalculable debt to those earlier writers on whose works I have drawn – the principal writers being mentioned in the Bibliography. In addition, there are all the well-known and almost unknown reference books, whose enumeration would have been impossible here. To the authors and editors of all, I give my heartfelt thanks.

Two books, however, have been of outstanding help to me: Gordon Home's *Roman London*, now happily once more available to the general public, and Ralph Merrifield's *The Roman City of London*, a work that the author's scholarship and industry have combined to make outstanding in its class. Neither of these authors, of course, adumbrates my theory of the 'continuity' of Roman London, yet their own facts and theorizings have been of incalculable value to me in providing the essential background to my arguments. I must also thank Mr Merrifield for kind permission to quote two long passages from his book, as well as Professor E. Ekwall and the Delegates of the Clarendon Press for permission to quote from *London Place Names*. My thanks, too, to the Editor of the *Evening Standard*, for permission to quote from Mr David Wilcox's article on the discovery of the Roman house in Billingsgate.

My very special thanks must go to the following:

Professor C. E. Darlington, Sherardian Professor of Botany at the University of Oxford, who not only wrote me the first supporting letter that I received after the publication of my theory in the *Daily Telegraph*, but sent me the first-ever sketch map of Londinium Augusta based on what Dr Darlington most courteously called 'Harrisonian' principles.

Mr Jack Lindsay, classical scholar and historian, who not only generously read the proofs of this book, but also made valuable comments, now incorporated into the text.

Mr Jonathan Price, who commissioned my first London book, and who has encouraged me since to write more and more on 'the illustrious city'.

And finally, Mr Ernest Parkin, artist and cartographer, for the care and patience with which he drew the map of Roman London to my design.

It seems to me that the Sirens, like other old Hellenic ideals, are coming to honour again.

During their westward progress, they tarried long about the headland of Athenaeum, which is the southern horn of the Bay of Naples now called Punta Campanella, and about its islands. A snowy temple, one of the wonders of the western world, rose in their honour near this wave-beaten promontory – for promontories were sacred in oldest days from their dangers to navigation; colonnades and statues are swept away, but its memory lies embedded in the name of the village of Massa Lubrense (*delubrum*). A wondrous mode of survival, when one comes to think of it: a temple enshrined in the letters of a word whose very meaning is forgotten, handed down from father to son through tumultuous ages of Romans and Goths and Saracens, Normans, French and Spaniards, and persisting, ever cryptic to the vulgar, after the more perishable records of stone and marble are clean vanished from the earth.

Norman Douglas: *Siren Land*

Permission to quote the above passage was given to me personally by the author many years ago, when – the last time that I saw him alive – he dined with me at my house in Chelsea with his son.

M.H.

12

Author's Foreword

This isn't a preface – I dislike prefaces. It's just a word to the Reader.

Think of this book as a detective story, in which I played the Sherlock Holmes to a quarry that even the most hopeful would have said was lost beyond hope of recovery.

Or think of this book as a story of buried treasure, but different from other such tales in that the treasure was found first – the map afterwards. (There's never yet been a good treasure tale without a map somewhere in it.)

As with everyone else who has ever set out on an 'impossible' journey, I set out alone. My compass I made myself – or, to use newer metaphors, my oscilloscope, my Geiger-Mueller counter, my electron-spin-resonance spectrometer. The point to bear in mind is that I set out to find the lost city of Londinium – or, more 'officially', Augusta Trinobantia – and I had to devise an instrument to enable me to find it.

You will see that I succeeded; but you will see, too, that I succeeded because the tool that I invented proved itself in actual use. This fact should be carefully noted: if my tool – my direction-finder, my buried-treasure detector; call it what you will – vindicated itself in the apparently hopeless task of recovering the topography of Roman London, then it must, at the same time, have vindicated itself as a tool of far more general application. In other words, what it has done for me, in helping me to recover and map the Roman city of London, it can do, equally well, for any other researcher who wishes to recover, say, York or Lincoln or Colchester – or, indeed, any other city of 'Romania' which has been inhabited continuously since Roman times.

But those attempts are for others. I set out to find and re-map what, over a thousand years ago, Bishop Helmstan of Winchester knew as 'the illustrious place, built by the skill of the ancient Romans, called throughout the world the great city of London'.

Already, though, between the writing of this foreword and its revision on a hot June afternoon of 1970, something has happened to bring a hoped-for – but quite (I admit) unexpected – confirmation of the main hypothesis on which my theory was based: that is, the hypothesis that Roman London had survived the defeat of the Londoners at the battle of 'Crecganford' (almost certainly Crayford, in Kent), dated by the *Anglo-Saxon Chronicle* as at A.D. 457. In the *Evening Standard* of 5 June, 1970, there was a detailed report of the discovery of a Roman house at the corner of Lower Thames Street and St Dunstan's Hill, near where, in 1848, a Roman bath-house was excavated.

A passage or two, extracted from the article, will sufficiently indicate the importance of the find:

'The amazing discovery of the remains of a Roman town house opposite Billingsgate Market has established for the first time that Romans still lived in London in King Arthur's time.

'Archaeologists are comparing the importance of the find . . . with the Midas [*sic*; *sc.* Mithras] temple found in the early 1950s.

'Dating of pottery found under ash in the furnace for the house's under-floor heating shews that Romans were living there after A.D. 450.

'This means that the Romans were living in London long after the collapse of the Roman empire – living in their centrally-heated home near the Thames at a time when the Saxon invaders were living in huts in Essex.

'Mr Peter Marsden, who directed operations for the [Guildhall] museum, said: . . . "it seems that although Saxons were settling near London at Mucking before A.D. 400, the City was able to remain an island of civilization in a sea of Saxon barbarism for some time, and was even able to trade with the eastern Mediterranean".'

I say in my book that I hope that my 'New Archaeology' may assist traditional archaeology, and that traditional archaeology may assist the new. Here, then, is a proof that these archaeologies may indeed render mutual assistance. My hypothesis has been confirmed by the spade and shovel of the traditional archaeologists of the Guildhall Museum.

There can no longer be any misunderstanding of that hitherto mysterious passage from the *Anglo-Saxon Chronicle*:

'Breten ieg-land is eahta hund mila lang, and twa hund mila brad; and her sind on þæm ieglande fif geþeodu: Englisc, Brettisc, Scyttisc, Pihtisc, and Boc-læden.'

(The Island of Britain is eight hundred miles long, and two hundred miles wide; and there are in the Island five peoples: English, British, Scottish, Pictish and 'Book-Latin'.)

That 'people' to whom the Saxon invaders gave the name 'Book-Latin' can have been only those who, within the impregnable Roman cities – London, York, Exeter and many others – preserved the essential *Romanitas* of the collapsing empire: Roman in thought and speech and culture.

So far, I have been able to apply my new archaeological method to the study only of London's *Romanitas*. Here, then, Reader, available to you for the first time in about fifteen hundred years, is my Guide to the Roman City of Londinium Augusta.

M.H.

:Y TO MAP REFERENCES: WESTERN HALF OF CITY

»NDINIUM, chief town of the Province of Maxima Caesariensis, in Britannia Inferior ('Southern itain'), was given, at some date between A.D. 337 and 368, the honorific title of Augusta Trino- ntia – 'Augustan city of the Trinobantes' – from which latter name was derived the mediæval roy Novant,' with all the fanciful Trojan legends to which that erroneous name gave birth om inscriptions and the recovered names of official institutions, London, in the latter days of e Imperial occupation, seems to have been known indifferently as 'London' or as 'Augusta' – rely both. The Treasury of London was known as the 'Augustine' Treasury, and the Christian elate, whose palace I have located far to the east of the (walled) city, was known as the 'Augustine pe' (*papa*).

Almost entirely rebuilt after the plenary destruction by Queen Boadicea (Boudicca) in A.D. 61, d rebuilt several times after that, notably under Hadrian, London was originally another of the pical Roman 'square-built' cities (*civitates quadratae*). Its present irregular shape – I talk now of e City of London, within the wall – was imposed on it by the Roman military engineers, devising 'central defensible citadel' in the face of threatened invasion. Every Roman city of whatever size d importance was provided with such a ruthless restriction of area for defensive purposes. Besides e wall, as we have it, my researches have revealed the existence of a complicated pattern of inner fences, to which the proven existence of a number of *viae sagulares* (defensive inner roads) give assailable testimony. These roads are drawn as double dotted lines, marked at intervals with S. The defences of London were far more elaborate than has been thought; the 'citadel' (that we w call London-within-the-Wall) being completely surrounded by a moat. The Cripplegate Fort s also moated, and there were defences of an elaborate nature at Temple Bar, Holborn Bars and ile End.

Buildings shown are only roughly to scale, since their location is known, their dimensions and ientation not, save in a very few cases. The Roman streets have been shown wider than they ust have been simply for the sake of clarity.

Stars (*) indicate eating-houses, cook-shops, Heavy points (•) taverns, etc.

GATES

. Porta Litoralis — Ludgate
. Porta Occidentalis — Newgate
. Altera Porta Aquilonica — Aldersgate
. Porta ad Circlum — Cripplegate

MILITARY ESTABLISHMENTS

. Guard-house (*castellum* near Walbrook Bridge)
. Legionary post
. Legionary post
. Praetorium of South-West (river) fort. Also guarded *collybus* or money-exchange
. Barracks
. Barracks
. Legionary guard-house protecting *Fiscus* (Imperial Treasury)
. Barracks of Reserve troops (*Gregarii*)
. Barracks of Chrysosaspides (Emperor's personal guard, so called because they carried gilded shields)

16. Legionary H.Q. and barracks
17. Barracks, Ordo (town-council) and Imperial metal stocks, principally tin and lead
18. Barracks and offices of the *sacomarius* controlling wages in London
19. Barracks
20. Barracks and offices of the Aediles (superintending police, markets and public works)

TEMPLES

10. Mars
11. College of the Arval Brothers, priests of Mars in his ancient aspect of 'Semo' (seed, fertility)
17. Bona Dea
18. Serapis ⎱ always built ⎰ NB that these four
19. Isis ⎰ together ⎱ Oriental deities
20. Antinoüs — have their temples
21. Mithras — close together
22. Diana
23. Jupiter Dolichenus

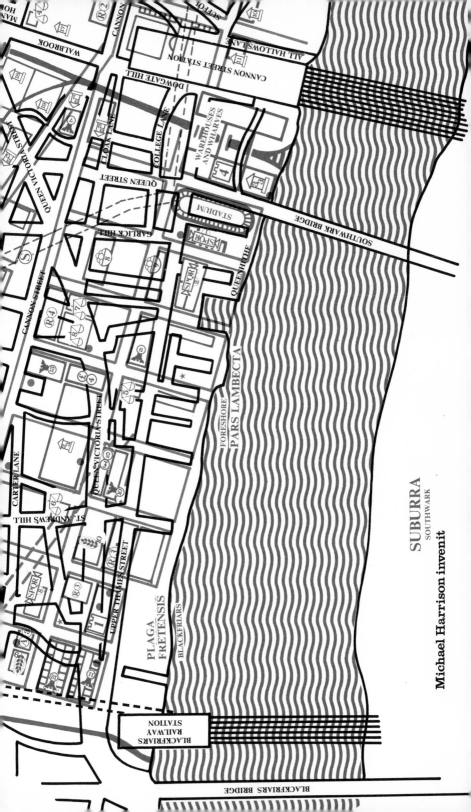

SUBURRA
SOUTHWARK

Michael Harrison invenit

24. College of the *Salii* – 12 priests, 'The Leapers,' dedicated to the service of Mars Gradivus
25. Temple of Mars attached to the Senate of London
26. Semo Sancus
27. Mars Gradivus
28. Diana
    Matuta* (*slightly to south of above*)
29. College of *Salii*, of temple of Mars No. 27
30. College of Fetiales, priests who sanctioned treaties, declarations of war, etc., somewhat akin to the mediæval heralds
31. Artemis the Bear Goddess
32. Bel-Sabazios (modern 'Bell Savage' or 'Belle Sauvage')
33. Temple of Artemis Venatrix (the Huntress), with attached College of Venatores, her priests in the 'Huntress' aspect. Elsewhere served and worshipped as Bear Goddess
    *Not marked on map

GRANARIES AND/OR WAREHOUSES
6. Warehouse and/or granary
7. Granary of fort
8. Granary of fort
9. Granary and annona (public food distribution)
10. Warehouse and/or granary

MARKETS
8. Monthly market (*trinundinae*)
9. Wine market (*macellum vinarium*)
10. Market
11. 'Market on the Western Hill' (*macellum ad cornulam occidentalem*)
12. Market
13. Market: this one was obviously part of the great Cattle Market (*forum boarium*) immediately to its south

WEIGHTS, MEASURES AND CUSTOMS
4. Office of the Collector of the *Stipendiarius*: fixed imposts payable in money; *vectigalis* being imposts payable in kind
5. Office of Salt-fish Control (*sacomarius salsamentarii*)
6. Office of City Health Inspector (*statio sacomarii medicinalis*)
7. Army Pay-office (*statio militum merentum*)
8. Office of Overseers of Grain (*statio sacomariorum messis*)
9. Office of Market Inspector (collection of market dues, control of weights and measures, etc.)
10. Office of Market Inspector

PUBLIC RECREATION
2. Training-school for gladiators (*sedes lanistana* – 'St Swithun Londonstone')
3. Bazaar (*vendita ad Senatum Populumque*)
3a. Baths
4. Public swimming-bath and/or place for washing clothes (*piscina* has both these meanings)
5. Baths
6. Public art-gallery (*pinacotheca*)
7. Baths (*on the north side*) attached to the *fas* (centre for public notices – *on the south side*
8. Bath-house

SPQR STATE ADMINISTRATION AND CONTROL
1. 'Ad gemonias' – steep stairway down which convicted criminals were thrown to death (The name survives in 'St James's (Garlick hithe))
2. 'Ad Socios' – headquarters of the *Socii* or Company of *Publicani*, whose name survived into the late Middle Ages as 'the Soke of Queenhithe.' The *publicani*, usually members of the Equestrian Order, were official farmers of the public revenue. Their chief offices were in one of those parts of London which were later ceded as 'bases' to the Roman Empire, on London's becoming an independent city-state: hence the mediæval name of 'Romelands.'
3. All-sports Centre – where one could watch every type of athletic display, including boxing and wrestling (*pancratium superlatum* whence 'St Pancras Soper Lane)
4. Administrative council of the City (*gubernacularia comitia* – see page 195)
5. Council of the Governor's legal assessors, the *juridici* (*aula juridica* – 'Old Jewry')
6. Basilica of Justice. (The Lord Mayor administers justice today on the self-same site)
7. Office of the Treasurer of the City (*saccararius*)
8. Municipal control and police headquarters (*collegium aedilum*)

FORTS
1. Fort and military lock-up (*antrum*) guarding estuary of the Fleet River (*Fretum*) and

Careful measurements of the great 'Cornhill' Basilica, made since the 'forties of the last century, as rebuilding of existing structures has made archaeological examination possible, now enable us to state its dimensions with confidence. It was the position of the two flanking streets, of the street which ran 'through' it, and of parts of the streets which have become Lombard Street and Cannon Street, which enabled me to reconstruct the 'grid' on which the Roman town-planners had laid out the once highly regular street-pattern of London. East and south-west Londinium use the same co-ordinates; the north-west is slightly 'tilted,' to allow for the presence of rivers and internal docks, notably a small dock where Paternoster Row and Amen Corner are today.

Reconstructing the eastern side of Londinium, though, is more difficult than reconstructing the west. The very strong military element in the east – military roads, legionary posts, temples, not only of Mars but of such Oriental cults as worship of Cybele, Antinoüs, Dionysos and the Cabiri, and the established presence of at least two military lock-ups – indicate that this part of London was felt, for centuries after the passing of the original Pax Romana, to be under the possibility of attack. The defences inside the city came as far back as Lime Street (the *limes*, or boundary, of military control); and as, immediately to the east of Lime Street, we find a *via militaris* (Billiter Street) – a street strictly reserved to military uses – it is clear that, if western Londinium was the 'civil' side of the city, then the eastern part was definitely the military side. It is perhaps not too bold to suggest that the civil part of London ended—so far as shops, etc., went – a little to the east of modern Gracechurch Street.

The establishment of the Roman 'grid' has been most useful in showing that, whilst the wider modern streets seem to diverge importantly from their Roman originals, many of the smaller streets – I instance St Mary-at-Hill and Great St Helen's; All Hallows Lane (by modern Cannon Street station); Watling Street – follow almost exactly the direction of the originals. My theory here is that the bigger, more important streets of Roman London had bigger, more important buildings on them, and that when these collapsed (perhaps not earlier than the sackings under the Danes), they left great piles of rubble blocking up the roads – rubble that there was no longer an efficient municipal control to clear away. Pedestrians therefore, skirting these rubble heaps, made new roads; whilst, on the smaller streets, the wood and stucco buildings, even if they did fall, were easily swept up.

Thames foreshore: Blackfriars (*Plaga Fretensis*)

1. Fort guarding docks, warehouses and customs offices, etc., at entrance to main tributary of the Thames: the Walbrook. This fort was immediately to the north of the Temple of Artemis Venatrix (No. 33)

FINANCE

2. Imperial treasury (western branch) (*fiscus*)
3. Exchange for banking, money-changing, etc. (*collybus*)

PRISONS

3. Remand prison serving Basilica of Justice (*lautumiae juridicae*)
4. Military lock-up (*antrum*)

PUBLIC FOOD CENTRES (*Annonae*)

. Annona serving west of city

GATES

4a. Porta Fluminea   Moorgate
5. Porta Bissulca ('The Two-way Gate')
                                Bishopsgate
6. Alta Porta ('The High Gate')   Aldgate
* There must have been also an eastern rivergate, about where the Tower of London is now

MILITARY ESTABLISHMENTS

1. Office of the *Sarcinarius* (military storekeeper and quartermaster) for the eastern gate. (The western *sarcinarius* was in modern Snow Hill and so just outside the walls)
2. Barracks
3. Barracks and military lock-up (*antrum*)
4. Barracks
4a. Military administration and barracks
5. Legionary barracks

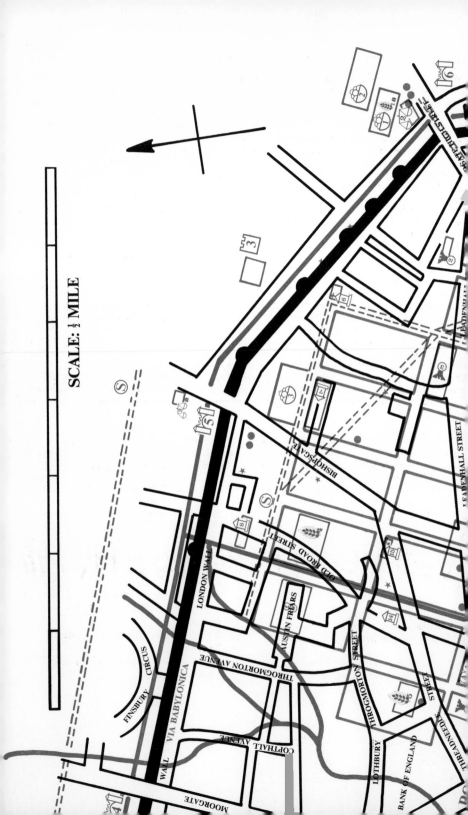

SCALE: ½ MILE

TOWER HILL
AD PATIBULAS
THE GALLOWS

COLLIS PALATINUS

FENCHURCH STREET STATION

FENCHURCH STREET

TOWER OF LONDON

FENCHURCH STREET

BILLITER

VIA MILITARIS

GREAT TOWER STREET

PALATUM BELLONORUM

BILLINGSGATE

ST. MARY AT HILL

EASTCHEAP

MONUMENT STREET

ROMAN LONDON BRIDGE

GRACECHURCH STREET

SHOPS

SHOPS

FISH STREET HILL

PONS SUBLICIUS

LOWER THAMES STREET

KING WILLIAM STREET

ARTHUR STREET

MAURICE POUNTNEY LANE

LAURENCE POUNTNEY LANE

ST. SWITHIN'S LANE

BIRCH

STREET

LONDON BRIDGE

Ernest Parkin delineavit

6. G.H.Q. of the *Dux*, the G.O.C. London District
6a. Barracks of (?) Praetorian guard

TEMPLES

1. Mars Gradivus (united, possibly, with that of his sister/daughter/wife, Bellona)
2. Temple of the Three Mothers (attested by many relics found in London)
3. Mars Stator (or, as I have suggested, a London form: Mars Standens). The presence of a temple dedicated to this god just at the edge of a *via sagularis* confirms my remarks about the 'on guard' aspect of Roman East London: for Mars Stator (or Standens) was the protector of Roman military limits, and particularly of Roman courage in the face of the enemy. It was Mars Stator who held the Romans firm in the face of Sabine attack – and he was so called because he *stopped* (*sto*) the Romans from fleeing
4. Temple of the Cabiri, Samothracian demon gods. The presence of a temple here may indicate that troops exotic even by Roman standards were garrisoning the eastern defences
5. Dionysos-Bacchus. The Greek and Roman gods of wine were equated in the ecumenical theology of Rome
6. The only Christian establishment that, so far, I have been able definitely to identify. The Palace of the Bishop of London (*sedes Augustini Papae* – known, up to the Reformation, as 'St Augustine Papey')
7. Selene. (A clay head of this goddess is in the Guildhall Museum)
8. Mars
9. Temple of Cybele (*fanum magnae matris*). Her self-emasculated priests were known as *Galli*, and Galley (or Gully) Hole, Row, Quay and Dock are names found near the successor to the *fanum magnae matris* – 'St Magnus Martyr'
12. The Bearward's depot – Keeper of the Sacred Bears of Artemis
13. Temple of the Glory of the Emperor and of Jupiter Nicaeus, God of Victory (another decidedly military deity)
14. Antinoüs
15. Artemis
16. Mars Gradivus

GRANARIES AND/OR WAREHOUSES
1. Granary and/or warehouse
1a. Granary and/or warehouse
2. Granary
3. Granary and/or warehouse
4. Granary and/or warehouse
5. Granary

 MARKETS
1. Market
2. Monthly market (*Trinundinae* – 'Three Nuns')
3. Market (by the Customs-house)
4. Slave-market (*macellum mangonum* – 'Slave dealers' market')
5. Market
6. Slave-market (*venalicium*)
7. Market and offices of market-officials

WEIGHTS, MEASURES AND CUSTOMS
1. Taxing-office of the Aediles (*sacomari aedilicii statio*)
2. Customs-house, douane (*ad mulctam*)
2a. Customs-house, douane (*ad mulctam*)
3. Customs-house, douane (*ad mulctam*)
4. Customs-house, douane (*ad mulctam*)

® PUBLIC RECREATION
1. Bath-house

SPQR STATE ADMINISTRATION AND CONTROL
9. (?) Governor's palace (this is still being excavated, but it is a building of most imposing dimensions

FORTS
3. Fort

 PRISONS
1. Convict prison (*lautumiae poenitationis*)
2. Military prison (*antrum*)

 FINANCE
1. Mint and/or metal refinery (*officina Honorin*
2. Banker's offices (*ad danistam*)
3. Treasury (*fiscus*), eastern section
3a. Offices of Imperial Treasury officials
6. Treasury of London (municipal, not Imperial)

Ⓐ PUBLIC FOOD CENTRES (*Annonae*)
1. Annona

Introduction

The year is A.D. 130. The place is London. A man, wearing a carefully pleated white *toga praetexta* (the toga with the purple border to show that he is a magistrate) and scarlet boots (to show that he is a senator[1]) stands with his back to the Forum Civile, gazing down the wide and gently sloping street which leads to London Bridge.

The man is Sextus Julius Severus; he has just been appointed by the Emperor Hadrian to succeed Marcus Appius Bradua as Imperial Legate, or Governor, of the Province of Britain.

Let us imagine a sunny day in May, in which the still sharp sunshine of early summer (or late spring) strikes sparkles from the armour of the Legate's military staff, amongst whom the appearance of the *magister equitum*, the Field-Marshal of Cavalry, is surely the most splendid.

The strong yet manageable winds of May have carried the Legate swiftly from Rotomagus – Rouen – to the port of London, and now, before entering the praetorium on the north-western corner of the Forum Civile, the Legate stands watching the pedestrian traffic in the city's principal street, and, beyond it, the waterborne traffic passing through the arches of the great wooden bridge.

By his side, the Notarius, his Secretary of State, points out the various important buildings which line the street, though even the most important (including the Governor-General's palace, set aside for his personal use) are dwarfed by the vast Basilica at his back – a tall building some 505 feet long: only 8 feet shorter than the present St Paul's Cathedral.

[1] Which is why the Pope wears scarlet shoes to this day.

Looking down the gently sloping Via Gradiva, which local pronunciation will, in the course of centuries, turn into 'Grace-church Street', the first object to catch the Legate's eye is the massive statue of gilded bronze which stands on the left of the Bridge Approach, the *ostium pontis*, that later ages will come to call 'Oystergate'. Severus has already seen this huge statue glinting in the May sunshine as he was coming up the Thames, but now, as he looks down on it from the eminence of the Forum Civile, he catches, for the first time, something of this city's importance – no statue as well-executed and large as this would have been erected, he reflects complacently, save in a city of note. His pride in his appointment grows – this is no disguised exile, as jealous friends have hinted, and as he himself has half believed.

To consolidate the peace that the vigorous, brilliant Hadrian has secured for a Britain menaced by the Brigantes, Sextus Julius Severus has been sent by an emperor who does not appoint to sinecures.

The Brigantes had revolted, and had then destroyed the legion sent to subdue them. The circumstances in which Legio IX Hispana – 'the Unlucky Spanish' – had been destroyed were still unknown; the legionaries had marched north against the fierce Yorkshiremen, and the legionaries had been killed, almost to a man. That had been in A.D. 119. In the following year, the then Legate, Quintus Pompeius Falco, had received a despatch telling him that not only were reinforcements on their way, but also that the Emperor Hadrian himself was accompanying them, to clean up a deteriorating situation that, the Emperor knew, needed his own sure 'Napoleonic' touch.

Hadrian took the battle-toughened Legio VI Victrix with him, and did not stop even when he had taught the cocksure Brigantes a lesson. He moved farther north, to the country of the Picts and Scots – even less willing to accept Roman discipline than the Brigantes. Now, with the remote northerners 'contained', Hadrian was to astonish even his most fervent admirers by the magnitude of his planning. Not London and York, but Britain itself was to have a wall: that 'Hadrian's Wall' which still stands as one of the most impressive monuments to Roman enterprise which have survived to this day.

Here now, in the sharp sunshine of a London spring, is the man whom Hadrian has chosen to maintain the peace that the Emperor has given to Britain. It is at the huge gilded statue of the Emperor that Sextus Julius Severus is gazing, as he stands with his staff at the top of Gracechurch Street.

The obsequious Notarius – there has long been a tradition that such pliant administrators should be recruited from amongst the Spaniards, in whom a large admixture of Phoenician and Carthaginian blood has given a usable talent for civil administration and the less sensitive forms of finance – points out the various buildings of the Via Gradiva to the Legate.

On the left-hand side, to the east of the Forum, is the *legionaria aula*, barracks of the detachment of men from Legio XX Valeria Victrix – 'the Governor's Guard'. Over the gate of their barracks the gilded boar, their regimental badge (which will become a famous British pub-sign) twinkles.

Farther south, by a few paces only, is the temple of Juno Lucina, and below that, at the corner of 'the first turning on the left' (now Fenchurch Street), is the most impressive Temple of Dionysus-Bacchus, itself only a few paces from the sinister little chapel of the Cabiri, the Samothracian demon-gods whom the more exotic elements of the Roman army prefer to 'healthier' gods such as Mithras or Jupiter Dolichenus.

The block between the Temple of Dionysus-Bacchus and the next street on the left is occupied by a row of five-storied houses with shops beneath – the Insula Veneta, though whether so-called because of the blue wash with which the plaster had been treated (*venetus* = blue) or because traders did business there (*venditum* = a sale), the Notarius does not say.

'And that tall building farther down on the left?' Severus asks. 'Is that not another legionary post just before it, at the corner of the street – let me see, the second street down on the left?'

'Yes, Excellency: the *castellum legionariorum militum*, guarding the Imperial Treasury – the tall building, beyond. It is well guarded, Excellency, and it is within easy access of the river and, of course, the Customs House, where you landed, sir.'

'What have the two guard-posts to do with each other?'

'Nothing, sir. They are not even of the same legion. The post by the Forum Civile has the duty of guarding your Excellency in particular, and the praetorian buildings and Basilica generally. The legionary post down there, sir, has the job of guarding the *fiscus*. There is a lock-up attached to each post: the *antrum* of your guard, sir, is along the road which goes to the eastern gate – the one they call the High Gate; the *antrum* for the Fiscal Guard is in the street at the corner of which they have their barracks.'

'This street is called, I believe, the Via Gradiva?'

'Because, sir, the Temple of Mars Gradivus is just around the corner, in the street on your right. The river runs along the street – they call it Via Lambecta, for that reason – but the street ceases to be called Via Gradiva when it reaches the Fiscal Guard's barracks; after that, between the *fiscus* and the bridge, it is called Via Fiscalis.'

'And the very splendid temple right by the bridge, on its left-hand side, just beyond the statue of the Divine Hadrian?'

Gazing straight ahead, the Secretary says, 'They really *do* concede the divinity of the Emperor here, sir! The British, I mean. They need no convincing of the godlike qualities of a general who avenged Legion IX; who sent a dozen savage tribes away with fleas in their ears; and who has given this island a peace that it never hoped to see again.'

The Legate says sharply.

'Are you implying that *I* need convincing of the divinity of the Emperor?'

'The gods forbid, Excellency!' says the Notarius, smoothly obsequious. 'I merely remarked that *these barbarians* did not. But to answer your question, sir, the very splendid temple by the river that you have just pointed out is that of the Magna Mater. . . . They even have a vast, formless rock inside; though this was not brought from Phrygia, but from an island to the far west – one of the Tin Islands. There is, indeed, Excellency, little in Rome which is not reproduced here, though admittedly on a more modest scale.'

Half angry at what he thinks is a none-too-skilfully concealed insolence, the Legate merely grunts, and points to the right. He can see, towering above the creamy-red tiles of the temples and secular buildings, the heroic group of statuary topping the 'Jove and Giant' column that London, in common with all Roman cities, has erected in what we now call Thames Street, and which, in those days, was probably called by a Latin equivalent, such as Via Tamesana. As he has been carried in his litter for the quarter of a mile which separates the river-stair from the Praetorium, all that the Legate has been able to see through the silken curtains have been shop-fronts, temple doorways and the curious faces of those who have halted to watch their new Governor-General go by.

An ambitious but confident and supremely competent emperor has appointed him to this, one of the 'trap jobs' of the Empire – that sort of job which either makes or breaks a man, and usually has the not undeserved reputation of doing the latter. Severus, an ambitious man himself, is determined that the appointment as Imperial Legate to this troublous and remote island shall not break him. He will, he vows, understand these British – both the tamed and the untamed – and perhaps, through that necessary study, come to understand their country and its special problems.

So there he stands, looking down the Via Gradiva – that the locals, so his aide-de-camp has already told him, pronounce 'Gradzi'a' – and takes his first lesson in London topography.

'Over to our right, beyond the Forum, sir, is the city's biggest market, this side of the city's central river.'

'The name of this river . . .?'

'It's curious that you should ask that, sir, for in fact the river, which is a tributary of the Tamesa, has no name – at least, none of which I've ever heard. Both we Romans and the locals simply call it "Vallatum", because, I suppose, it's banked and palisaded its entire length, from the Thames to the northern gate. You see the masts there, sir, on the right, a little way down the street – at the back of that block of flats and shops? That is a small dock, which leads off the canal which runs along the Via Lambecta. The dock is called the *portus corbitensis*, because small merchant vessels discharge there, their cargoes being taken straight into the big market at the other side of the Via Mercenaria.

'I mentioned that just around the corner of the Via Lambecta

– the first turning, there, on the right – is the Temple of Mars Gradivus, which gives this street its name.

'On the other side of the Via Lambecta – you can see the pediment from here, sir – is the Temple of the Glory of the Emperor. You will observe that, with the statue of Hadrian and the "Jove and Giant" column, we have a right-angled triangle, with the acute angle of the base pointing luckily to the east.'

'Indeed?' Severus notes with interest, for he has all a Roman's ingrained respect for *numen* and the unalterable rightness of omen and ritual. This, he reflects happily, may well turn out to be a fortunate appointment, in more senses that one. 'And what lies behind that tall, plain wall?'

'That section of the city we call the *cancellarius vicus*, Excellency, because it is cut off from the ordinary comings and goings of the population: it is the main dock area, and it was considered wiser to reserve it for official use. There are two more such restricted areas – both to the west of the city: one on the river, the other beyond a tributary called the "Fretum". It's sixty years ago since the Britons burnt this city to the ground, and massacred some seventy thousand people – but, all the same. . . .'

'I understand,' says the Legate. 'The ships put in at this *cancellarius vicus*, unload their cargoes, put them into the warehouses . . . and so on?'

'Yes, Excellency. The *cancellarius vicus* abuts on the Vallatum – the main river which runs into the Thames – and it makes it easy to ship goods throughout the city: along the Vallatum I mean.'

'I see a tall wall by the river.'

'That is the embankment, to prevent flooding. This city, sir, is one big marsh, and every building that you see is erected on piles – even the road on which we are standing is built on a foundation of wooden piles. Were there no embankment, there would be nothing dry in this city save the Forum behind us and the basilica of the *ordo curialis* on the other hill to the west.'

'Is the *cancellarius vicus* reserved entirely to the activities of a dock?'

'Within the walls . . . yes. And, as with the other *cancellarii vici*, the military are there too. But to the left of it, as we look at it, Excellency, there is another large market – this city is full of markets.'

'The basilica behind us is certainly large. I cannot recall ever having seen a larger, save in Rome or Milan. Would you say, Notarius, that this city is as important as some would have had me believe?'

'Every bit as important, sir,' says the Notarius, eager to restore himself to the Legate's good graces. 'It is important by location. At the head of the Province's largest river, it must inevitably be its most important harbour. It is also something of a holy city to the locals.'

'Have we not Romanized them yet . . . ?'

'To the extent that they speak Latin with a strong British accent, and twist our Latin words most barbarously to the form that they find easier to say . . . yes. But they worship their own gods, and keep to their own customs. Otherwise they are Roman. London is, as I said, a holy city to them. Even if Rome were to abandon it, these Britons – Romanized or not – would keep it going.'

'There is money here?'

'A lot,' says the Notarius, whose job it is to see to the money of London. 'I have pointed out the Imperial *fiscus* just ahead, to the left. Behind us, on the other side of the hill, there is the main Treasury of London, whose *praepositus* I shall have the honour of presenting to your Excellency this afternoon.

'There are the various *aeraria*, scattered throughout the city, and there is another very important *fiscus* on the Tamesa, on the other side of the Vallatum, by that large tributary of the Tamesa, the Fretum.'[1]

The Legate looks over what he can see of his charge – the city looks beautiful, peaceful and exceedingly prosperous in the May sunshine. Across the river, above the huddle of red roofs, the signal-tower on what is now Knight's Hill begins to flash its bronze mirror. A shorthand-writer at the Legate's side draws out his 'government issue' wax-tablet and stylus, and waits to take down the message. The wooden back of the tablet bears a circular government brand: PROC. AVG. DEDERVNT/BRIT.

---

[1] Latin *fretum* = 'estuary'.

PROV., 'Issued by the Imperial Procurators, Province of Britain'.

His stylus darts over the wax, and, at the Notary's bidding, the *amanuensis* reads out what he has transcribed.

'All quiet on the northern border, sir. The Wall reports no barbarian sorties of any kind. The Pax Romana is maintained throughout Britain.'

'Good!' says the Legate. 'Gentlemen, let us go inside. It may well be May, but it is still cold.'

The reader, whilst accepting this imagined conversation as the traditional convention of a writer, may well ask: 'But how is it possible to be so certain that Gracechurch Street was, in the days of Roman London, called "Via Gradiva", and that, on this street – whatever it was called – were the temples, barracks and blocks of flats which have been described in such detail? Have the archaeologists of the Guildhall Museum dug up the remains of these buildings? – identified them beyond doubt? Has a map of Roman London been found which now enables us to give the names of the streets and of the buildings which lined them?'

The answer is that, though the archaeologists of the Guild-hall Museum have been busy, and have dug up and clearly marked on the map the remains of many a Roman building and roadway, they have not positively identified any other buildings than the Temple of the Glory of the Emperor (which was identified by Roach Smith in June 1850), the Basilica at the top of Gracechurch Street, tentatively identified in 1848, and positively identified in 1880, when the old buildings of Leaden-hall Market were pulled down, and – perhaps – the Temple of Mithras, discovered[1] in 1953.

The fact is that the method now available to us for locating the buildings and streets of Roman London is not archaeological at all, but based on the theory that the majority of London names are of Roman origin, being merely the modern survivals of Latin words – much modified, it is true, by the passage of some 1,500 years, but nevertheless recognizably Latin. In this book the theory will be explained in detail, but here it is necessary only to say that, if we can find the Latin original

[1] *See* the author's *London Beneath the Pavement* for a full account of this important discovery.

behind a modern London name, we can state without argument that such-and-such a Roman building stood in such-and-such a London district. To give but one example: the modern London name 'St Botolph' is derived from the Latin word, *multa* (or *mulcta*), 'a customs house, *douane*', and enables us to say that, where the various 'St Botolph' churches now stand, were once the Roman customs-posts at the gates – or 'Bars' – of the city. This is what we shall call in this book the 'New Archaeology'. It will not supplant the old archaeology, but rather will complement it in an ambitious endeavour to recover the lost facts of Roman London. The spade of the archaeologist will still be required to uncover the *material* remains of vanished Londinium, whilst the New Archaeology will be able to say just what those remains formed part of in the days when Roman buildings lined the streets of Roman London. It is clear that, so far, traditional archaeology has not been able to do much more than uncover the plan of a Roman building, plot the line of a Roman street or wall; recover the pattern of a Roman river-embankment; tell us something of the construction of the revetments within which the Roman engineers contained London's many rivers and streams. Except for three buildings – two temples and a law-court – traditional archaeology has always found itself unable to state not only *what* the various buildings of Londinium were, but also *where* they were; whereas the New Archaeology can not only state decisively that London had, for instance, at least four public picture-galleries – *pinacothecæ* – but can state, equally decisively, where those *pinacothecæ* were located.

There is nothing like a handful of examples to show what this 'New Archaeology' is, and how it works.

Take the various City of London churches which are 'dedicated' to 'St Andrew'. In this book – where, for the first time, the theory and application of the New Archaeology are explained and demonstrated – it will be shown that the *siting* of these various 'St Andrews' is strong confirmation that our interpretation of the name is correct. But, for the present, let us confine ourselves merely to observing what the name 'Andrew' *really* means (and it has nothing to do with the saint who was crucified upside down).

Antrum is a Latin word meaning 'cell, lock-up', etc., and the locative of the word, *antro*, simply means 'at the lock-up'. The original Latin word *antro* on the lips of the British-speaking Londoner of Roman days, was 'softened' to 'andro', just as the modern American has softened the English word *pretty* to 'priddy'. (We shall see, in the course of this book, that the sound of T, when it fell between vowels, was almost always softened to D in the speech of the Roman Londoner.)

Well, to get back to *antro*, softened to *andro*: this sound, after its original meaning had been forgotten, was accepted, by a now Christianized London, as the name that we spell 'Andrew', itself a corruption of Latin *Andraeus*.

We see here that we now have found, in the original of the various 'St Andrews', a clue to the nature of the Roman building which first occupied the site of each 'Andrew' church: a lock-up. Later I shall explain that there is evidence that these were not civil, but military, lock-ups, always attached to (or under the control of) one of the legionary detachments scattered throughout London. If we were making a map of Roman London, we could begin by marking, wherever we found a church 'dedicated to St Andrew', the site of an *antrum*, a Roman military guard-house or lock-up.

Philology and etymology – the sciences of words' meaning and origin – are now getting on for two hundred years old, and we do know a great deal of what has happened to the *meaning* of words and the *sound* of words in the centuries over which we may trace the development of both meaning and sound.

We know, for example, what happened to the words of Latin when they came to be pronounced by non-Latin peoples – especially do we know, and especially are we concerned with, the pronunciation of Latin words in the mouths of Celtic speakers, such speakers as made up the bulk of London's population for centuries after, say, A.D. 61, the year in which Rome's grip really tightened on Britain. In modern Welsh there are at least eight hundred words directly derived from the Latin, and the same is true of that allied modern *p*-Celtic language, Breton. Allowing for the fact that many of these words borrowed from the Latin are the same in both these Celtic tongues, we still have some thousand Latin words, adopted by Celtic speakers, whose development, from Latin into modern *p*-Celtic (Welsh or Breton), we may trace at practically every stage.

This gives us the vitally important knowledge of what happened to Latin *sounds* in the mouths of the Londoners of British race. We know that they wrote and spoke Latin, but, more importantly, we know that they pronounced it in their own fashion, and it is the twist that they gave to Latin sounds, in Latin words, which has influenced the development of the original Latinisms into names which are now typically 'London'.

The reasoning behind the theory of the New Archaeology is simply this: if we know, from modern or ancient Welsh, what happened to Latin words when once the Celtic speakers got hold of them, then we should, *assuming that a modern London name is a word of Latin origin,* be able, from our knowledge of the history of Welsh sounds, to discover the Latin original.

In fact, we can do just this. And to this new tool of research, the modern London names, formerly thought to be of 'Anglo-Saxon' origin, yield up their Latin originals easily. Sometimes the names that we are examining are the names of streets, sometimes the names of churches, sometimes the names of taverns. All have proved, not only to have their origins in the Latin of Roman London, but to be the certain evidence by which we may locate every type of Roman London institution, from a public swimming-pool to a slave-market; from a Public Assistance office to a legionary barracks; from a snack-bar to the temple of some Roman god.

What the spade of the archaeologist uncovers are fragments of walls, broken drains, perhaps a tesselated pavement, the base of a pillar, maybe its foliated capital. Sometimes richer rewards await the archaeologist: a marble sarcophagus, a memorial inscription, a tombstone erected by a London gladiator's sorrowing wife, a tavern jug with the 'address' scratched on it, 'London – next-door to the Temple of Isis'. But these things are rare, and they are getting ever rarer. The new buildings go down so deep that they excavate everything out of existence: beneath the skyscrapers is now only the primeval clay.

It is fortunate that, just as conventional London archaeology had reached, as it were, its last gasp – having nothing more to excavate, since what remained was too hard to get at – the New Archaeology should be devised to offer a different (and, as it has turned out, far more effective) way to reconstruct the London of anything from 1,500 to 2,000 years ago. The New Archaeology has made it possible to do what traditional archaeology could never have done: re-map Roman London *almost completely*. I confidently trust that we may – not at once, not altogether; but eventually, and in large part – mark out the lines of the Roman streets, *naming them* as we go; putting the various public and private buildings along them, and indicating the purpose of each building. What is more, because I feel that we may indicate the purpose of so many Roman London buildings of which only unrecognizable fragments remain – and most of which have disappeared altogether – I believe that we can reconstruct the pattern of Roman London life. We shall be able to say now how Roman London was organized, how it was governed; what its social and economic patterns were. All these things the New Archaeology – which will be fully explained in this book – enables us to do. What it promises us is the exciting prospect of being able to reconstruct and re-map cities and towns for which traditional archaeology can do little. So long as the old names remain – and they do remain, richly, in London – we shall be able to recapture much of a past which, up to the present, has seemed to have vanished beyond recall.

What must be borne in mind is that there is no guesswork in this finding Latin originals in London names; the rules by which we work were discovered and published years ago by eminent students of the Welsh language, such as Morris-Jones, Loth, Baudiš and many others. In the course of my own research into the pedigree of London names, I have observed that the usage of the London 'Welshmen' – it would be more correct to call them 'Britons' and their Celtic language, 'Brittonic', but 'Welshmen' links them more closely to us – differs at times from that of those who spoke the Ancient Welsh recovered from old manuscripts; but the differences between 'London Old Welsh' and 'classical Old Welsh' are few and unimportant. We shall note them as we come to them.

What the theory expounded in this book holds is that the

names in a Roman London were pronounced in a manner typically Celtic by a population whose native tongue was the ancestor of modern Welsh. The theory further holds that London stood out against the attacks of the 'Saxons', preserving its autonomous government, its peculiar customs and culture, its 'pagan' religion, its Latin language (at least for official purposes) and – which most concerns us here – the Latin names of its public buildings, its temples, its baths, its treasuries, and so on. That these names in later centuries were 'interpreted' as the names of saints and so forth, after their Latin origins had passed completely out of the memory of men, does not alter the fact that, however changed, the majority of London names are Latin names – and the fact that we use them today is the strongest possible evidence for the assumption that London never collapsed: that London, on the contrary, survived the 'Saxon' assault, and maintained its integrity and continuity to the present day. The evidence of London names proves this.

Locked away in these London names are the evidences of Roman foundations and institutions. For instance, the name of the church of St John Zachary (spelt more correctly 'St John Sacre', in 1378) is clearly derived from the name of the *saccararius*, the City Treasurer, whose office, we may assume, once occupied the site on which the church stood until its destruction by fire in 1666.

The Temple of the Glory of the Emperor was identified in 1850 through the finding, by Roach Smith, of part of the dedicatory inscription, on a large fragment of stone unearthed by the workmen. As the stone was found in Nicholas Lane, the assumption is that the temple stood there. More, traditional archaeology cannot – *and dare not* – say.

But the New Archaeology has a great deal more to tell us. Take the evidence of the name 'Nicholas Lane'. Here, hardly altered from the original, is the Latin *Via Nicalis* – 'Victory Street', the allusion being to an epithet of Jupiter, *nicaeus* (from the Greek Νικαῖος), 'He who grants victory', '. . . the temple of Jupiter, whom they call Nicaeus,' says Livy – and so they called him in London, as the name 'Nicholas Lane' proves.

We know, then, that what Roach Smith found – a partial

inscription dedicating a temple to the 'numen of the Caesar' – was the inscribed lintel from a temple of Jupiter Nicaeus, a favourite – one might almost say *the* favourite – divinity with the victory-seeking rulers of the early Roman Empire.

Thus we have found, not only a temple dedicated to Jupiter Nicaeus, but its firmly-evidenced location.

Not all Latin names have remained as relatively unaltered as Saccararius, Nicaeus, Annona, Praetorium – the last two have given us, respectively, the various 'St Annes' and 'St Peters'.

Sometimes, as in Blow Bladder Street, the former name of that part of Newgate Street where it joins Cheapside, the Latin original is not at all apparent – certainly not at first glance.

But remembering the Celtic trick of 'softening' P to B, and dropping the vowels from unaccented syllables, we see that the strange word, 'Blow Bladder' is, in fact, nothing but the Latin word, *propolaria*,[1] from *propola* 'a retail shop', and so we see that modern (up to the 18th century) Blow Bladder Street is simply the corrupted form of Via Propolaria, 'The Street of the Retailers'.

This is important. At the end of the Middle Ages, the shops of Cheapside, especially at the northern end, were literally world-famous. No visitor to London would miss seeing these splendid shops, whose carved fronts, painted and gilded, were an outstanding glory of the City. It is evident, from our interpretation of 'Blow Bladder', that Cheapside's importance as a shopping centre began in the earliest days of the Roman occupation of London. We shall see, too, that the splitting up of London into 'spheres of influence', centring commerce and retail-trading about the Cattle Market at what is now St Paul's, and centring law and administration and larger-scale trading about from what is now the Guildhall area to beyond the cross-roads at Cornhill; this division, established in Roman times, persists to this day. What there is of retail trading in the City of London is confined almost completely to Cheapside, whilst all of original walled London to the east concerns itself with the less material forms of trading. The City's law is administered by

[1] Propolaria > Pro'plaria > broblaria > blobladia > bloblad'a – marks the progressive change from *propolaria* to Blow Bladder.

the Lord Mayor – as the successor of the *praefectus urbi* – at the Guildhall, where the proximity of such names as Basinghall Street and St Michael Bassishaw testify that here, too, was a basilica. Other evidence that the justice of the City was administered here in Roman times, as it still is today, will be given later.

But the point that I wish to emphasize here is that London has had a continuous history, and though that history has not survived for all periods – hence the myth that London 'died' between A.D. 457 and A.D. 597 – there is ample evidence, outside the pages of the surviving historical record, to support the claim that London, in its names, its customs and its social, juridical and commercial organization, has never 'stopped for one minute'. The continuity is unbroken from, say A.D. 61, the year after the Boudiccan revolt, to the present day.

One striking example of this continuity may be given here. The last man to be executed in public in England, Michael Barrett, the Fenian, met his death outside Newgate Prison. The vast crowd which witnessed this historic hanging – including the nineteen persons who were crushed to death as the mob pressed nearer to the scaffold – accepted without comment that Barrett would be hanged where he was hanged, 'because that was where they hanged them in the City'.

Now, this area – just outside the City's western gate, but still within the *pomoerium*, the 'defensive belt' which circled every Roman city – had always been used for judicial executions. In nearby Smithfield, William Wallace had been executed, and here, too, were burnt the martyrs under the later Tudors. The evidence of certain names in this area makes it quite clear that this area, just to the west of Newgate and Aldersgate (Alder = *altera*, 'the other' [Northern] gate), had been set aside as a place of execution by the Roman government itself. There were two principal 'Golgothas' of Roman London: one in what we may call the western Smithfield district, the other in the eastern Smithfield area by the Tower of London – for both the evidence of the name is decisive, though the names vary slightly, because of differences in London pronunciation between eastern and western usage.

There was a street on Tower Hill (a traditional site of

31

execution up to the beheading of Lord Lovat in 1745) which was called Petty Gales, sometimes Petty Wales. In the parish of St Bartholomew the Great (a Roman crypt lies beneath the present Norman church), in West Smithfield, we find another Petty Wales, whilst very near, in the parish of St Mary Alder-mary, in Cripplegate Ward – that is, within the area of what we shall later describe as the 'Cripplegate Fort' – we find a Petty Cales Lane.

These three variants of the same word – Petty Wales, Petty Gales and Petty Cales – are all derived from the Latin *patibula* (Later Latin *patibulas*), meaning 'gibbets'. When Tacitus tells how Suetonius Paulinus was counselled by military strategy to stand aside and let the ravening forces of Queen Boudicca fall upon unwalled London and massacre those who had elected not to go with the Roman general, the historian describes the terrible massacre in four tense words: *caedes, patibula, ignes, cruces,* 'slaughter, gibbets, fire and torture!' It may well be that it was Queen Boudicca, and not the Romans, who first set up gibbets at Smithfield – but, in that case, the Romans continued the practice, for our modern names, Petty Wales, Petty Gales and Petty Cales, are all derived from the Latin phrase *ad patibulas*, 'at the gibbets', and not from any Celtic word.

As our 'Ordnance Survey' of Londinium progresses, we shall find that few gaps will remain in our knowledge, once we shall have come to the end of our search for vanished Roman London. Baths, the stadium, barracks, treasuries, temples, cook-shops, granaries, taverns, wells, bridges, defensive works of every land: we shall identify all these and site them with accuracy. But, in doing this, we shall do something more: we shall recreate the social, administrative and commercial activities of what, in its Roman heyday, was one of the great cities of the Imperium, and one which was unique in that it was the only Roman *municipium* of its size which lay so close to the western edge of the world.

Our New Archaeology offers us the fascinating prospect of being able to prepare – possibly for the first time in history – a detailed map of mighty Londinium, then, as now, the greatest city in the Province of Britain.

In advancing the theory that the majority of modern London names have their origin in Latin words, I must make clear what is implied in that claim—

a. London, once 'named' internally, has known no break since; London names, once given, have continued to be used until the present day; and

b. those present London names *of Latin origin* have come down to us, modified, in the first place, by the now carefully recorded idiomatic pronunciation of the 'Welsh'-speaking inhabitants of Londinium, and, in the second place, by a completely individual London usage, to which successive immigrant elements – Greeks, 'Anglo-Saxons', Danes, Buccinobantes (Germans – *foederati*, under their king Fraomar), Sorbs from the Slav Baltic (settled in the district around their 'capital', Salisbury, but doubtless migrating to London, as all provincials have tended to do for the last two thousand years), Irish, Scots, Picts, Atticotti, and all the rest. They have certainly modified the original Latin – the wonder is that so much of the original structure of each maltreated Latin words survives. (To know how much words *may* be maltreated, I have only to observe that I heard the porter, as the train came in, announce the name of the station. 'A.C.!' he said. 'A.C.?' an American in my carriage asked, in complete puzzlement, looking for the name-board – which, of course, was out of sight. 'A.C.,' I said. 'That's how they pronounce "Hayward's Heath" locally!' Consider the tremendous prestige of such a street as the 'Via Militaris', which has altered so little that we still call it 'Billiter Street'.)

The proof that I shall offer in this book will be what we may well call a 'circular' one: in demonstrating that most of the older London names are of Latin origin, I shall claim that I am proving that London has enjoyed an unbroken continuity as a city, from the time of its Romanization in the first century A.D. to the present day. But as I shall also try to prove this continuity by other evidence, I shall, I trust, be proving my claim that there has been no need for the original Latin names to have altered, save for the inevitable changes which affect every word in the course of time.

I talk of continuity, and I think of it, perhaps, as something not so much *flowingly* continuous, as a river is continuous, but rather of the quality of a steady progression, from one moment to the next, which has yet in it a tendency to a 'repeat pattern'. The same things – given a sufficient length of time – tend to recur. ('For there is no new thing under the sun.')

Accidental or not, this 'repeat pattern' is obvious and striking. An example: I was walking down Southampton Row the other day, when I noticed that the Lyons teashop, which had served cups of tea and toast ever since I can remember, had gone, and that in its place was a spanking new café, obviously owned by persons of Italian descent. I was not wrong: the name on the fascia was 'Amandini'.

Just another Italian name? Well, yes. Just another Italian name. (It should properly be written 'Degli Amandini' – 'of the Amandinus family'.) But where had I seen this name – this 'just another Italian name' – before?

I remembered a stone sarcophagus found in 1869, buried to the north-west of the north transept of Westminster Abbey.

The beautifully cut letters on the side of the sarcophagus spell out the dedication:

MEMORIAE · VALER · AMAN
DINI · VALERI · SUPERVEN
TOR · ET · MARCELLUS · PATRI · FECER

('In memory of Valerius Amandinus: Valerius
Superventor and Valerius Marcellus made
this for their father')

This 'Italian' name which appears above the new-furbished café in Southampton Row is, at least by adoption and usage, a well-attested London name. It not only appears on the sarcophagus of Valerius Amandinus – dating from not later than A.D. 200 – but turns up again as part of the name of a church in Foster Lane: 'St Vedast and St Amandus'.

I shall show later that this 'St Vedast' is, in fact, no more than the Latin phrase, *di fasti*, the (official notices of the) days on which court cases were heard, and refers to the time when 'St Vedast', with Foster Lane, was part of the Forum Boarium.

Why 'St Amandus' should have attached itself to 'St Vedast'

34

I am not prepared, at this moment, to say, but it is curious that a name which appears first on a second or third century sarcophagus, turns up again as part of the name of a mediæval church – and then turns up once more to adorn the fascia of a modern café in Southampton Row.

In reading this book, there are only a few important facts which should be borne in mind if the reader is to understand the theory put forward, and to follow the reasoning which will support that theory. The most important fact is that the mass of the inhabitants of Roman London were Britons – the people who are the racial and linguistic ancestors of the modern Welsh – who spoke an early form of the Welsh language, of which, happily, we know a great deal.

These 'proto-Welsh', if so we may call them, had idioms of pronunciation which are still characteristic of the Welsh which is spoken today, from Patagonia to Pwllheli, from Pittsburgh to Portmadoc. Of these idioms of pronunciation, that with the most far-reaching influence is the change of M to a sound between F and V, whenever M falls between two vowels or between a vowel and such a 'sonant' as N. Thus, Latin *columna*, 'a column', becomes, in early Welsh, *colofn*: the M between U and N having become F. Again, the name of a Roman London street, Via Militaris, 'Military Road', becomes, in 'London Welsh', *Gwi' Vilitar'*, because the M falls between an A and an I, and so changes to V – the name further developing through the centuries, until we reach our modern form of 'Billiter Street'.

Other characteristics of Welsh pronunciation will be noted as they occur, but what *must* clearly be borne in mind is that the rules governing the changes which come over Latin words adopted by Welsh have been carefully studied and recorded in minute detail. To the cultured Roman ear of the imported civil servant or military or naval officer, the average Londoner's treatment of Latin words must have sounded as odd as the average Indian's or Pakistani's treatment of English words sounds to the cultured modern English ear. Yet the Indian or Pakistani *is* speaking English – albeit with his own idiomatic pronunciation.

It is essential to remember that, for all his barbarous

pronunciation, the Celtic Londoner of anything from 1,900 to 1,400 years ago was speaking Latin – and the Latin words that he used, the Latin names to which he referred, he has transmitted to us in a completely *unbroken* continuity covering nearly two millennia. Today, behind such 'obviously English' names as 'St Botolph' and 'Do Little Lane', we may – once we know the rules governing the change from Latin to Welsh, so far as importations of Latin words into Welsh are concerned – disinter the Latin original, and discover which Latin temple, say, stood once on the site of a modern London church.

The reader does not need any specialized knowledge of philology – indeed, he or she does not need to know any philology at all. The derivations of modern London words will be explained as we go; and, without any scholarship at all, the reader may join me in what must be amongst the most fascinating quests of all time: the search for, and the certain discovery of, one of the most famous cities of the Roman Empire, whose plan – if it ever existed – has been lost for centuries.

We shall, with the aid of a new archaeological tool – 'etymological archaeology' – dig up buried Londinium. We shall find out which gods were worshipped in London, and which gods were not. We shall even solve the vexed problem: Where was Roman London Bridge?

What we shall get from this search will be something which, only five years ago, would have seemed beyond the wildest hopes of even the most adventurous scholarship: an 'Ordnance Survey' map of Londinium – that this map exists today, printed in this book, has been made possible only by the new archaeological tool that this book introduces to the public.

So far as the material remains of Londinium are concerned, little survives today – and of what is found little is judged of sufficient 'importance' to be permitted to endure. Land is too valuable to allow the crumbling foundations of a Roman building to occupy even a few square feet of the modern city's overpriced acreage. A hastily snatched photograph for the *Illustrated London News* and *The Times*, a few hopelessly pleading letters to the newspapers – 'Can *nothing* be done, Sir, before it is too late, to save this irreplaceable relic of London's Roman past . . .'. So they go on: the discoveries, the photographs in the

Illustrated London News and *The Times*, the brave, utterly useless letters. . . .

Along comes the bulldozer, and down go the piles, and up go the tall erections in the new Kliptiko school of what is still called 'architecture'.

Of the uselessness of trying to save anything from the past which ranks in importance only second (or third or fourth or fifth or sixth) to such 'priorities' as widening a road for 'essential traffic', I have only too humiliating an experience.

Nor was it even a Roman relic that I was trying to save: merely a 1620 house and thirteenth-century arch – the latter, the last surviving fragment of the vast Priory of Holy Trinity, founded by Queen Matilda, wife of Henry I, in 1108, and 'dissolved' by Henry VIII in 1531. By one of those strange accidents, the gate of the Lady Chapel, which led to the yard of the Mitre Inn in 1746 (Rocque's map shows it), had been built into the rear wall of the Smyrna Restaurant, where I ate rich Greek food before the war. A fire gutted the Smyrna, but still left the arch intact. I wrote to the Lord Mayor, on May 23, 1967, suggesting that the arch be preserved, and giving my reasons. A passage or two from the Town Clerk's answer will sufficiently indicate the fate inevitable for such letters as mine:

4th July, 1967

Dear Sir,

Entrance Arch of the Lady Chapel of the Priory of Holy Trinity Church [sic] *and 72 Leadenhall Street.*

Your letter of the 23rd May, addressed to the Lord Mayor, with suggestions for the preservation of the above properties, has been laid before the Improvements and Town Planning Committee.

The Committee consider that in regard to the entrance arch, the arch has no great architectural significance, and further, is not listed as being of architectural or historic interest under Section 32 of the Town and Country Planning Act, 1962. I understand, however, that the arch is to be recorded by the Museum staff prior to demolition and may be commemorated by a plaque at a later date.

The Committee sympathizes with the suggestion to remove

the façade of 72 Leadenhall Street to a site in Aldgate High
Street, but it is the view of the Corporation's officers that the
timber elements of this façade may[1] not stand such removal.
The site in Aldgate High Street is much wider than the
present site, and structural problems could arise in obtaining
a satisfactory 'graft' on to existing façades.

72 Leadenhall Street is listed as Grade III under Section
32 and therefore not likely to be preserved, in that buildings
within this Grade are considered to have little intrinsic value.[2]

The Aldgate High Street site forms part of the Haydon
Square redevelopment area at present under consideration,
and accordingly will be required for development purposes
in due course.

May I assure you that the Corporation does take steps to
help in preserving buildings in the City in appropriate cases
but the Committee do not feel they would be justified in
carrying out the proposals suggested by you in this instance.

Yours faithfully,
(Signed)
Town Clerk

In restoring Roman London to a detailed reality, however,
we do not need even a momentary glance at, or assessment of,
a few feet of crumbling wall – momentarily spared from the
bulldozer's all-obliterating surge. So long as the names of
London survive, if only in the written record, we have the
means, as I shall show, to restore Londinium to a living reality,
as not even the most inspired of traditional archaeologists could
do. Nothing remains today of Londinium save a few Roman
crypts and basements: St Bartholomew-the-Great, St Mary-le-
Bow, St Etheldreda, a subterranean room on Tower Hill
– a handful of other buried chambers, of which one (St Mary-
le-Bow) may be a Roman stipendiary magistrate's court.
Above ground: a few feet of London wall, the remains of a
bastion at Newgate, the remains of a *castellum* at Cripplegate,
another on Tower Hill, not much in all.

---

[1] Their word, not mine!
[2] 'Little intrinsic value.' I pleaded for this perfectly preserved house because, a
'jutty' building of the type condemned and forbidden to be built following the Act
of 1629, it had escaped every fire of London, including those of the war of 1939–45.

On the other hand, in the hundreds of London names is the rich evidence of the buried but not irrecoverable City of Londinium Augusta.

When I was a boy, Christmas crackers used often to contain what were apparently blank sheets of paper, marked only with a small printed x. One got one's father or uncle to touch this x with the glowing tip of his cigarette, and lo! the paper would char . . . and then a tiny spark would move purposefully over the surface of the paper, tracing out a veritable likeness of Mr Lloyd George or General Pershing or Marshal Foch.

It seemed miraculous to a small boy, and indeed, in a manner of speaking, it was. Just so may we, upon the blank, un-Roman surface of modern London, let our light trace out the streets and buildings, forts and elaborate defensive works of that splendid city of which our dim, seedy formlessness is the lineal descendant; that Londinium Augusta which had hardly ceased being a completely Roman city when, in 839, Bishop Helmstan of Winchester told how he had been consecrated 'in the illustrious place, built by the skill of the ancient Romans, called throughout the world the great city of London'.

Let us now examine, for the first time in over a thousand years, the topography of that 'illustrious place'.

Chapter I
The problem of
London's 'disappearance'

So far as the historical record is concerned, the last *surviving* mention of London as a Roman city, A.D. 457 and its first mention as a 'Saxon' city in 597 leaves a gap of 140 years to be explained away.

In the explaining, two principal schools of opinion have made themselves heard. The first holds that, after the battle of Crecganford (almost certainly Crayford, in Kent), the 'Saxons' captured, sacked and emptied London – the 'evidence' for the supposed desertion resting on the somewhat negative 'proof' supplied by an almost complete absence of 'Saxon' remains amongst the antiquities dug out of the London soil. This school of opinion believes that, following the visit of Augustine to the court of Aethelberht, King of Kent, the 'Saxons', returning to a ruined, deserted London, were forced to – and did, in fact – build London anew. It follows, of course, that they had to find street and district names for a city whose original Roman names had vanished from men's memory.

The acceptance of this theory that modern London is a 'Saxon' restoration of a Roman city which had almost ceased to exist necessarily imposes the corollary theory that all the older London names – save for a few which are 'demonstrably Celtic' – are Anglo-Saxon in origin. It is the acceptance of the theory that London began anew with the 'Saxons' which has inspired such scholars as E. Ekwall to trace all such older London names to Anglo-Saxon originals. As I shall show, in the course of this book, the originals of most of the older London names are Latin – but I shall return to this subject later.

The other school of opinion – of which, perhaps, the late Sir

Lawrence Gomme was the most distinguished representative –
holds that London did *not* fall after the defeat of the Londoners
at Crecganford in 457. *The Anglo-Saxon Chronicle* states clearly
that the defeated Londoners 'fled to London'.

This other body of opinion holds further that, not only did
London not fall to the 'Saxon' invaders, but that, further, it
preserved its characteristic Roman culture – and Gomme and
others point to the inferences to be drawn from Pope Gregory's
reference to Londoners, in a letter to Augustine, as 'hostile to
Christianity', a significant remark which is elaborated by Bede
when he writes that the Londoners had 'their own High
Priest'. The Londoners, in fact, so resented the attempt to
impose Augustine's companion, Mellitus, on them as Bishop of
London, that they rose in considerable tumult, and sent
Mellitus packing back to Canterbury.

Behind her impregnable walls, so the alternative theory
goes, Roman Londinium preserved her Latin–Celtic culture,
and when the 'Saxons' did finally enter Londinium, a little
before 600, it was as friendly neighbours, now in solemn treaty
alliance with the independent city-state of Londinium Augusta.

I was faced – as many historians before me had been faced
– with the necessity of determining which of these two theories
was supported by the more convincing wealth of evidence. The
trouble seemed to be that there was so little evidence either
way. Then, by one of those happy accidents which, fortunately,
occur so often in research, I saw that there was not only much
evidence in favour of the theory of Roman London's survival,
but that the quantity – no less than the quality – of this evidence
completely demolished the opposing theory that between
Roman *Londinium Augusta* and 'Saxon' *Lundene Byrh* stands the
gap of a century-and-a-half of a ruined, deserted London in
which nothing happened, and in which every link with
London's imperial past had been broken. I saw that such an
opinion as that of the Royal Commission was no longer
tenable:

> 'The walled towns of the south-east, out of reach of the
> Picts and out of mind of the Saxons, may thus be thought to
> have lingered on almost as "reservations" for the secondary

Roman-British population. The silence of history in regard to them is probably just; London in the year 500 can have mattered little to anyone save a few decivilized sub-Roman Londoners'.

C. E. Vulliamy is even more positive that nothing remained – he does not even concede 'sub-Romans', but imagines a ruined London in which a few *sub-human* squatters share the ruins with foxes and wolves.

We may say good-bye for ever to these theories: I shall, in this book, show that *the majority* of the older London names demonstrably survive from the times of the Roman Empire, and prove – especially by their impressive numbers – that Roman London triumphantly survived both the departure of the Eagles and the coming of the Sons of Woden.

The survival of Latin names *from every part* of London can mean only that these names were in continuous and unbroken use, and this can mean only that we may claim for London an equally uninterrupted continuity of existence – certainly an existence unbroken by those mysterious 'Lost Years'.

Here I shall anticipate a later chapter of this book, and give one typical example of what may be done in getting a modern London name to yield up the secrets concealed in its true meaning. But before I go on to give this example, I cannot stress too strongly what I have said before, that, in finding the Latin originals in the modern London names, I have used only *fully attested etymological principles* to be found in the works of such distinguished etymologists, philologists or historical phonologists as Loth, Morris-Jones, Grandgent, K. Jackson, J. Baudiš, R. Thurneysen, A. Pogatscher, K. Luick, C. G. Rice, Max Förster, etc. I must emphasize that I have invented no theory of word and/or sound development to provide myself with a convenient method by which my own arguments might be supported. So let me return to the example, but once again stressing that *all* the classic rules of etymology and phonology have been strictly observed by me.

Cannon Street is one of the City of London's principal thoroughfares, and is known to millions more than the City workers who use its railway terminus each day. Because

Cannon Street was once known as 'Candlewick Street', the more fanciful school of etymologists have invoked the theory that this street was formerly a centre of the candle-making business. Let us, using our new tool of Etymological-Archaeology, see just what the origin of 'Cannon Street' is.

Our method, in this and all other cases, demands that we find, in old charters and other sources of information, the earliest forms of the name that we examine. London, it is apparent, began to lose its strongly Roman character at the period of the Danish invasions, and the earliest recoverable forms of our London names are necessarily separated by some centuries from any recognizably Latin originals.

Nevertheless, by going back over a thousand years, we can recover forms of the names separated from Latin originals by not more than, say, three or four hundred years, and so that much less altered that the modern forms of the names.

Let us see now what happened to the original Latin words which lie behind that familiar modern name, Cannon Street.

The earliest forms of the name, as recorded, with their dates, are as follows:

Candelwrichstrete	1180–7
Candelwrichtestrate	*circa* 1200
Candewyllestrate	*circa* 1200
Candelwrithestrate	1190

and so on, the changing name developing to:

Candelwiccestrate	1259
Canwynstrete	*temp*. Henry VIII
Canninge Street	*temp*. Elizabeth I
Candlewright Street	17th century
Candlewicke Street	

Observe, first, that the form, 'Candlewick' (i.e. 'Candelwiccestrate') is not encountered before 1259, whilst 'Candlewright' is an earlier form surviving into the seventeenth century.

Let us sum up the inferences to be derived from a study of the changes which have overtaken the original name – changes that we can study *only* over the past eight hundred years and from a form which had already moved considerably away from its origin.

a. The name cannot be derived from Latin *candela*, 'candle', since we know what happened to this word in the mouths of the Celtic-speaking population of Britain. *Candela* developed into *canuill*, *canvil*, etc., in Old Welsh – the language that the majority of Roman London's inhabitants spoke.

b. Dickens records the survival (on Mrs Gamp's lips) of an alternative London pronunciation to 'candle' – i.e. 'cangle'.

c. It is attested that Latin *cancellarius* developed into British (Old Welsh) *cangellawr*. An alternative London pronunciation to this appears to have been, *candellawr* – see Mrs Gamp's pronunciation, above.

d. We may now, with some confidence, trace the origins of the earliest form of the name which has come down to us, i.e. Candelwrich (strete):

$$Candelwrich < Candelawr\text{-}'ic < Cangellawr \ wic$$

The last clearly derived from a Latin original: *cancellarius vicus* – 'the fenced-off area', 'the boundary district', 'the out-of-bounds area'.

e. The name makes it clear that the Dowgate 'dock' area – lying at the back of the present Cannon Street Railway Station – with its customs-house (St Mary Bothaw, as I shall explain later), quays, etc., was fenced-off from the 'Town' proper, and that the original Cannon Street was a road which bordered the northern side of this 'restricted area', access to which was to be had (as is at present the case with the London Docks) only by 'duly authorized personnel'.

To give every derivation in such detail would prove tedious to most readers, and the pedigree of London names will be given fully only in exceptional cases. However, representative derivations will be found in the Appendix.

Before we turn back to the origins, not of London names, but of my theory, we should note here that this examination of the name 'Cannon Street' has clearly demonstrated what such study is capable of yielding. We have, in this one example, not only revealed the presence of a 'fenced-off' dock area at

45

Dowgate and the estuary of the Walbrook, *of a size not previously suspected*, but we have also had a strong hint that the great Hanseatic mercantile headquarters on the Thames, the 'Steelyard', was merely the inheritor of an important dock-and-wharfage complex which had existed at Dowgate since Roman times.

There were at least two other *cancellarii vici*, 'walled-off areas', and from their position, taken in conjunction with that of the Dowgate *cancellarius vicus* (Cannon Street), we may, again with some confidence, suppose that there was a pattern of these *cancelarii vici* which disposed them all around the 'federated' City, even though the memory of each *cancellarius vicus* has not always survived in a modern London name.

Incidentally, we may observe, in taking note of two other *cancellarii vici*, that their names, surviving into modern English, clearly support my contention that dialectal differences of speech obtained even within the narrow limits of Roman London, though it is just possible that the different forms that Latin words take when surviving into modern English may be due, not to dialectal differences, but to the fact that the same word was adopted into London Latin at different periods – cf. modern English 'penthouse' and 'appendix'; the former is the Latin word *appendix*, adopted into medieval English through early French; the latter, the same Latin word, adopted unaltered at the time of the English Renascence. My own opinion, however, is that the different forms, surviving in modern English, of words originally Latin, are evidence of the use, in Roman London, of dialects as markedly different as those which, in the London of up to 1939, distinguished the speech of, say, Grosvenor Square from that of the Whitechapel Road.

Now, just as the Latin word *mul(c)ta*, 'customs-house, douane', appears as the English names, Botolf, Botolph, Bottle, Bothaw and Bolt, so does the Latin phrase, *cancellarius vicus* take on at least three distinct forms.

We have already seen that it has produced, in our own times, 'Cannon Street'; but *cancellarius vicus* has also, over the centuries, become both 'Chancery Lane' and 'Chandler's Rents'. In the first case, the change from *cancellarius vicus* has not been so great as that which altered *cancellarius vicus* to 'Cannon Street'; in the second, the change, though less than that which produced 'Cannon Street', is more than that which produced 'Chancery Lane'.

Mediæval references to Chancery Lane (Chauncelleres Lane, 13 Ed. III; le Chaunceler Lane, 7 Ric. II; Chaunsler Lane, 6 Hen. VIII, etc.) should always be taken in conjunction with references to 'Chanceleresdich', apparently an embanked tributary of the Fleet River, in what is now Holborn.

One reference, quoted by Harben, is most important: 'Land of Simon fab' (i.e. Simon Smith) in parish of St Andrew Holborn, extending from '*fossatum quod vocatur*' Chancelleres dich '*versus ecclesiam conversorum*' south, to Symon's (*sic*) house north, 31 perches in length (511½ feet).

The '*ecclesia conversorum*' – Church of the Converts – was part of an establishment for the shelter and support of converted Jews, which stood where the Rolls Chapel was later, and where the Record Office stands today. The *fossatus quod vocatur Chanceleres dich*, 'the ditch called 'Chanceleres'' ', was apparently the western boundary of the street from which modern Chancery Lane has developed, or perhaps it would be more correct to say that the origin of Chancery Lane was a street (or, may be, only a footway) which ran along the eastern bank of the embanked 'ditch' or *fossa* (*fossatum* is the medieval form) joining then, as it does today, Holborn and the Strand. It is also highly significant that an alternative name to 'Chanceleres dich' was 'Doge[1] brook'; the significance becoming apparent, not when we consider that 'Took's-court' is a small turning off nearby Cursitor Street, but when we consider that both 'Doge' and 'Took's' are almost certainly derived from the Latin *dux*, properly a lieutenant-general, a general of division, but used, in the later days of the Empire, to mean a general officer of even higher rank: what we should now call a 'full general'. The word *dux* has become in Italian both *duca* and *doge*; and something very similar seems to have happened in London Romance, where *dux* has yielded both *Took's* and *Doge*.

What, then, we must assume for the origin of present-day Chancery Lane is the name of a western *cancellarius vicus* – a

[1] The 'g' is hard. The word sounded like 'dogger'.

47

'walled-off area' – which lay at the edge of the *pomoerium* centred about 'Temple Bar', and whose defensive function is apparent, first from the fact that the *cancellarius vicus* included an embanked stream ('Chanceleres dich'), and second from the fact that the military establishment of a Roman general was to be found adjacent to the stream. It is plain that the *cancellarius vicus* of 'Chancery Lane' was a 'restricted area' over which the *dux* had complete authority.

Elsewhere we shall see that the gate to the City, which we now call Temple Bar, had a bath, a restaurant and a bank, as well as the expected customs-house, attached. And that the peculiar military character of this City entry survived until long after London had ceased to be a Roman city is evident from the fact that it was still open – that is, unbuilt-upon – land when the Knights Templar, over six hundred years after the Battle of Crayford, took it over as their *manège*, small arms school and archery ground.

A name alternative to both Chanceleres Lane and Doge Brook appears in records from about 1200 onwards. This is 'Newstrete' (1227). Medieval scribes had no doubt that they were translating correctly into Latin when they wrote, for instance, 'In "novo vico" called in English "Newstrete" ' (1232), and in the reign of Edward I, there is a reference to a tenement 'Novâ Stratâ' (in New Street). All the same, the alternative name is not derived from Latin *novus* or *nova*, 'new', but from *novalis*, 'ploughed land, meadow', – for the entry at 'Temple Bar' marked the western limit of the city, beyond which the *territorium*, with its kitchen-gardens and grazing grounds extended.

The other *cancellarius vicus* whose former existence we can assume through the survival of its name, is witnessed by the name of a small alley, running west out of Addle Hill (*vicus aedilicius*, 'Aedile Street') at No. 7, opposite Knightrider Street, to Wardrobe Court and St Andrew's Hill, in Castle Baynard Ward. The Wardrobe (see page 193) was, of course, the successor, under the English kings, of the western *fiscus*, the senior Imperial Treasury of London. The name of this small alley – preserving the memory of an original *cancellarius vicus* – is Chandler's Rents. Hatton calls the alley 'Church Hill or

Chandler's Rents', but in Rocque the two names belong to distinct streets: the east-west street being named 'Church Hill', whilst the north-south street is called 'Chandler's Rents'.

'Chandler's' is plainly just another *cancellarius vicus*, and this 'strictly reserved area' obviously stood in relation to the Blackfriars 'River Fort' as the Cannon Street *cancellarius vicus* stood to the port of Dowgate.

As 'Blackfriars' *militaris thesaurus* ('Military Treasury') served, amongst other important Roman London institutions, both the Imperial Treasury of west London and the Forum Boarium, with its important public offices, we may well assume that the 'Chandler's Rents' *cancellarius vicus* ranked above that of the Cannon Street 'restricted area'.

Though I have not yet been able to identify, by means of a modern name, any of the other *cancellarii vici* of Londinium, the certain discovery of three attested districts of this type at 'key' places – a western City entry and two docks – gives us leave to feel sure that Roman practice, at least so far as London was concerned, was to establish a *cancellarius vicus* at all or most of the 'key' places of the 'federation' City.

No better example could be found than a *cancellarius vicus* at Cannon Street to demonstrate how traditional archaeology and the new 'etymological archaeology' may assist each other in arriving at the historical facts of London.

Here is what traditional archaeology has to say about the area that I have stated to have been a *cancellarius vicus*, a 'strictly reserved area', much of whose contents – and something of whose constructional nature – we may recover from the evidence of street names within this area. I quote from *The Roman City of London* (London, Ernest Benn, 1965) by Ralph Merrifield, a 'scholarly' yet immensely readable work for which I can find no superior in its class. Here is what Mr Merrifield, who is Assistant Director of the Guildhall Museum, has to say about my *cancellarius vicus*:

'A great structure which, from its size and the massive character of its walls, must have been an important public building, stood on the site of Cannon Street Station and

Bush Lane, but we have as yet no evidence of its nature. The discovery of numbers of tiles stamped PP. BR. LON on the site in 1868 suggests that some branch of the provincial government was concerned with its construction. Several wooden drains were found running beneath the foundations towards the river, and it is possible that this building also was a public bath-house, on a grander scale than is known elsewhere in London. It was set into the gravel slope of the river bank with its floors at different levels, and evidently had considerable architectural pretensions. A striking feature was the massive platform of ragstone and flint concerete, parallel with the river. The building was evidently not constructed before the Flavian period, for the cement floor of the large compartment to the north overlay a rubbish pit of that date. In 1964–5 . . . the plan of an east wing of quite a different character was recovered west of Suffolk Lane. This contained a series of small and uniform rooms between two corridors. It overlay pottery of the Flavian period, but apparently continued in use until late in the fourth century.'

It is evident, from this passage, that more than mere hints of the unusual character of the Cannon Street building complex had come to the archaeologists of the Guildhall Museum, as they excavated all about Cannon Street, Bush Lane and Suffolk Lane, and carefully noted what they found.

But, apart from the undeniable evidence of the name 'Cannon Street', with its obvious derivation from *cancellarius vicus*, there is the very important contributory evidence of the names of streets (or lanes, they are hardly more) within the 'reserved area'.

For instance, the Suffolk Lane mentioned in the passage quoted from Mr Merrifield is a Latin word which certainly confirms his archaeological deductions, made from the excavations on the site. Here we have a Latin word hardly altered over nearly two millenia: *suffultus*. And note, please, what this Latin word *suffultus* means! – 'propped underneath, propped up, to be supported, put under by way of support'. If this is not an allusion to the fact, noted by Mr Merrifield and his fellow-archaeologists, that this building 'was set into the gravel slope of the river bank at different levels', I do not know to what it could allude.

In the 'reserved area' there is a Martin Lane – a temple of Artemis, without doubt. There is a Ducksfoot Lane, of which the first part – Latin *dux*, 'general, military commander' – tells us that here, as in the *cancellarius vicus* at Temple Bar, the 'reserved area' was under the command of a military officer of general's rank. There is a Crooked Lane, which is modern English for Latin *via cruciata*, 'street of Torture', which, taken in conjunction with the fact that Laurence Pountney Lane, once the site of the *lautumiae poenitationis*, 'Convicts' Prison', is adjoining, clearly marks the 'reserved area' as one in which the Roman government exercised its harsher functions.

The presence of a Miles Lane indicates the presence of a riverside market, for 'Miles' is the very corrupted form of Latin *macellum*, 'a market', through a medieval form *myghel*.

Mr Merrifield is right indeed to suggest that 'some branch of the provincial government was concerned' with the establishment of this 'reserved area'.

In passing, it should be noted that Cannon Street, whose original course was the northern boundary of the *cancellarius vicus*, follows exactly the line of the Roman street, and even total modern rebuilding of the site has quite failed to obliterate, on the map, the regularly rectangular outline of this important area which was built immediately to the east of the Walbrook, and obviously in intimate relation with a tributary of the Thames along which, and along whose own tributaries, boats could move to all parts of Roman London.

But hear further what Mr Merrifield has to say about another area that our new 'etymological archaeology' has identified, on the evidence of the modern name, as a *cancellarius vicus*. I refer to the *cancellarius vicus* whose memory is preserved in the name of the small alley, Chandler's Rents, which runs from Addle Hill, *opposite* Knightrider Street, to Wardrobe Court and St Andrew's Hill.

Again I quote from Mr Merrifield:

'Equally puzzling is the mysterious long wall of Knightrider Street, which extended for at least 400 feet, and probably for more than 580 feet, cutting through the filled-in gravel quarries of an area which seems to have contained few buildings. The foundations had in places been laid in a boarded trench, for impressions of the vertical timbers have been observed. The wall was of ragstone with some courses of tiles, and was pierced in two places by brick culverts for the passage of water. No trace of any transverse wall adjoining it has ever been seen, *so it seems more likely to have been a boundary or precinct wall than part of a large building'.* (My italics.)

'Here, then,' adds Mr Merrifield, 'are two structures, obviously of importance, which cannot yet be identified. . . .'

Before this book is finished, I trust that we shall have gone far towards identifying, by our new archaeological discipline, this and many other sites.

It is yet too early to embark upon the complete re-mapping of the imperial city of Londinium Augusta . . . but we have made a good start. Normal archaeology – in this case, that of Professor Grimes – has already told us that on the river, The Walbrook, which bounded the east side of the Cannon Street *cancellarius vicus*, a temple of Mithras stood. Our new archaeology, as we shall see, will supply the names of many other London gods.

Chapter II
The Birth of a Theory

It was in the early part of 1964 that work on my book, *London Growing*, came to a halt, so that I could decide which of the two possibilities – London sacked by the victorious troops of Hengest and Aesc, after the battle of Crecganford in 457; or London, embattled but secure from assault behind its massive and (in the result) impregnable fortifications – I must adopt in continuing the history of London's development.

I have already explained that it had occurred to me that, could it be proved that Latin names in London had survived in any considerable numbers, this would be strong evidence for London's having preserved her life throughout the 'Lost Years', 457–597. On the other hand, I had never encountered London names which had struck me forcibly with their 'Latinity', save for one or two, such as Oystergate, at London Bridge – which seemed to echo Latin *ostium*, 'entrance, gate, etc.' – and Cloak Lane, whose resemblance to Latin *cloaca*[1], 'drain, sewer, etc.' had been remarked upon by an eighteenth-century reader of the *Gentleman's Magazine*.

I therefore turned to a study of the older London name in a most open frame of mind. I was not seeking evidence to support an attractive theory that I had decided to adopt; I was merely seeking something which should guide me in choosing between two opinions in regard to London's past.

I decided to begin my search for surviving Latin names – which, if found, would, I realized, be in deceptively English guise – in a part of the City of London that archaeology, after the end of the 1939–45 war, had conclusively shewn not only to be of Roman foundation, but also to have been constructed

---

[1] *kloak* is modern Swedish for 'water-closet'.

by Celtic London's imperial masters quite early in the Roman occupation. I refer to the so-called 'Cripplegate Fort', about which a few words must be said.

The bombing of the Cripplegate area of the City during the war made it possible for archaeological research to uncover a citadel of early date in the north-west corner of Londinium. What made this discovery doubly interesting was the fact that the citadel had been built before – and obviously independently of – the walls which enclosed the habitable area of Londinium, variously estimated to lie between 350 acres (Gordon Home) and 380 acres (Henry Harben).

Careful excavation by experts from the Guildhall Museum and elsewhere made it clear that the Romans, probably in the period soon after the rising of Boudicca (Boadicea) in A.D. 61, but just possibly *before* the Queen of the Iceni sacked and burnt London, had built a small square fort in the area now bounded roughly by Noble Street, Falcon Street and Castle Square, on the west; by Hart Street, on the north; by Aldermanbury on the east; and by Love Lane on the south.

A glance at a map of London will shew that the typical Roman 'grid-iron' lay-out of the streets is still apparent in the present street-plan, where the northern half of Wood Street represents the original north–south main street – the *cardo*, 'hinge' – while Addle Street and Silver Street together form the original *decumanus maximus*, the principal east–west street.

The south–north street – the *cardo* – led to and emerged through the 'Cripplegate'; there should, therefore, be traces of other gates in Falcon Square, in Wood Street – by the church of St Alban – and in Aldermanbury, at the junction of Addle Street.

Evidences of the great antiquity of this 'first settlement' survived, in plain view, until fairly recent days. Strype speaks of the venerable age of St Alban's Church, and the buildings adjoining the present church's predecessor – rebuilt in 1634, it was burnt down in the Great Fire of 1666, and once again rebuilt, by Wren, in 1685 – were commonly supposed to have been the palace of King (whom Stow calls 'Saint') Athelstan, crowned at Kingston, September 4, 925.

Strype, calling attention to the undoubted antiquity of

St Alban's Church, remarked on 'the early work shewn in the building, the Roman bricks inlaid in the walls, the turning of the arches and the heads of the pillars'. This makes it seem probable that, if the original 'St Alban's Church' was not the converted south gate of the primitive Roman citadel of London, then it was constructed of materials from the gate. And it may be that the sharp curve north that the modern east-west street – Addle Street – takes on meeting Aldermanbury may be accounted for by an original blocking of the road, when the no-longer-used east gate of the citadel crumbled into a pile of stones and brick.

For it is no idle speculation which lets me state that both the east and south gates of the 'Cripplegate Fort' were eventually dismantled. We know that, much later on in the Roman occupation – I completely reject the theory that it was *after* the Roman occupation – the City was walled, the walling taking in the fort at Cripplegate. But we now have evidence, thanks to the new discipline of 'etymological archaeology', that the internal faces of the fort – that is, the east and south faces – were pulled down and replaced by *lilia*: Roman defensive devices whose purpose (and whose discovery by my archaeological method) will be explained later.

There is one exceedingly odd fact about the 'Cripplegate Fort', to which, by a regrettable oversight, I did not call attention in my book, *London Growing*. It is this.

If one looks at an old map of London – say, Norden's map of 1593 – one sees that the grid-iron lay-out of the fort to which I alluded on page 54 was little less deformed then than it is now. Silver Street and Addle Street curve and wind well away from their original straightness – evidently the warping of the streets in the original Roman 'grid-iron' is no modern happening.

Yet, if one turns to the *Plan for Rebuilding London* that Wren prepared after the Great Fire, one may see that the master-architect has straightened out all the wavering streets and alleys of the 'Cripplegate Fort', restoring the original Roman straightness and making clear the grid-iron plan from which the present pattern is derived.

Now Wren was an antiquary of considerable attainments, in an age in which archaeology had hardly begun to assume the disciplines of academic research. His conclusions, drawn from the finding of cinerary urns under the ruins of Old St Paul's, may now – and happily – be confirmed by the evidence drawn from the name of an adjoining street.[1]

Did Wren, then, arrive at the conclusion that the Cripplegate area was originally laid out by Romans? Or were there still standing, in his day, sufficient remains of Roman structures to make the Roman origin of this area obvious?

I ask this question because I believe that there were Roman, or at least Romanesque, buildings which did survive in London to a remarkably late date, though whether they survived as late as Wren's time, I should not care to say.

But certainly it seems that there were buildings in the time of Elizabeth I which must have had their origin in a period before even the Norman. If you study carefully the famous London map of Ralph Agas, you must be struck by the 'classical' appearance of certain big buildings, especially in the neighbourhood of the Guildhall and the church of St Michael Bassishaw. These buildings cannot be displaying the neo-classicism of the Renascence, for, as far as we know, no classical architecture in England predates the uncertain classicism of John Thorpe – yet here, in the Agas map of the mid-sixteenth century, are undoubtedly buildings of classical architecture. If they were not classic in the manner of the Renascence, they must have been classic in the manner of the Romans of Londinium. Were they, in fact, Roman buildings which had survived? Or, to be more accurate, were they Roman buildings which had survived above ground, as there are Roman buildings surviving to this day which are below ground?

At any rate, Wren, whether by intuition or by archaeological deduction, or through his being possessed of information from a source now lost, 'corrected' the modern street-plan of the Cripplegate area, and restored to its lay-out its original Roman character.

A fascinating speculation arises from this fact that Wren restored the Roman character of the Cripplegate area in his plan for the rebuilding of London. Was Wren in possession of a

[1] Alsies Lane < *elysii campi*, 'burial ground'.

Roman map of Roman London – or, at least, a map from a time when London still retained the hardly altered street-plan of Londinium Augusta? I remember the words of an eminent New York dealer in rare manuscripts and printed matter, Mr Louis Feldman: 'Paper is the most fragile thing in the world – you can burn it, throw it away, let the water get at it, so it dissolves. Yet nothing survives as paper does. It lasts longer than stone or bronze . . . and when anyone tells me that a manuscript or book no longer exists in this world, I just go on looking, pretty confident that, sooner, or later, it'll turn up. *Nothing* lasts as paper does.'

Bronze or brass can, however, last pretty well – though the vulnerability of metals is due to the fact that they may serve so many more pressing purposes. Wars, with their need of metal, are most dangerous to the survival of metal objects – and only chance would have made a map, engraved on metal, survive from the days of Londinium to the days of Wren.

Perhaps there was a map on vellum, but there is another possibility: a stone carving or a mosaic in some ancient church. A marble map of the city was displayed in both Rome and Ostia. Had Londinium such a map – and if so, did Wren see it? It is impossible to say now *why* Wren restored Roman London in his plan to rebuild the City; we can only record the fact that he did – and wonder *why* he did.

It was at this area of undoubted Roman origin that I determined to search for Latin names, surviving to the present in their more familiar English garb.

The sounds of speech are constantly changing, even within a single lifetime, even within the experience of a single speaker. No man speaks exactly as his father spoke before him; no man, in his later years, speaks exactly as he spoke when young. On the other hand, changes are rarely individual: the changes belong to the mass of speakers as a whole, and it is this fact which enables us, in tracing the development of a word, to perceive that changes in pronunciation appear to follow ascertainable laws. What is even more important, we see that certain well-defined speech-habits will be transferred by a body of speakers from one language to another. To take but one example: when London was a Celtic-speaking city, its inhabitants had a trick of putting a violent accent on the first syllable of a word, and letting the unstressed remainder of the word wither away. It was in this way that the name Augustinus (St Augustine) became, first *Aug'stin'* and then *Au'stin*.

Happily, contemporary written evidence of this trick of pronunciation has survived. On a bonding tile, found in Warwick Lane, Newgate Street, and now to be seen in the Guildhall Museum, a disgruntled tile-maker once 'worked off his grouse' against a fellow tile-maker who, apparently, was not pulling his weight in the tileworks.

Written in well-formed 'rustic' uncials (proof of the high degree of literacy amongst Roman London's artisans) is this denunciation of a mate's 'lead-swinging':

AVSTALIS

DIBVS XIII

VAGATVR SIB[I]

COTIDIM

('Austalis has been clearing off on his ownsome every single day this past fortnight.')

There are two evidences here of London speech-idioms: the first is that the name 'Augustalis', which in this context we may translate 'Londoner', has been contracted to 'Austalis', the intervocalic G of 'Augustalis' having been first softened to a glottal stop (as used by the modern Cockney) and then elided altogether; the second is that *sibi* ('by himself, on his ownsome') has been contracted to *sib'*. The decay of the final syllables contributed importantly to the unique character of Latin words adopted into Brittonic.

This trick of accentuation was carried over from the Celtic-speaking London to the Anglo-Saxon-speaking London, and, indeed, is a characteristic of London speech to this day.

Another trick of pronunciation, common amongst the Celts of fifteen hundred years ago, and still a marked characteristic of Celtic speech-habits, was the trick of changing an M, whenever it fell between two vowels, to a sound[1] which is written V in

---

[1] Phonologists represent it by the Greek letter β (beta).

58

Breton, F in Welsh, and which – as we shall see – is represented by B, F or V in some of the names in London which have come down to us from our Roman past.

It is not my intention to confuse the reader by attempting to introduce a short course in etymology and phonology within my account of how I re-mapped Londinium Augusta, but I do call the reader's attention to this so-called 'lenition of inter-vocalic M', for, in my search for surviving Roman London names, it has provided the most significant clues to the Latin words behind modern names.

It is as well here to recall the stages through which the names of Roman London have passed before reaching their present stage of development. But first of all, it is important to note the initial stage of that development: *Latin words, given a provincial pronunciation by local officials, and then pronounced by the Celtic-speaking Londoners as though they were Celtic words.*

Fortunately, as I have said, we know a great deal of what happened to Latin words introduced into the vocabulary of Celtic-speaking peoples – especially of those Latin words which were adopted by that Brittonic speech which has developed into Modern Welsh. So we know what happened to the Latin names in London when the Celtic-speaking Londoners pronounced them.

Here are some common Latin words – note how they were modified by being taken into Brittonic (or Old Welsh), *the native tongue* of the mass of London's inhabitants in the time of Roman rule.

Latin word	Meaning	Old Welsh
fuga	flight	*ffo*
agricola	husbandman	*aircol*
tribus	clan, Tribe	*tref*
columna	column	*colofn*
argentum	silver	*aryant*
arma	arms (military)	*arff*
signum	sign	*swyn*
civitatem	city	*ciwawd*
Romani	Romans	*Rufein* or *Rumein*
Caritatem	charity	*cardawt*

Latin Word	Meaning	Old Welsh
episcopus	bishop	escop
benedictio	blessing	bendith or bendigo
cera	wax (noun)	cwyr
sagitta	arrow	saeth
bucca	water-pot, mouth	boch
Dies Martis	Tuesday	Diu Maurth
saccus	purse	sach
vesper	evening	gosper
intervenio	intervene	athrwyn
Constantinus	Constantine	Custennhin
stabellum	stable	ystafell
mensis	month	mis
coxa	hip	coes
nuptialia	nuptials	neithiawr
imperator	field-marshal	{ amherawdr ymherawdr
descendo	descend	dyscynn
ascendo	ascend	escynn
templum	temple	temhyl
tempus	time	tymp
caldus	hot	call
solidus/sol' dus	shilling	swllt
vinum	wine	guin
verbum	word	berf (not gwerf)
memoria	memory	myfyr
testis	witness	test
abecedarium	horn-book	agwyðawr
stella	star	istwyll
Aegyptus	Egyptian	Aipht
Graeca	Greek (f.)	Groeg
sanctus	{ 'state property' holy (religious)	seith or sant
cocina	cook-shop	cegin
punctum	point	pwyth
colonia	{ self-governing town	colun
manica	sleeve (of a tunic)	maneg

Latin Word	Meaning	Old Welsh
piper	pepper	pubyr
diabolus	the devil	diawl or diefil
Aprilis	April	Ebrill
altus	high	alt
serpens	serpent	sarff
caseus	cheese	caws
scala	step, stairs	yscawl
porta	door	porth
portare	to carry	porth
fontana	fountain	finnaun
taberna	tavern	tafarn
calamus	pen	calaf
cubiculum	sleeping-room	cudigl
grex	crowd, gathering	gre, grega
gladius	sword	cledyf

Many of the speech-habits of these early Londoners have been carried over to a London which now speaks English and not Old Welsh, as I have pointed out. See, for instance, what happened to the Latin word *templum* in the above list.

The Londoner of, say, A.D. 500 pronounced it *temhyl* – and 'Gissa tiggid va Tem'l', says the Cockney of today, as he asks the booking-clerk for a ticket to Temple Station on the District Railway.

The list of Latin words given above demonstrates the principal Celtic idioms of pronunciation which have changed Latin words such as *monumentum* into Old Welsh *mynwent* – a pronunciation that London usage eventually developed into 'Fyfoot (Lane)'.

Without wishing to load on to the reader all the phonological rules governing the changes of Latin into Old Welsh, I still feel it important that the reader should be given the opportunity to observe the principal Celtic speech-characteristics affecting the alteration from Latin into Welsh. Here they are:

1. 'Lenition' of intervocalic M, which changes the M into a sound variously rendered by B, V or F when the M falls between two vowels. Note that the preceding vowel may belong to the preceding word. For instance, Breton *merc'h*,

'girl, daughter'; but *va verc'h*, 'my daughter, my girl', and not *ma merc'h*. Exceptions to this rule – e.g. *Diu Marth*, 'Tuesday', from Latin *Dies Martis*; 'Merthyr,' from Latin *martyrum*, are few and are governed by rules which need not concern us here.

2. Consistent dropping of the last syllable[1] – this causing an eventual dropping of what has then become the last syllable. This speech-habit has most important results. For instance, by dropping the final A of the word *arma*, a form *arm'* was created. But the untrilled R being ignored, the word *arm'* was considered to be *ā'm'*, and, if a vowel followed as the beginning of the next word, the M became intervocalic, and *a'm'* became – as it did become – *arff*, the M being 'lenited' to a spirant (i.e. the sonant became a spirant.) Eventually, the *arff* form of *arma* was used in all cases, whether or not the word was followed by a vowel.

3. Metathesis – the habit of inverting consonants or even syllables within a word – is a potent cause of word-change in all languages. From a *graffito* at Pompeii we have *lerinquas* written for *relinquas*, and all who speak English are familiar with the pronunciations, *articifer* and *ossifer* for *artificer* and *officer*, respectively. Examples from Old Welsh are Latin *axilla*, 'armpit', becoming Old Welsh *ascell*; Latin *verbum*, 'word', becoming Old Welsh *berf* (through an intermediate form, *verb'*); Latin *cavitatem*, 'emptiness', becoming Old Welsh *ciwawd* – the syllable AWI in the Latin word being inverted into the syllable IWA in the Old Welsh word.

4. Suppression of the nasal before a dental. This is a phenomenon common to all the Indo-European languages, and is governed by rules which are not needful to be detailed here. Examples from Old Welsh are Latin *pontem*, 'bridge, causeway', becoming Old Welsh *pot* (but note modern Welsh has restored the nasal in *bont*); Latin *contrarius* becoming Old Welsh *cythrawl*. As all other Indo-European languages, Old Welsh is not consistent in suppressing the nasal before the dental: e.g. Latin *planta* becomes Old Welsh *plant*. (This inconsistency is observable in English, where we have both *tenth* and *tithe*.)

[1] Cf *sibi* > sib', as noted on page 58.

5. Change of intervocalic G to a glottal stop,[1] with eventual near-elision of the stop. This is a speech habit to be found in many languages. It is characteristic of all the Scandinavian languages, and is particularly noticeable in modern London speech. A typical example from Old Welsh is Latin *sagitta*, 'arrow', becoming *saeth* in Old Welsh.

6. Consonant alternations – again common to most Indo-European languages. Typical, and important, examples are:

L/R alternation – e.g. Latin *contrarius*, Old Welsh *cythrawl* (compare Old French *lossignol*, Modern French *rossignol*, etc.)

K/T alternation – e.g. Latin *benedictio*, Old Welsh both *bendigo* and *bendith*; Latin *venalicium*, Old London both *wenlok* and *wulnoth*; Latin *Marc-us*, Old Welsh *Martel*. (Compare Old English *helpmake*, Modern English *helpmate*, etc.)

P also alternates with both T and K, as in all other Indo-European languages.

7. T, especially when intervocalic, is vocalized to D, as in modern Cockney and American-English – e.g. Latin *catena*, 'chain', Old Welsh *cadwyn* (Modern Breton, *chaden*); Latin *nota*, Old Welsh, *nod*. However, this is by no means a consistent feature of the change from Latin into Old Welsh, for very often the T is retained – e.g. Latin *paratus*, Old Welsh, *parawt*, whilst, seemingly almost as frequently, the T disappears altogether – e.g. Latin *fontana*, Old Welsh, *finnaun*; Latin *Antonius*, Old Welsh, Anhun.

8. Two Latin sounds which have aroused much controversy are V and C – the latter when it precedes E or I. From the evidence of such Old Welsh words as *kell* (Latin *cella*), *cegin* (Latin *cocina*) and *dyscynn* (Latin *descendo*), it would seem that C before either E or I was consistently pronounced as K in Roman Britain, whenever it occurred in a Latin word, but exceptions are found, e.g. *sarzin* < *sarcinarius*. The 'official' Roman-British pronunciation of Latin V is more difficult to determine, since it appears in Old Welsh words, taken from the Latin, as both F (Old Welsh *berf*, metathesized from *verb*' – for *verbum*) and GW (Old Welsh *guin*, Latin *vinum*;

---

[1] Cf Augustalis > Austalis, as noted on page 58.

Old Welsh *gwers*, Latin *versus*; Old Welsh *gwein*, Latin *vagina*). Thus it would seem that Latin v was pronounced – at least by the provincial British – with two sounds: one resembling our GW, the other resembling our consonantal w (or, to be more precise, initial WH, as the Scots pronounce it in such English words as *which*, *white*, *whether*, etc.). In London, as an inscription makes clear, v was sometimes pronounced as B.

9. Initial s in Latin became an aspirate – or rough breathing – in words adopted into Old Welsh; e.g.: Latin *Sabrina*, 'the Severn', Old Welsh *Hafrenn*; Latin *saliva*, Old Welsh *haliw*; but this remark applies only to Latin words adopted early into Old Welsh. Later, the Latin initial s was imported, unchanged, into Old Welsh; e.g.: Latin *scala*, Old Welsh *yscawl*; Latin *sc(h)ola*, Old Welsh *ysgol*; Latin *spolia*, Old Welsh *yspeil*; Latin *serpens*, Old Welsh *sarff*.

In the above highly synopsized account of the sound-changes undergone by Latin words imported into Brittonic (or Old Welsh), enough information has been given to enable the reader to follow the changes from Latin to Old Welsh – and to understand how it will be possible to deduce, from a modern London name, the probable original Latin form.

London Brittonic (or London Old Welsh) will, in future, be referred to here as 'Old London'. As my arguments develop, it will be noted that sound-changes in Old London do not always conform exactly to those established for the change from Latin to Old Welsh – but this is simply because Old Welsh has been minutely studied, whilst Old London has never been studied at all. (This book sees this highly localized form of the Brittonic or Old Welsh speech noticed for the first time.)

For instance, Old London differs from Old Welsh in that the former seems to be far more consistent in its lenition of inter-vocalic M – that is, the change of between-vowels M to a sound midway between a B and a v. For, where Old Welsh changes Latin *monumentum* into *mynwent* – with lenition only of the medial M – Old London has lenition of both initial and medial M: *fyfoot*.

There are also vowel mutations as a Latin word is adopted

into Old Welsh. A common one is the o/ɪ mutation, which means that stressed Latin o becomes stressed ɪ in Old Welsh; e.g. Latin *moneta*, Old Welsh *mynet* – later Old London *mint*; Latin *confessio*, Old Welsh *kyffes*; Latin *molis*, Old London *fill*. Other typical Celtic sound-mutations will be noted as they occur.

Now to return to my first search for Latin survivals amongst our London names.

Since, at the time, I accepted the findings of the London archaeologists, and believed that Roman London had had its origins, at least in the military sense, in the newly-discovered 'Cripplegate Fort', it was in this area, I reasoned, that the Roman names, if they had survived at all, would be likely to be found.

I did not use a modern map, preferring the 1677 London map of Ogilby and Morgan, not only because it is the result of the first really careful survey of the City by modern standards (Faithorne's map is good, but not up to the Ogilby and Morgan standard), but also because it contains a number of place-names which have either been altered or have been swept away. The Ogilby and Morgan map, in short, took me back three hundred years on the way to the London origins that I was seeking.

In 1677, both the walls and gates of London still stood, and many a tiny, obscure alley is shewn on the map that one would seek in vain today. I turned, with my magnifying glass, to the network of streets and lanes within the north-west angle of London's walls. I was looking for Latin words – or names which might once have been Latin words – amongst the familiar London names.

Several caught my eye, but I resolved to begin in as orderly a manner as I could: by going to what our modern archaeologists (but I remembered that Wren had agreed with them!) had stated to be the very centre of the original Roman citadel of London.

I sought the *decumanus maximus* of the small, square fort – that Via Principalis which is today represented by Addle Street and Silver Street: the principal east–west road of the Fort, just as

65

E

Wood Street follows (roughly) the line of the *cardo*, the principal north–south road.

Now something then did strike me – and that was the queer name, Addle Street, whose origin has usually been given as *aethel*, 'noble', and in a way this derivation is correct.

But – *pace* those opinions which hold that everything started with the Anglo-Saxons! – *aethel* itself, I believe, is but a 'Saxon' pronunciation of a Latin word; and this was the word that I thought I saw staring at me through the familiar English disguise: *aediles*. Was Addle Street, I asked myself, the only slightly altered Via Aedilicia – the Street of the Aediles?

For it was here, in the *decumanus maximus* of the citadel – in what we may well call the nerve-centre of the 'Cripplegate Fort' – that we should expect to find the mansion-house of the Aediles, the men in any Roman city 'whose business it was to maintain the streets and public buildings, and probably to exercise some control over private building enterprise'.[1]

For a first tentative dip, my net had fished up, I thought, a small but very promising haul. But if one swallow doesn't make a summer, then one likely-looking find doesn't establish a theory.

But what that find had done was this: it caused me to consider the organization of a Roman town – any Roman town – and recall the essential officials that one would expect to find running it.

Now the body – corresponding to our borough or city council – which actually ran a Roman town was the *ordo*[2], and here – yes! well within the fort – was Oat Lane. Was I on the right track? Let me try to find the recollection of an almost equally important Roman organization: the *annona*.

The *praefectus annonae* of any Roman town or city of the Empire was a state-appointed official whom we may call Director of Food Supplies – especially of the food issued free to those for whom the state felt bound to make provision.

I wondered if the various churches dedicated to 'St Anne' – but particularly the church of St Anne, Gresham Street, near the Guildhall – preserved the name of the various offices of the *praefectus annonae*, scattered through the Roman city of Lon-

[1] Gordon Home, *Roman London*.   [2] *Ordo amplissimus*, 'Senate'.

dinium? An argument from accepted etymology could, I felt, be honestly used here to support my belief that 'St Anne' derived from the institution of the *annona*.

The argument is this. In Late Latin, a new genitive form was created, in popular usage, for various short words (mostly disyllables) ending in A. Thus, for the classical Latin genitive of *scriba*, 'scribe, writer' – i.e. *scribae* – Late Latin coined a new genitive, *scribanis*, which generated a new nominative/accusative, *scribanem*, which is the origin of modern French *écrivain*.

Amongst the words provided with the new genitive form was the name Anna, revered amongst the (pagan) Romans as that of Anna Perenna, a personification of the Eternal Year, whose festival was celebrated on the Ides of March (15th) – that is, the first day of full moon in the new year, as the Romans reckoned time. *Anna*, the genitive of whose name in classical Latin is *Annae*, got the new genitive, '*Annanis*' – and it is easy to understand how, even in Roman times, *annanis* would have become confused in the popular mind with *annonae*, so that the 'free hand-out' of the Annona became credited to the goddess of plenty, Anna Perenna, and the offices of the *præfectus annonae* might well have come to be thought of – or even, literally, to have become, shrines of Anna Perenna: *fani annanis*, Shrines of 'St Anne'.

There were, as I looked, several other names which hinted, in their form, at a Latin origin. The other half of Addle Street, for instance, is now called Silver Street; but two early forms of the same name, 'Selvernestrate' (the first recorded mention, *temp*. Edward I) and 'Syrverstret' (1440), might, I thought, have echoed an original Via Severina, named, perhaps, in allusion to the Curator (Treasurer of the Municipium) who had his office there, after one of two Emperors – Severus I or Alexander Severus II – who put a Curator in charge of the municipal senate, and thus struck the death-blow to Roman free institutions.

Two church-names in the 'Cripplegate Fort' area interested me: St Alban's and St Agnes. Now, respecting the former, it should be recalled that all metals, under the Roman Empire, were the property of the state, and it is possible that this 'saint's name' – 'St Alban's' – is made up of the Celtic word for 'tin', *stannum* (which would have become *stan*' in London speech) and the Latin synonym, (*plumbum*) *album*. '*Stan*'-*album*' might have yielded a later 'saint-alban'. If this theory seems a little far-fetched, it has a curious support in the fact that a variant from of *stannum* was *stagnum*, and that our second church, St Agnes, was an equally ancient church of the Cripplegate district. Indeed, to add further confirmation, St Agnes was often called St Ann & St Agnes, a name in which one would have to be very deaf not to hear the echo of both *stannum* and *stagnum*. Were the churches the descendants of the warehouses in which the Cornish tin was stored in Londinium's citadel? *Stannum* is also echoed in nearby Staining Lane.

All the same, however hinting of ultimate success these apparent echoes of Latin names were, my honesty had to compel me to admit that so far I had found nothing but hints and echoes. I was still, apparently, far from that positive proof by which my theory must stand.

However, when I turned my attention to the name 'Cripplegate' itself, and to the name of nearby Golden Lane, I began to feel myself on firmer ground.

What I needed, though, to prove my theory, were names which did not merely lend themselves to being 'turned back' into Latin names, but names which, when they had yielded their Latin origin, plainly named some plausible object, street or district *in a plausible place*. Such possible derivations as 'Via Severina' from a thirteenth-century 'Selvernestrate' would not prove anything, for there is nothing in the nature of the *decumanus maximus* of the 'Cripplegate Fort' to make it imperative that it was named 'Via Severina'. In truth, it could have been called anything.

Stow, who liked legends – and the more fanciful, the more he liked them – tells us that Cripplegate was so-called because of the cripples who congregated about it. Why they should have gathered more thickly about that gate than about London's other gates, Stow does not say. He simply gives us the legend, and expects us to be as satisfied with it as he appears to be.

Unfortunately, persons expecting much greater respect as historians have perpetrated legends concerning the derivation of 'Cripplegate' quite as fanciful as that of Stow. We need not concern ourselves with such other legends.

The original Latin name of the gate that we now call Cripplegate can be found, very little altered, in that part of the *Laws of Æthelred, c.* 978–1016, entitled *De Institutis Lundonie*, where 'Ciryclegate' – or the first part of the name, rather – seems to be an only slightly modified pronunciation of *circlus*, a contracted form of Latin *circulus*, but a form attested in Vergil, nonetheless.

The name, therefore, means no more than 'The Round Gate', or, more exactly (since *circlus* is a noun, and not an adjective) 'The Ring'.

Nearby Golden Lane once had a name which gives strong support to the supposition that the 'Cripplegate Fort' was originally an isolated citadel. Now called Golden Lane as being 'nicer' than Sucking Lane, this street, connecting Barbican and Old Street, was once known as 'Soukinge Lane', a name which clearly betrays its Latin origin.

A glance at the map shews Soukinge Lane (Golden Lane) as a way which was apparently an extension of the line, running due north, of the western wall of the 'Cripplegate Fort'.

Stow – and here we have no reason to disbelieve him – says that Soukinge Lane marked the City boundaries by the 'City posts' – a theory to which the name 'Goldīg Wellestrete' in a St Paul's deed of 1217–43 may give some support, if 'welles' refers to an ancient *lilium* fortification – 'welles' being synonymous with 'lily pots', to which we shall come presently.

However, to return to 'Soukinge', the name preserves the original pronunciation with remarkable fidelity. *Succingulum*, 'a girdle, a belt', is hardly altered in 'Soukinge Lane'. The fact that, in later times, the City boundary was marked by Soukinge (Golden) Lane sufficiently confirms the original form of the name as *succingulum*, 'the girdle' (of the City).

Passing over, for the moment, such highly suggestive names as Aggett's Lane (? *equites*, 'the Knights'), Figstrete, Fig-Tree Alley and Fig-Tree Court (? the *vicarius*, whose palace we might expect to find in Cripplegate Ward) and St Olave (? Latin *ulva*, 'sedge' – cf. one of the names of St Ann(e)'s:

'St Anne in the Willowes'), I come now to what was the first piece of really convincing proof yet to reward my search: that now vanished alleyway called 'Lilypot Lane', which lay at the south of the 'Cripplegate Fort'.

Lilypot Lane runs west out of Staining Lane to No. 7 Noble Street, in Aldersgate Ward. It follows roughly the line of the southern wall of the 'Fort', either along the outer face of the wall or along the inner. (But most probably outside the wall's face.)

Though the name of the lane south of the Fort and in the other similarly-named lane in Aldgate Ward is written as one word, 'Lillipot', in earlier occurrences it is spelt as two words, *Lily Pot*, *Lillye Potte*, the latter form preserving the original Latin pronunciation in a truly remarkable way.

For 'Lily Pot' – better still, 'Lillye Potte' – was originally *ad* LILII *pontem*: 'where you cross the sunken *chevaux-de-frise*'.

First, the word *lilium*. As used by Caesar, it means a 'sort of fortification, consisting of rows of pits [?"welles"], in which were driven stakes, sharp at the top and rising only four inches above the ground'. *Pons*, of course, means not only 'a bridge to cross a river', but any other kind of device by which men may cross – thus *pons* may be a gang-plank, a cutting through an embankment (as we shall see when we come to Philpot Lane) or even a floor in a tower. The *lilii pons* which gave the Lillye Potte Lane of later days its name was obviously some sort of bridge – swing? draw? – by which one might cross in safety the ha-ha planted with sharp stakes – those vicious spikes that Roman military humour (never of the most subtle type[1]) called 'the lilies'.

It is curious how closely the later form, Lillye Potte, follows the Latin *lilii* (pronounced *lil'ye* – with consonantal Y). 'Potte', of course, is simply Latin *pontem* (accusative case of *pons*), with the N nasalized before T – as we noted on page 62 and the final '-em', as was usual in post-Republican Latin and always in London Latin, so lightly pronounced as to be unheard.

Now the finding of this *lilium* defence to the south of the Fort – indeed, along its southern wall – is of extraordinary

---

[1] The zareba of thorn-bushes and brambles, thrown around a temporary encampment, was known to these rough lads as 'Grandma's pudenda'.

importance, for many reasons. In the first place, because one might well expect to find a *lilium* in that position – that is, following the line of a wall – here is strong confirmation that our derivation of Lillye Potte from (*ad*) *lilii pontem* is at least probable. In the second place, it enables us to state something of the relationship between the Celtic people of Londinium and their Roman masters. In this way.

Either the *lilium* defence was a substitute for the wall or an addition to it. The latter seems unlikely, for whilst the citadal was completely walled, it would have been encircled not with a *lilium*, but with a wide ditch – the *fossa* (*fos*, in London British), the remains of which, some 11 feet wide, have been found on the northern face of Cripplegate.

What I think happened was this: when the north-western and south-eastern corners of the 'Cripplegate Fort' were joined to the wall encircling London, the original southern wall (and possibly the eastern wall also) were demolished, either wholly or in part. The *castrum*, however, though now unwalled (its two outer walls being now included within London Wall), was still kept separate from the rest of enclosed London by means of a ditch of stakes. The memory of this separate citadel, which survived to medieval times – 'In this year [886] *gesette* Alfred *Lundenburh* and gave the *burh* (translated into Latin as *arcem*, i.e. citadel) to Aethered the ealdorman to hold' – was strong enough to transmit many more evocative names than merely 'Lillye Potte'.

The occurrence of the name, Lillipot Alley, north out of Leadenhall Street at Billiter Street in Aldgate Ward, seems to suggest that this type of fortification was adopted in other parts of London. Certainly, on the map that I was now tentatively preparing, I felt justified in marking a *lilium* fortification along the western half of the southern wall of 'Cripplegate Fort'.

Once I had begun to look for 'Latin' names, I found many, though one, hidden under the modern name of Milk Street, I mistook for a Hebrew one – *melek*, 'king'. On the other hand, I still think that Maiden Lane, formerly known as Kyrone Lane, is derived from the genitive plural of the Greek word for 'maiden', *korè*. I shall have more to say on this point when we come to consider the cult of Artemis, the Bear Goddess, in London.

I felt sure that I had identified the site of the Temple of Dionysus-Bacchus in the (now demolished) church of St Dionis Backchurch, for 'Bacchus' becomes 'Bach' in Old Welsh, and the fully attested Old Welsh habit of dropping Latin final -us would turn 'Dionysus' into 'Dionys'.

Several other temples – or their vicinities – I safely identified, and the result of this preliminary testing of my theory I thought safe to published, not so much because I felt that I had got undeniable proof that my theory 'held water', as they say, as because I felt it necessary to air my theory: to let other people examine it, pass judgment on it, and either support it or disprove it. I wrote to Sir Colin Coote, then Managing Editor of the London *Daily Telegraph*, for whose newspaper I had written over many years, and briefly outlined my theory. By return, Sir Colin invited me to contribute an article of about 2,000 words. I wrote this, and a few days later had the satisfaction of seeing the article appear on the leader-page of the *Daily Telegraph*.

The reception was oddly mixed, though – as I have found is almost invariably the case – those who disagreed with me wrote to the Editor of the newspaper, whilst those who felt drawn towards my theory wrote to me. Amongst the latter was Dr C. E. Darlington, Sherardian Professor of Botany at the University of Oxford. He disagreed with my then derivation of 'Fore Street' – with which, I, too, have since disagreed! (It is derived from Latin *foras*, 'without, outside', and is, in fact, the same word as is found in Moor Gate and Moor Fields.) But with my theory in general, he wrote to say that he was in complete agreement, and, in sending me a rough sketch-map with all of my tentative identifications (save, of course, Fore Street!) marked in, Dr Darlington may claim to be the undeniable first to have attempted the re-mapping of London on my new 'etymological-archaeological' principles.

I continued work on the investigation into London's names, correcting several original surmises as I became better acquainted with the etymology of London nomenclature. For instance, I quite discarded the supposition that Milk Street was derived from the Hebrew word for 'king', *melek* – doubtless the proximity of Milk Street to Old Jewry had tempted me to guess at a Semitic word as Milk Street's original. The word, 'milk', in Milk Street is almost certainly connected with *militem*, 'soldier'. It may well be the survival of *vicus militaris* – 'Soldiers' Quarter' or 'Soldiers' District' – but whatever the original phrase from which 'Milk Street' is derived, certainly the Latin *militem*, 'soldier', formed part of it.

But the detection of this error concerning Milk Street – finding, as I have said, that it is derived from a Latin, and not a Hebrew, word, – benefited me greatly, for it caused me to look more closely at two neighbouring names: Old Jewry (the street) and St Lawrence Jewry (the church at the entrance to the Guildhall).

Because many Jews did have their residence or place of business, up to the expulsion of 1291, in Old Jewry, it had never been questioned that 'Old Jewry', as the name of a London street, referred to a former occupancy by persons of the Jewish faith. 'St Lawrence Jewry', the church, was so-called, it was as unquestioningly accepted, because of the proximity of the church to the street named Old Jewry.

Now, however, both these 'unquestioned names' were about to be critically examined by me in the searching light of 'etymological archaeology'. The results of this critical examination were, to say the least, astonishing.

Let me retrace the steps by which I arrived at my unexpected and, as I said, astonishing conclusions.

I had noticed that there were two churches 'dedicated to St Lawrence' (actually, the 'saint' to which one is dedicated is spelt 'Laurence', and not 'Lawrence' – but they are, as we shall see, the same). One church, we have already noticed, is that of St Lawrence Jewry, at the entrance to the Guildhall; the other is the church of St Laurence Pountney, near the River Thames, on the south side of Cannon Street, that is to say, at the south-eastern corner of that 'restricted port area', the *cancellarius vicus*, whose name is hidden in that of modern 'Cannon Street'.

Now, 'Old Jewry' is not a new name, though the word – as a collective noun for Jews – is. Had there been a Jewish quarter in Roman London, it would have had some such name as *judaicus vicus* or *vicus judaeorum;* and though D, between vowels

73

in Latin words, can change to R in London Latin (and so to London British), as we shall see, *judaeus*, 'Jew', in Latin, gives *Idew* in Old Welsh; and *judaeorum*, then, whilst it *might* yield 'Jewry', would, much more probably, yield some such word as *idewwy*; whilst *judaicus* would almost certainly yield something like *idewch*.

I had already tentatively accepted the hypothesis that the Guildhall had been the site of centralized London's government since Roman times – we shall come to the proof later – and it seemed to me not unreasonable to assume that, as the Lord Mayor ('regent' of that revered Lord of London of which Welsh writings tell) judges offenders in or near the Guildhall, his Roman predecessors might well have judged offenders in or near the same place.

Now, when a prisoner is awaiting trial, what does one do to him? – what does one have to do to him? One has to lock him up until he be ready to appear before the justiciary. And what does one do when he has been found guilty of a crime meriting less than the death penalty? One either fines him or sends him to work out a sentence of imprisonment.

Now there are several words in Latin for our word 'prison'; and most of the Latin words are derived from the places where those prisons were first sited, just as out word for a boy's prison, 'borstal', comes from the name of a village outside Maidstone, where the first of such juvenile prisons was established.

The common word for 'prison' in Latin is *carcer* – which became (though derived from *carcerem*, rather than from *carcer*) Old Welsh *carchar*. A place of (usually temporary) detention or a 'lock-up' was *antrum*, which, in the phrase, *antro*, 'at the lock-up', provides the first part of the name of a London church, 'St *Andrew* Undershaft' – the last word being the early English equivalent of the Latin phrase.

A *janiculum*, as the name of a prison, was named after that famous military prison in Rome, and has given us the military slang for punishment: *jankers*. But the 'grander' Latin word for prison – again named after two famous prisons in Rome, – was *lautumiae*.[1]

---

[1] The original meaning of the word is 'stone quarries' – one may easily understand why! Other forms of the word are *latomiæ* and *latumiæ*.

The nominative plural of first declension nouns – those ending in A – is formed, in classical Latin, by changing the A to AE. Thus *nauta*, 'sailor', becomes *nautae*, 'sailors'.

But, in Late Latin – that highly 'unclassical' idiom which became the *'koinè'*, the common speech throughout the Roman dominions as the Empire began to break up – we have a new form of nominative plural for the first declension nouns. Instead of singular, *scala*, 'stair'; becoming plural, *scalae*, 'stairs, staircase', we have plural, *scalas*. As the word *lautumiae* must have shared in this change, we may assume a Late Latin form, *lautumias*.

Now, in London British, *lautumias* would regularly become, either *lawdom*, *lawdoff* or *lawdoms*. In regard to the last, it is rare that the original Latin final s is retained in Brittonic (or Old Welsh), but this retention is not unknown, and examples are: Latin *Iudas*, Old Welsh, *Iudas*; Latin *bilis*, Old Welsh *bustl* (metathesis); Latin *laxus*, Old Welsh *lais*.

The D/R/ or R/D consonant change is common enough,[1] but, in fact, to American ears, the average Englishman *always* pronounces the intervocalic R as though it were D. Readers of *Esquire* and other American publications will not need to be reminded that when a character in a story says 'veddy', instead of 'very', we know, beyond a shadow of doubt, that we are listening to an Englishman. We may take it, then, that the changes from original Latin *lautomiae* went like this:

LAUTUMIAE > LAUTUMIAS > LAWDOMS > LAWROMS

– the last bringing the original word near enough to 'Lawrence' or 'Laurence' that we should recognize the fact that 'Lawrence' is, in fact, derived from Latin *lautumiae* or *lautumias*, 'prison', the word always being given in the plural, as with our 'scissors' or 'trousers'.

If, then, 'St Lawrence' originally meant merely 'prison', what did 'Jewry' and 'Pountney' mean, as meaningful suffixes to 'St Lawrence' (or 'St Laurence')? I felt that the answer would be found in my examining the topographical positions of the two churches. St Lawrence Jewry's original had obviously

[1] And persistent. Modern Nursted and Perry Street – villages in Kent – were Nutsted and Pett Street in the mid-eighteenth century.

been some institution in close relation to the Guildhall, or, to be more plain, a prison (*lautumiae*) intimately connected with the justiciary of Londinium, whilst the original of St Laurence Pountney had been a prison at some distance from the law-courts of central London, but, I noticed, most conveniently placed on the river highway which led to the slave-markets of Gaul and Italy and Africa.

I thought that, taking the two similarly-named churches to have originated, in each case, from a prison, we might assume that the name 'Jewry' had an original connection with Latin *jus/juris*, 'the Law', which left it pretty well inevitable that 'Pountney' was nothing but* *poenitationis*, 'of punishment'.

We may, though, be a little more exact in naming the institution which was the original of 'St Lawrence Jewry'. The Legate – *legatus Augusti pro praetore* – shared his power, in the government of an imperial province, with a Procurator, but the Legate took precedence, and it was he who exercised supreme control (under the Emperor) of both the military and the judicial systems of the province.

As 'Lord Chief Justice' of the province, the Legate was assisted by trained lawyers, the *juridici*, who were appointed directly by the Emperor. Out of these *juridici* was selected a legal council to assist the Governor in his judicial decisions: this body may be fairly compared with the present Judicial Committee of the Privy Council, and in time these specially-nominated *juridici* came to be knows as *assessores*, 'assessors'. Appointments which were within the Legate's own gift were those of the *comites* or attachés. The rank of *comes* (the word means, literally, 'companion, mate') varied considerably, according to the context in which it was used (cf. our use of the rank, 'captain' in Army or Navy or the sports). In the Roman army, *comes* was the title held by that commissioned officer roughly equivalent to our full general; as the rank of a young man of good family 'attached to the person of the *legatus Augusti pro praetore*', we could probably best express it by calling the young man 'the Governor-General's *aide de camp*', or by saying of him that he was 'on the Governor-General's staff'.

These appointments to the rank of *comes* of the Governor were eagerly sought after by young Romans of good family who wished, as Gordon Home says, 'to acquire the knowledge of administrative methods and practice'.

It is clear that if, in his capacity as Chief Magistrate, the Governor-General of the Province had his *basilica* where, approximately, the Guildhall now stands, and if his *juridici* had their college close by, then we might expect the original of 'St Lawrence Jewry' to have been, not *lautumiae juris* but *lautumiae juridicae*.

The equation, then, is plainly this:

St Lawrence Jewry = *lautumiae juridicae*,
     'Prison of the Jurists' – i.e.
     'Remand Prison'
St Laurence Pountney = *lautumiae poenitationis*,
     'Prison for Punishment' – i.e.
     'Convicts' Prison'

There is, unfortunately, no need to suppose that the sentenced Londoners served their sentences 'up the river', at the *lautumiae poenitationis*. They were almost certainly shipped off to the Roman cities of the Continent, to take part in gladiatorial combats, or, if they were exceptionally fortunate, to be sold as slaves. Later, I shall identify two of London's slave-trading centres.

Well, to return to my search, I felt now that I had almost found convincing proof of the validity of my theory; but I could not reject the conviction that I still lacked the really positive proof that I needed, not less to convince myself than to convince others.

I had not, I can say it now, found this final, clinching proof by the time that I had finished my article for the *Daily Telegraph*. It was not, indeed, until I began to consider the origins of that ubiquitous 'saint', Botulf of Icanhoh, to whom so many London churches are 'dedicated', that I realized that I had, at last, found the positive proof so long sought.

I had found the key to the re-discovery of that great city of the Romans, Londinium Augusta.

Chapter III

The Convincing Proof –
'St Botolph of Icanhoh'

The fact that a church, named after St Botolph, stands outside all the main gates of London, and outside some gates of many of our other ancient cities, has been 'explained' by telling us that St Botolph (or Botulf) of Icanhoh, a seventh-century[1] East Anglian saint, is 'the Patron Saint of Travellers' – a bit of fancy which is usually further embellished by the informant's adding that

> 'The dangerous roads of the olden days gave rise to the custom of saying a prayer to St Botulf before setting out on a journey. In consequence, small shrines of St Botulf were erected outside the gates of a city, so that travellers could ask St Botulf's blessing for a safe journey, and leave an offering at his shrine. From these shrines, the present churches dedicated to St Botulf have arisen.'

It is a pretty tale, but it is, alas, only a fable. Let us see now what was the truth that I found behind this tale.

I began to interest myself in St Botulf, the Abbot of that Icanhoh, in East Anglia, whose site has never been identified; that Saint *'quem singularis vitae et doctrinae virum . . . fama circumquaque vulgaverat'*;[2] who, in most mysterious circumstances, was appointed, at some unknown date, the Patron Saint of travellers – a sort of home-bred St Christopher.

Do I mean that there was no such person as Botulf, the East Anglian abbot of a famous monastery in the seventh century?

[1] He is called 'an eighth-century saint' on the board outside St Botolph Aldgate, but in the anonymous life of Abbot Ceolfrith of Wearmouth, it is stated that he visited Botulf some time after 669.

[2] 'whom, alone amongst men, the fame of whose life and teaching was bruited everywhere abroad'.

Certainly not. I have no reason to dispute his existence. All that I say is that the many churches 'of St Botolph' are neither 'dedicated' to him, nor, in fact, named after him.

What, however, is undeniable – and therefore of immense importance in my quest for Londinium – is that *outside* each City gate is a church of St Botolph . . . just as *inside* each City gate is a 'Saracen's Head' tavern. I felt that there was an important connection between these two facts; but let us deal with that of the 'St Botolph' churches first.

Suppose, I asked myself, 'St Botolph' were not the name of an East Anglian saint, but simply a Latin word which had become so corrupt in the mouths of generations of 'sub-Roman' Celtic Cockneys that it had come at last to be identified – in sound at least – with the name of the East Anglian abbot?

But if the church of St Botolph at each gate had not begun as a church, as what had it begun? What would one expect to find at a City gate? Well, there were several things. I decided to examine the name, 'Botolph', by the established rules of etymology, to see whether the name itself would not answer my question.

At that time, I used to come up to London Bridge Station each morning, and as I walked down the cobbled slope, my ears were daily assailed by the blast of a three-man band. In the man who thrust his collecting-box into the faces of the hurrying commuters, I did not realize that I had, not merely my clue to the mystery of St Botolph, but the certain proof that the solution I was to find was the correct one. For in the jargon of his trade, the man with the box was employed to 'bottle' the audience. And 'Bottle' is a common variant in old records of 'Botulf', 'Botolfe', Botolph', and all the other spellings.

Well, it was time to apply the already well established rules of etymology to the name 'Botolph'. (Or, not to confuse the reader with a modern spelling, 'Botolf', or 'Botulf'.)

The examination of the name proceeded like this:

1. Suppose that initial B stood for an original 'lenited' M?
       ——that would give MOTOLF
2. Suppose that final F (or PH, as it is now spelt) stood (as it stands in such Latin-into-Old Welsh words as Latin *turma*,

Old Welsh *torf*; Latin *arma*; Old Welsh *arf*, etc.) for a Latin word ending in M?

—————that would give MOTOLM

3. But there is, besides the 'full' forms, 'Botulf' and 'Botolph', a much more syncopated form, 'Bottle'. Suppose we syncopated MOTOLM?

—————that would give MOT'LM

4. T and L, when they come together in a London word, often change places. Suppose we changed the positions of T and L, in the name 'Botolph', or, as we have now written it, MOT'LM?

—————that would give MOL'TM

5. Here we have clearly the Latin phrase *ad multam*, 'alongside of the Customs Office'; for *multa* or *mulcta* is Latin for 'fine, penalty, amercement' – and is here used for our modern word 'customs'.

6. To save space, the mutations of the vowels, in the change from Latin to Old Welsh, are ignored. However, the mutations are perfectly regular.

7. '*Bolt* Court', off Fleet Street, and St Mary *Bothaw*, preserve variant pronunciations of Latin (*ad*) *mul(c)tam*.

The 'dedication to St Botolph' of so many churches sited at City gates turns out to be no more than the echo of the Latin name for 'customs post' – where the *mulcta*, the levy, was paid by persons entering or leaving the City, or a customs duty was paid on imported or exported goods.

This, then, was the positive proof that I had sought: a Latin derivation, found 'strictly according to the rules', which, when found, could not fail to be the correct solution of the etymological problem.

This was what I meant a little while back, when I said that the man encountered 'bottling' the audience had given me, not merely the clue to the solution of the 'St Botolph' mystery, but had also offered me the certain proof that the solution that I was to find would be the correct one.

For what the musicians' mate was doing was 'to bottle' the passers-by – that is, to put a levy on them; to fine them; to 'mulct' them, in other words. Starting out from the one Latin phrase, *mulctam facere*, 'to levy a fine', London speech habits had arrived at variants of the one word, 'Botolph', 'Bolt', 'Bottle', etc., but had given two distinct meanings to the word: 'to rattle a collecting-box (successfully)' and 'the Patron Saint of Travellers – St Botolph'.

A really beautiful proof that there were customs-houses at the 'Bars' of London, as well as at the main gates – or, if you prefer to have it stated differently, a proof that the Bars of London were a sort of 'advance gate', a gate of the *pomoerium*, as distinct from a gate of the City – came to me by chance, after I had finished the first draft of this book.

I had, for a number of reasons, assumed that the Bars – Holborn, Temple, almost certainly Norton Folgate, and so on – were supplied with these 'sub-customs-houses', though my principal reason for assuming so was that I believed that all wheeled traffic, being forbidden in London during the hours of daylight, would have had to be dealt with by a different set of customs-officers, *multatici*, than those who dealt with the pedestrian traffic entering the City gates.

I had surmised the existence of a customs-house in or near Fleet Street (Via Fretensis) from the presence, in that street, of a Bolt Court, which seemed to be to be but a variant on Botolf (Botolph) or Bottle.

However, the existence of a *coquina*, 'cook-shop' in 'The Cock Inn', and a *danista*, 'banker, money-lender', in 'St Dunstan's', at Temple Bar inclined me to believe that in imperial or immediately post-imperial times there was an important business centre at the top of Fleet Street, and this, I thought, argued the presence of a *mulcta*, a customs-barrier, around which the business centre had grown up.

The proof to which I referred above came to me in an advertisement, printed in *The Intelligencer*, June 22–30, 1665, and quoted in Henry Sampson's *History of Advertising*, 1874:

'This is to certify that the master of the Cock and Bottle, commonly called the Cock alehouse, at Temple bar, hath dismissed his servants, and shut up his house for this long vacation, intending (God willing) to return at Michaelmas next, so that all persons who have any accounts or farthings [i.e. tokens issued by the landlord] belonging to the said house,

81

F

are desired to repair thither before the 8th of this instant, and they shall have satisfaction.'

It is of no consequence that the master of this inn closed down to take his chance of flying the Plague, then raging throughout London; but it is of great consequence to find that The Cock was once called The Cock and Bottle, for this can only mean that its name originated in a Latin phrase, *coquina a(d) mulctam*, 'cook-shop by the customs-house'.

The numerous 'Bottle' public-houses, then, must also take their names from a former propinquity to a customs-house, and it is interesting to reflect that The Leather Bottle at Cobham, in Kent, where both Mr Pickwick and I had our good times, was originally a *statio legionaria multaticia*; or 'military traffic control', I suppose we might translate it.

Cobham is only a mile or two outside Rochester – *Durobrivae*, which was also the name of the present Castor, near Peterborough – and this now insignificant village must once have been part of the elaborate defensive system that the very thorough Romans threw up around Rochester, as they did around London. Though this book is about London, and not about the Province of Britain, it is useful here to point out to researchers of the future that the detection of such names as 'Leather Bottle' outside a former Roman city or town[1] will help them to plot the circumscribing defences which, under the Roman system, evidently extended far beyond the centre protected.

What is more, a careful study of public-house names would, it is clear, be richly rewarding. To find out what the names of London's taverns were in, say, the twelfth century, would open up, I am sure, even more evidence than has so far come my way. I invite another enthusiast to 'have a go', as they say.

I had – at last – found the positive proof that I had sought. London names were descended from Latin originals – and therefore I had established that the identity of Roman-British Londinium had persisted throughout the 'Saxon' invasions and

---

[1] There is 'Bottle Farm' at Charing, between Maidstone and Ashford, in Kent.

the 'Lost Years', 457–597; and that, when, after a treaty of peace had been made *c.* 600, the East Saxons entered the City peacefully – and entered a Londinium where Latin was the official language and the gods of the pre-Christian Empire were still worshipped.

It was this fact – that my new 'etymological-archaeological' method had established – which explains the hitherto inexplicable statement of the Byzantine historian, Jordanes, who, writing in about the year 500, referred to the Province of Britannia as still part of the Roman Empire.

I had been satisfied with the proof that the interpretation of the name 'Botolph' had convinced me I now possessed; and armed with a good deal more assurance than I had had in what I may call my 'pre-Botolph' days, I decided to supply a further convincing proof by explaining the meaning of the name 'Saracen's Head', which, like that of 'St Botolph', is always found by a City gate or 'bar' – *and at no other place.*

As with the numerous 'St Botolphs', the explanation of the equally numerous 'Saracen's Heads' had to conform to the condition – if it were to be accepted as a valid explanation of the modern name – that the Latin name found would be self-evidently correct: that is, as 'St Botolph' had turned out to be the name of a Roman establishment, *at a place where it ought to have been found* (outside a City gate), so the explanation of 'Saracen's Head' must explain, not only what the name might mean, but explain also why a 'Saracen's Head' had to be found near a City gate – but *inside*, as the 'St Botolphs' were *outside*.

In all, I traced the existence of eight mentions of the name 'Saracen's Head' – obviously a most incomplete list, as there were at least nine principal City gates, besides a number of subsidiary ones whose positions, and possibly whose names, I hope to determine before I end my researches.

The eight references to a 'Saracen's Head' in the records of London are as follows. To each I have added the name of the gate or other entrance to the City with which each 'Saracen's Head' mentioned would have been associated.

1. *The Sarozens Hedd*   On south side of Aldgate, in a passage

leading to Poor Jewry Lane.

ALDGATE

2. *Sarsynshede*   A hostel, so named, in Fleet Street, in the time of Henry VI.

LUDGATE (but possibly within a 'bar' situate on the *west* side of the Fleet River, i.e. Temple Bar) near the *mulcta* represented by modern Bolt Court.

3. *Saracen's Head*   West side of Friday Street.

North-west entrance to 'Cannon Street' *cancellarius vicus* DOWGATE.

4. *Saresynes heved*   Opposite a tenement, 'Powlesbruerne', in parish of St Gregory-by-St Paul's. Mentioned in a deed, 20 Richard II, it may be identical with the Saracen's Head in Little Carter Lane, below.

CASTLE BAYNARD (river-gate)

5. *Sarsons Hedd*   South out of Little Carter Lane, in parish of St Mary Magdalene, in ward of Castle Baynard. Mentioned in a deed, 36 Henry VIII.

CASTLE BAYNARD (river-gate) – whether or not it is identical with No. 4

6. *Le Sarsrnesheved*   Tavern in parish of St Nicholas ad Macellas (St Nicholas Shambles) in ward of Farndon (now Farringdon), 1385.

NEWGATE

7. *Saracen's Head*   South out of Camomile Street, in Lime Street Ward.

BISHOPSGATE

8. *Sersyn Head*   North side of Snow Hill, west of St Sepulchre's Church (where Captain John Smith of Virginia is buried). This was probably the most famous Saracen's Head of all: immortalized by Dickens as the favourite coaching-inn of the fascinating Mr Wackford Squeers. As this Saracen's Head lay some distance

> *outside* Newgate, it must have served a
> subsidiary river-gate on the Fleet River
> – possibly a gate on Holborn Bridge, for
> there must have been a bridge there,
> even in Roman times.

Well, here is the very incomplete list of all the Saracen's
Heads that I have been able to extract from the London
records.

It is not difficult, when one collates the different forms, to
see that the original of this chain of development is a Latin
word:

SARSIN < SARCIN' < SARCINA = Latin 'package, bundle, load,
pack' – but, more precisely, 'Saracen's Head' comes, not
from *sarcina*, but from *sarcinae* (the Late Latin form was
sarcinas, whence 'Sarsyns' etc.), the baggage carried by the
soldiers, and thus different from that other type of soldier's
baggage, *impedimenta*: 'hanc legionus sub sarcinis adoriri', as
Caesar observes. The *sarcinae* were piled together before a
battle.

The name, 'Saracen's Head', then, has nothing to do with
either Saracens or with Heads, but was originally a *sarcinaria* –
the military store where the soldier could 'dump' his baggage.
He must have done this on entering a garrison town like
London, and picked it up – 'signing for it' – on being posted to
another command. This explains why the various 'Saracen's
Heads' are to be found *inside* a gate: if they were military stores,
they needed to be within a wall-protected city. The 'Head' of
'Saracen's Head', may come from *sedes*, 'dwelling, abode,
resting-place', etc., by the following possible development:
Latin *sedes*; Old Welsh, swyđ; Middle English, *heved*; Modern
English, *head*. Or there may have been an independent Old
London development of *sedes*, in which the initial s was replaced by H (Cf. Old Welsh *hafrenn* from Latin *Sabrina*; Old
Welsh *haliw*, from Latin *saliva*, etc.). But what seems most
probable to me is that the 'Head' of the name is nothing more
than *sarcinaria* pronounced *sarcinadia* – and so developing

85

inevitably into *Sarsons Hedd*, just as Latin *metiarius*, 'measurer, surveyor', has developed into the English surname Meatyard (pronounced today 'Mityud').

But whatever the origin of 'Head', there can now be no doubt that the origin of the 'Saracen's Heads' of London and other Roman cities is simply a Roman military store of specific use, where the *sarcinae* of the legionaries and auxiliary troops were stored.

We have thus established two 'features' of Roman London: the *mulctae* or customs-posts, just outside the City's gates, and the *sarcinariae* or baggage-stores, just inside. The pattern of Roman London's military and civil administration is beginning to emerge from all this speculation and enquiry.

But in identifying the various 'St Botolphs' with the Roman *mulctae*, we have also postulated the existence of a gate wherever we find a *mulcta* – a 'St Botolph'.

If, then, we find a 'St Botolph', recorded by Froissart as having stood halfway up Cheapside, we must look for a gate – as we must when we find a 'St Botolph' on the Thames before the reign of William the Conqueror.

One is not astonished to find that there was a gate on the river: there must have been several, if not many. But the hypothesis that there was, in Cheapside, a gate to account for a church of St Botolph led me to the most significant discovery of all: the multiple origin of London, implicit in the mediæval phrase 'The Londons', but not understood until it became clear to me that London – Londinium Augusta – developed, not from one Roman military area at 'Cripplegate Fort', but from certainly *five* such forts, with the strong possibility that there may have been as many as *six*.

As late as 1232, we find London referred to as a noun in the plural, in the title of the *Cronica majorum et vicecomitum Londoniarum*, 'The Chronicle of the Mayors and Viscounts [i.e. Sheriffs] of the Londons'; and we shall see that the memory of the City's multiple or corporate origin survived in London consciousness far beyond the thirteenth century.

Yet who had suspected that London was – is, I suppose one could well say – a federation of smaller 'Londons'?; a federation which is, to a large extent, reflected today in the grouping of the City's Wards, which owe their origin to the federal character of London herself.

In discovering once more this forgotten fact, I was first led to suspect the federal character of Londinium by this finding of a 'St Botolph' recorded as having been halfway up Cheapside; my suspicions were confirmed after I had grasped the significance of the various 'St Peters', scattered about the City. It was where they were located which gave me the final, convincing proof that London had been multiple in origin.

Chapter IV
The Five – or Six? – Londons

The Roman Empire was originally a federated assembly of farmers' small-holdings, and it was as a levy of property-conscious, neighbour-suspicious, stranger-envious farmers that Rome first went to war – and first broke upon the notice of history. Just as American millionaires – at least of pre-1939 generations – invariably 'recollected' the days when they sold newspapers at the street corner, so did Rome, in her rise to world-power, in her imperial splendour, and even in her nostalgic, revengeful, plotting decline, remember her rustic origins. From beginning to end, the Roman Empire was a culture of farmers, who had laid down their scythes in order (under a multiplicity of economic pressures) to conquer the world.

Roman Law is the law of the market-place – and the Roman consciousness of Rome's rustic origins has transmitted itself to millions who neither speak Latin nor know much of Rome herself. If the President of the United States of America says that he *stipulates* that such-and-such a nation's rulers shall do such-and-such a thing, the man is unconsciously recalling the fact that the Latin word *stipulare* means 'to seal a (farmer's) bargain', by breaking a *stipula*, 'a straw'. If we hear that this or that ruler has 'promulgated' a law (he usually, I find 'promulgates' a *decree*) he is bringing back memories of Rome's earliest past, when the word *promulgare* came into use – a word compounded of simple Indo-European words, and meaning no more than 'to press the milk (*mulg*) from the udder of a cow'. When the farmer who always stands at Rome's origins wished to 'think', he left the tent or hut in which he would be too much with his noisy family, and sought peace 'with the stars', *cum sideribus*, from which Latin phrase the verb 'to consider'

has been coined. The *templum* was an open space of land –
originally – which had been made 'holy' by the performance of
certain acts. Sometimes our farmer went here to reflect, and
from this habit arose the words 'contemplate', 'contemplation',
meaning to 'reflect within the *templum*'.

The fact that Rome was always snobbishly – and, perhaps,
we may say both sentimentally and superstitiously – aware of,
and attached to, her rustic origin is a fact of supreme importance
in understanding the character of the Roman people. From a
settlement of farmers in Alba Longa, a small tribe of Italic
settlers became a world-power; but whatever they did throughout their splendid history, the Romans always did, if not as
practising farmers, then as those who never forgot the rustic
customs on which their world-state had been elevated.

This is not a digression. What has been said above explains
why a Roman farm and a Roman fort and a Roman city were
invariably laid out in exactly the same fashion – that pattern
that we conveniently call 'grid-iron'.

With a bronze-coultered plough – since iron, being a 'new'
metal, could not be permitted to enter into the performance of
necessary 'numinous' acts – a furrow was driven in a straight
line from south to north, 'sightings' being taken with a primitive
but efficient surveyor's instrument called a *groma*: simply four
plumb-bobs hanging from each arm of a cross turning hori-
zontally at eye-level on an upright pole.

The south–north furrow, called the *cardo*, 'the hinge', was
crossed at right angles by an east–west furrow, the *decumanus*.
Around this cross a quadrilateral was drawn – still by means of
the bronze-coultered plough – and this was, and so emained
until long after the end of the Roman Empire, the pattern on
which farm, fort and *colonia* were laid out.

Even when the Roman troops, on a march through hostile
territory, halted for a single night, the camp was arranged in
the grid-iron pattern which, when the troops halted finally to
establish themselves in permanent quarters, would give them
the immutable ground-plan for their town or city.

Now, in ploughing the rectangular pattern of a collection
of peasants' small-holdings, a strip of uncultivated land was
left along the *cardo* and the *decumanus*, and – when the larger

plots became subdivided – between each successively smaller quartet of plots. On this 'no man's land', at each intersection of the path between cultivated plots, a small shrine was erected. As the point of intersection of the paths was called a *compitum* ('compter' in English, as we shall see), the small shrines were dedicated to the *lares* of the cross-roads – the *lares compitales* – and each was open in all directions, so that the *lares* of the farms about might have unrestricted access to the perpetually 'numinous' shrines.

At a distance of fifteen feet from each opening an altar was erected, on which, at times of festival, but particularly at the Compitalia – 'Harvest Home' – sacrifices might be made, as the neighbouring farmers renewed their agreements to be friends as well as neighbours.

Since a Roman camp was laid out in exactly the same way as a 'collective farm', the 'Cripplegate Fort' was similarly laid out. An aerial view of the vanished Roman military town of Caistor, in Norfolk, shews ideally how a Roman military establishment was laid out. But beneath the winding pattern of London's modern street-plan lies a series of rectangular, grid-iron layouts as precisely regular as that of Caistor.

The advantage of the grid-iron method of constructing a settlement is that, with the simple surveying instruments available to the Roman civil and military engineers, it was no difficult matter to add similar rectangles to an original rectangle, making a bigger camp or town, and pushing the centre of the original 'grid-iron' always away from the newer centre, along any of the diagonals radiating from the latest centre. The original 'grid-iron' is multiplied in area, say, four times, by having three similar rectangles added to the original rectangle. The original *cardo* and *decumanus maximus* become the principal crossroads of a district now only a *quarter* (hence the name!) of the enlarged city. The important point to remember is that, with their strictly legalistic minds, the Roman authorities insisted that certain official buildings of significance had necessarily to be in the centre of the city; and, as that centre shifted with the growth of the city, so the siting of the principal buildings (at least in the early years of the city's expansion) would tend to shift, too.

At the centre of each settlement, where the main roads – the *cardo* and the *decumanus maximus* – crossed, the commander's tent was set up. In a town, a substantial building, the *praetorium*, housed the city's governor, the *vicarius*; whilst, grouped around the *praetorium* were the various buildings connected with the administration of the city: the *basilica*, 'law-court', being one of the principal of these.

But it was the clue of the many *praetoria* which appeared to be scattered throughout Londinium which put me on the track of discovering the several smaller 'Londons' which had been combined to form 'Greater Londinium' – the Londinium as we know it.

The first clue came with my considering the church – no longer standing – of St Peter Westcheap. Its site, taken in association with its name, was highly suggestive; and a glance at the other four 'St Peters' shewed, in each case, a similarly suggestive siting *at important crossroads*. Was it possible that 'Peter' was a corruption of *praetorium*?

The derivation was certainly possible, by the well-established laws governing Old London:

PRAETORIUM > *PREIDYR

– but, just as there is a pun – the only pun – in the New Testament on the name of 'Peter': 'Thou art Peter (*Petrus*), and upon this rock (*petram*) shall I build my Church'; so there was the Celtic word for 'four', *pettor*, which survives in the Latin word *petorritum*, 'a four-wheeled carriage', and in the English name for a certain flag, 'the Blue Peter', as meaning 'a rectangular or four-angled shape'. It would be easy for a Celtic-speaking Londoner of Imperial times to think of the first part of the Latin word, *praetorium*, as somehow connected with *pettor-*, 'four-square, rectangular', because the *praetorium* usually stood by an open, square or oblong space. *Praetorium* would then become *p'aetorrium*, which would naturally develop in Celtic mouths to *peidyr* – to be accepted, later, as a local pronunciation of 'Peter' (i.e. *Petrus* or *Petrum*). It seemed more than probable that a church 'dedicated to St Peter' represented the site or the vicinity of a *praetorium*. But why so many *praetoria*? The explanation could be only that London had developed from several smaller 'forts', each with its own *cardo*, *decumanus maximus*, two *fora* and, of course, its *praetorium*. In that case, how many subsidiary 'Londons' had there originally been? The clue of the several 'St Peters' ought, I believed, to provide me with the answers to these important questions.

The number of 'St Peters' that I have been able to trace is five. They are as follows:

1. St Peter Cornhill — By the eastern BASILICA, whose impressive remains – it seems to have measured 505 feet in length, and was the second largest in the whole Roman Empire – have been positively identified and, to a large extent, surveyed. It should be noted here that the word *praetorium* could mean either the offices of the governor or the large 'square' on which such offices would normally stand.

2. St Peter the Less — On the Thames, at 'Pouleswharf' – centre of a huge Roman building complex, recently uncovered, in which I have already identified, amongst other things, THE TEMPLE OF JUPITER DOLICHENUS. This vast complex may well – and almost certainly did – house another, and riverine, fort.

3. St Peter le Poer — On the west side of Old Broad Street and thus still on that VIA PRAETORIA which is recalled by the name of St Peter Cornhill. Indeed, 'Broad' (Street) may well be another (later?) corruption of *praetoria*.

4. St Peter ad Vincula — In the Tower – and one may well hold that the name (that is, of 'St Peter') arose in the time when the Tower was a fort separated from the other London forts. In this case, the

Tower would have had its own *praetorium*.

5. St Peter Westcheap   At Wood Street. It must have been the *praetorium* of Phase II of the CRIPPLEGATE FORT.

Accepting the possibility that the names of St Peter Cornhill and St Peter le Poer are both derived from propinquity to the same *praetorium* – that at what is now the crossroads of Leadenhall Street and Gracechurch Street – we have four certain *praetoria* and one possible *praetorium* in Roman London. Our new 'etymological archaeology' has certainly changed the traditional picture of Roman London's development. We can say now, with considerable confidence, that the Romans developed their London, not simply from one modest north-west fort – the 'Cripplegate Fort' – but from certainly four, and possibly five, such forts, integrating them into a larger city only long after the individual foundations of the 'citylets'. That former interior walls, when pulled down, did not altogether remove the fortified character of the individual forts is proved by the survival of the names of the two Lilypot Lanes; by the significance of the name, Billingsgate (not at all connected with 'a Saxon family, the Billings'); by such names as Castle Baynard, Catshole, etc. – which will be explained in due course – and by the fact that a St Botolph's church – in other words, the *mulcta* at the southern entrance to the 'Cripplegate Fort' – survived long enough for its name to have been transmitted to posterity by association with a church built on or near its site.

Let us turn now to the fish-quay today named Billingsgate, on whom romantic etymology has fathered the improbable derivation as from 'a Saxon family named Billing'. It would have been much more plausible to have suggested a derivation from Birinus, Bishop of the West Saxons, for *Birinus*, through a form *Belinus*, might have developed into the form that Stow gives us when he says that the pile of ancient buildings near Billingsgate was known as 'Belliney's Palace', and adds that it was named after a British king, Belinus.

Stow is right when he says that the buildings were known as

'Belliney's Palace', not so correct when he says that they were named after King Belinus. 'Belliney', in fact, is *Bellona*, the Goddess of War, and the Latin phrase from which 'Belliney's Palace' is derived is *Bellonarium palatum* – *not* 'the Palace of Bellona', but rather 'the fortified embankment of Bellona': a fort and military arsenal in one.

The legend that the Tower of London was built by Julius Caesar, though fanciful, is not all *that* fanciful; as we shall see, not only is almost every name associated with the Tower (including that name) pure Latin, but also the significance of many names in and about the Tower proves two important facts: (a) the early date of the Tower 'fort' as one of the four (or five or six) 'Londons', and (b) the early date at which certain of the best known establishments of the Tower Hill district became 'features' of that historic London quarter. We have seen that Tower Hill, last used as a place of execution when Simon, Lord Lovat, was beheaded for his part in the Rising of 1745, must have been a place of execution as early as the first Roman settlement at 'the Tower', just as West Smithfield was also set aside for such purposes at an equally early date. Be it noted that, in both cases, the presence of a place of execution means that 'Tower Hill' and 'Smithfield' were both outside 'city limits' – that is to say, the forts outside which these two places of execution had been fixed were not yet absorbed with a 'federated London'. Indeed, the 'Smith-' of both the 'Smithfields' is simply the Latin *semotus*, 'cut off'.

Before we return to the consideration of the fortified area at 'the Tower', it should be noted that there is another striking piece of evidence that the 'Cripplegate Fort' was originally perfectly detached from the rest of London.

Alsies Lane and Elsyng Hospital lay, in medieval times, well within the City, in that part, north of St Paul's, which is bounded by the length of the Wall connecting Aldersgate and Newgate. Both 'Alsies' and 'Elsyng' are derived from Latin *elysii (campi)*, 'Elysian Fields' – a burying ground which bears the same name in Arles: *Les Aliscamps*.

Wren found many traces of this extensive burying-ground when digging the foundations of new St Paul's – the point to note here being that Roman urban and municipal law strictly forbade burials within the city limits. Therefore, when the *elysii campi*, the burying-ground, was used, it was not within the limits of a walled Londinium – the wall came later, with the 'federation' of 'all the Londons'.

But to return to our search for evidence that the Tower of London represents one of the original Roman 'forts' out of which Londinium grew; and to reinforce the evidence that Stow's 'Belliney's Palace' was originally the *Bellonarium palatum*, a great fortification (Stow remarks on its vast size) raised on piles at the Thames's edge: this word, *palatum* (or, rather, the adjective derived from it, *palatinus*) occurs again in the Tower area – and in a most curious context indeed.

Archaeological excavations beneath the Church of All Hallows Barkingside were made possible after the last war by the serious damage that bombing had caused to this ancient church. Amongst other discoveries made was what appeared to be a barber's shop of Roman times – for of the Roman date of the church's foundations there is no doubt. A Roman building certainly lies beneath the church, but of what nature was this Roman building? The spade of the archaeologist, alas, cannot supply the answer from the meagre evidence that he has turned up. 'Etymological archaeology', however, can put forward at least a plausible attempt at answering.

There are several churches in London with the 'dedication to All Hallows'. Let us see which Latin word, if any, we may trace behind the phrase 'All Hallows'.

Old Welsh *haliw* is derived from Latin *saliva*, the substitution of the H ('rough breathing') for the s (initial sibilant) being proof that the importation of the Latin word into Old Welsh occurred at an early date. In later importations, the initial s was unchanged in Old Welsh. *Haliw* is, therefore, an early borrowing from Latin.

Now, if Latin *saliva* gives Old Welsh *haliw*, the Old Welsh word which lies at the back of '(All) Hallows' must be a Latin word beginning *sal-*. We shall leave the consideration of this word's possible identity until after we shall have examined the name 'Barkingside', which has no meaning, if it be considered as a purely English name.

95

The derivation of *Bellonarium palatum* from 'Belliney's Palace' gives us the clue to the derivation of 'Barkingside'.

(The o of *Bellonarium* becomes the I of 'Bellineys' – or, more precisely, ON in the first word becomes IN in the latter, because of that vowel change typical of Brittonic Celtic speech known as the 'o-mutation'. It is this same 'o-mutation' which is responsible for such changes as, for example, Latin, *moneta* to modern English *Mint*; Latin *mola* to modern English *mill*.)

To return to *Barkingside*. The first two syllables, at any rate, are not difficult – once given the clue of 'Belliney's Palace' – to etymologize. As thus:

Latin *Palatini* > Old Welsh *Baratin'* > Old London *Barakin'*

– and so to *bar'kin'*, the last step before its anglicization to the now 'correct' Barking.

What, then, does 'Hallows' mean? Well, just as Latin *saliva* produced Old Welsh *haliw*, so 'Hallows' comes, through Old Welsh, from *Salii*, 'the Leapers' – the dancing priests of Mars Gradivus.

Dressed in brilliant reds and purples, crowned with the mitres of flamens, carrying archaic figure-of-eight shields on their left arms, that they beat with the stick carried in their right hands, the Leapers, in bronze armour, danced and howled their most ancient ritual through the cities of Rome.

What confirms our guess here that 'Hallows' is derived from *Salii* is that 'Barking' appears to be derived from *Palatini* – and in Rome herself the twenty-four Leapers of Mars were organized in two companies, or *collegia*, the *Salii Collini* and the *Salii Palatini*, the latter just such a title as we appear to have found concealed within the homely vocables of 'All Hallows Barkingside'. Of the two *collegia* of Leapers, that of the *Salii Palatini* appears to have been the much more ancient, since this *collegium* of Leapers was associated with the earliest Roman settlement on the Palatine.

If our etymology is correct, we have here the certain evidence that the *Salii* of Londinium were settled on or near the *palatum* of Bellona, who – as his wife, sister or daughter – was frequently associated with the god Mars. We should expect to find the names of Bellona and Mars in close conjunction – and, on Tower Hill and about, we do, in fact, so find them.

Apart from the almost certain identification of a great river-side fort-cum-arsenal, *Bellonarium palatum*, there is further evidence of the fortification of the Tower area in such a way as to make clear that that the 'Tower Fort', like the 'Cripplegate Fort', was not included within the general London area.

What makes this evidence so important is that it represents the second successful prediction that I made, based on my own interpretation of a London name, that such-and-such a building *must* have occupied a certain site. The first certain identification that I made by the new archaeological method was of Amen Corner; the second is that to which I shall now refer: the oddly-named alley, on Tower Hill, known in the seventeenth century as Cat's Hole (later Cat or Catt Alley). I said that this name was simply a metathesis of *castellum*, 'castle, fort, stronghold, fortified dwelling', and I pointed out that underneath the site of Cat's Hole must be a Roman military post.

Such a post – that a bronze plate now describes as 'Roman Guard-house' – was found at the exact site that I had predicted *from the evidence of the name*, and from no other evidence.

Another of London's 'forts' appears to be – if the name, 'St Peter', of a church in Castle Baynard Ward, indicates the former existence of a *praetorium*, 'commander's house' (and therefore a *via praetoria*) – Castle Baynard itself.

It was in this Ward of the City, that the vast wall, over 400 feet in length, already mentioned, was recently uncovered, as was an equally vast 'raft' of Roman concrete, of such formidable strength, that the demolition contractors had some difficulty in removing it.

'Castle Baynard' seems to be *castellata balnearia* – the 'castellata' referring to the fact that a great public bath lay within a fortified area. The presence of a *praetorium* would imply that this fortified area, as one would expect, was laid out in the typical Roman grid-iron pattern.

But may not this vast 400 feet wall – which certainly implies a building complex of no ordinary dimensions – have included, besides a great public bath (the *balnearia*), such typically Roman buildings as temples? Certainly, as I shall try to shew in the next chapter, there was a temple here to Jupiter Dolichenus.

97

G

Until the late Middle Ages, Baynard's Castle – how strange that the name survives now only in the name of a modest public-house! – rivalled the Tower as the most heavily fortified part of the northern river bank. Traditions die hard indeed! – for, if we are correct in our assumption that 'Baynard's Castle was originally one of the 'Forts' that we have surmised, then the mediæval fortifications of Baynard's Castle were merely the continuation of a fortified condition which had lasted un-broken since the Romans first built a walled defence at the confluence of the Fleet River and the Thames. This part of the Thames foreshore was also known as 'Pouleswharf', and the church whose name may imply a former *praetorium* was known as St Peter the Less. To reinforce the assumption of a former *praetorium*, there were also a Peter Key (Late Latin *cayus*, 'house' = Classical Latin *casa*) and a Peter's Hill. Stow tells us that the corner house at the upper end of Peter's Hill, towards the north was called Peter Key in his day, though he adds that it was also called 'Petres Taverne be Poules cheyne'.

I have, so far, left one other mention of 'St Peter' out of my list of the 'St Peters' (= ? *praetoria*) to be found in London: Peter's Court, in Ironmonger Row, Cheapside. It almost certainly owes it name to that same *praetorium* from which St Peter Westcheap took its name; but there is just the bare possibility that St Peter's Court records another *praetorium* further east, established as the 'Cripplegate Fort', losing its inner walls, was expanded to take in more of the London which had enclosed it on the east and south. I think that St Peter's Court, Ironmonger Row, was named after the *praetorium* of the 'Cripplegate Fort', but, as I said, there may have been another *praetorium* further east, between the *praetorium* commemorated in the name of St Peter Westcheap and that commemorated in the name, St Peter Cornhill. If so, this other *praetorium* was perhaps where the Guildhall now is, especially if, as I believe, the Guildhall is the direct descendant of the palace of the *vicarius*, and that both Basinghall Street and the Church of St Michael Bassishaw preserve, in a not-too-corrupted form, the Latin word *basilica*, the 'hall of justice', which was as-sociated with that *lautumiae juridiciae*, that we have recognized as the origin of the name of 'St Lawrence Jewry'.

Summing up, we may say that there is now ample evidence that London began as a collection of small forts – possibly, and almost certainly, placed strategically around the limits of a London sacked by Boudicca (Boadicea) in A.D. 61. These forts were linked later, and the linking may well have been very late in the Roman occupation of Britain: it may be even after the rescript of Honorius had recalled the Eagles in 410.

But the probability is that London, in common with the other European cities of the Empire, was walled in that disastrous third century when almost every Roman city seemed to its anxious inhabitants to be the target of barbarian raiders. As A. Ledrun[1] wrote in 1900, 'To put an end to incessant pillage, the Gallo-Roman towns sacrificed their faubourgs, and, retrenching their extent, surrounded themselves with strong walls, which were very often supported on sculptured blocks taken from destroyed edifices. Le Mans, like the towns of Senlis, Tours, Autun, Bourges, Fréjus, etc., girdled itself with ramparts flanked with strong towers, of which important remains still exist, along the River Sarthe. The *enceinte* of Le Mans enclosed an area about 500 by 200 metres'. With the exception of the size, all these remarks would apply equally to Londinium.

It was this ruthless 'cutting back' of the Roman cities to a heavily fortified nucleus which accounts for their irregular shapes, so greatly contrasting with the Roman military engineers' and architects' ideal of the perfectly regular *civitas quadrata*. However, my discovery of the modulus on which the street-plan of London was laid out enables us to appreciate the original regularity of the city, and to understand how military expediency erected the walls where they might do most good; and so gave to London the shape that it retains to this day. It is clear, from the extensive suburbs of this 'reduced' city, that Londinium thrived as well outside as inside the new walls, and – save in the mid-fourth century – London must have escaped those more devastating barbarian assaults against which she had so strongly (and irregularly) walled herself.

Here, then, we have the origin of the mediæval phrase, *Londoniae*, 'the Londons'. But even in late mediæval times, the multiple origins of London were still very visible to the Cock-

[1] Quoted in T. R. Lethaby, *Londinium*.

99

neys. In particular, the 'Cripplegate Fort' retained its obviously independent character into modern times. I quote from an earlier book of my own, *London Growing*, this passage:

'The Saxon Chronicle, under the year 886, has this: "In this year *gesette* Alfred *Lundenburh* and gave the *burh* to Aethered the ealdorman to hold."

'John Earle, pointing to the Latin paraphrase of this passage, "*dux Aethered . . . custodiendi arcem . . .*", points out that *burh* was a citadel; that the Latin *arx* makes that clear; and that the passage means that "Alfred established a military colony . . . that we have here an account of the military occupation of Tower Hill".

'They thought that Earle was wrong sixty years ago; we know now that he was wrong – but not in thinking that Alfred gave the citadel of London into the guard of Aethered. *Burh* does mean "citadel", and that the citadel survived until Alfred's time, and for centuries after, is proved, I think, by a name to which, so far as I know, no other historian of London has called attention.

'This is the name of a tenement in "the parish of St Margaret de Friday strete", which occurs in *The Calendar of Wills in the Court of Husting, London*, edited by Dr R. R. Sharpe. The tenement has two names: "Le Burgate" and – in 1427 – "Le Castell on the hoop", which means, "has a circular sign, bearing the representation of a Castle".

'Now it is clear that this property in the parish of St Margaret Moses, which stood at the corner of Friday Street and Pissing Alley – *piscina*: either a swimming-pool or a fishpond? – was named in direct allusion to the Cripplegate Fort.

' "Le Burgate" means "near (modern French *lès*) Burgate" – and here "Bur" = older "burh", whilst "gate" may mean either "entry" or "the way to".

'The fact that the sign of this property bore the representation of a "castell' clearly identifies the word "Bur" (burh) with "castell" – *castellum*, "a fort, stronghold".

'The perhaps first citadel of London, then, was standing until late medieval times, and the reference in *The Calendar of St Paul's Documents* (23 Henry VIII) to the "clensyng of certaine ruinose houses in Aldermanbury, sometime the palace of Saincte Aethelbert Kyng . . ." may well refer to the remains of Roman buildings within the citadel. It is clear that this "stronghold" of London continued to be preserved – and undoubtedly used – until almost the end of the mediæval period.'

This was written before I had fully examined my theory of a 'federated London', but my remarks on the survival of the 'Cripplegate Fort' still apply. It only remains to add that, thanks to the work of the archaeologists of the Guildhall Museum and other such establishments, the foundations of one of London's original forts have been revealed, and may be inspected by all.

Chapter V
The Gods of Roman London

To the methods – and the results – of traditional archaeology, we owe much information on the nature and the number of the gods worshipped in Londinium. Statues, votive tablets, coins, references on tombstones – all these have given us more than a mere hint of the depth and complexity of Roman London's religious belief. One should stress the depth, no less than the complexity, because, as F. M. Stenton points out in his *Anglo-Saxon England*, 'it was the conservative heathenism of the men of London which frustrated this [i.e. Mellitus's] first attempt to establish a local bishopric. In view of their attitude, it is hard to believe that any tradition of Roman Christianity still persisted in the city . . .'. Bede, writing in the following century, remarks sourly that the Londoners 'had their own High Priest', as he accounts for their angrily flinging out Mellitus, the Bishop whom King Aethelberht had imposed upon them. Mellitus, though he had returned from attending a Roman synod held by Pope Boniface IV on February 27, 610, bearing letters from the Pope to Laurentius and King Aethelberht, could win neither respect nor even tolerance from the Londoners, who expelled him from their city in 616. We shall see presently why – and the 'conservative heathenism' of the Londoners was only partly responsible for their bitter animosity against Mellitus; though the principal reasons, having been revealed purely by the methods of 'etymological archaeology', have – obviously – been ignored by historians.

Traditional archaeology has shewn us that the Londoners worshipped Mithras, Dionysius, Serapis (the Egyptian God of the Harvest), Minerva, Mercury, a river god, possibly to be identified with the Celtic river-divinity Nodens (or Lug);

Cybele (if the evidence of what appear to be castrating forceps is acceptable), the Three Mothers, Diana and Isis – the existence of a temple of the last-named being confirmed by a scratched inscription on a jug: *Londini – Ad Fanum Isidis*, 'London – just by the Temple of Isis', where, presumably, was situate the tavern from which the wine-jug came.

But 'etymological archaeology' can greatly reinforce that slender list, and though traditional archaeology has, so far, found only one building which may reasonably be assigned to uses of a particular faith – the Mithraeum in Walbrook (found in 1954/5[1]) – our newer archaeology may prove the existence of London-worshipped gods without any relic of their worship having been discovered; further, this new archaeology may recover the knowledge, and even the position, of temples of which no recognizable fragment now remains. In confirming what traditional archaeology has already discovered about the gods of Londinium, our method takes us much farther; widens our view of the past beyond the dreams and hopes of those whose only instruments are pick and shovel and sieve.

What our method has found stresses the validity of my remark about the depth and complexity of the religious sentiment of Roman London. Already we can prove that Londoners of, say, fifteen hundred years ago, were worshipping – besides those pick-and-shovel-identified gods mentioned above – the following:

Dionysus-Bacchus
Artemis, the Bear Goddess
Mars Gradivus
Satus
Juno Moneta
Belin-Sabazios
Semo Sancus Dius Fidius
The Cabiri (*Samothracian demon-gods*)
Antinoüs
Bellona
Bona Dea

[1] A detailed account of the discovery of this splendid relic of Roman London may be found in my book, *London Beneath the Pavement*.

Mars Stator (*Standens)
Jupiter Dolichenus
Jupiter Nicaeus
Anna Perenna
Annona Augusta
Apollo
Matuta
Selene

We may not only identify at least the approximate locality of the temples of all the above – and of the temples of other gods known to have been worshipped in Londinium, through the finding of some objects associated with their cults – we may also assure ourselves that these are by no means the last of the gods of Roman London whom our New Archaeology will recover from the obscurity into which almost all such Gods have fallen.

Of course, in proving the exact origin of our London names, we shall have to sweep away some notable myths. And we shall find our discoveries buried beneath some very pretty myths, indeed: as with the god Belin-Sabazios, whose names survives to this day under the more homely form of 'La Belle Sauvage'.

Belin was a Celtic divinity; Sabazios was one of the many 'surnames' of Bacchus, a London temple of whom was the subject of an Act of Parliament in 1965.[1] The combination of these two names – one Celtic, the other Roman – has not been hitherto recorded, to my knowledge, but the equating of Roman with 'barbarian' divinities in one double title, is not at all uncommon in the tolerant religious atmosphere of Roman belief: such double titles as Mars Thincsus or Jupiter Dolichenus are commonplaces, especially amongst military inscriptions.

Belin, then – whose name appears in that of the British king, Cunobelinus ('Hound of Belin') – was equated with Sabazios, and on the eastern bank of the Fleet River a temple was erected to Belin-Sabazios, on a site which is now to be described as 'at the bottom of Ludgate Hill, on the northern side of that street'.

One has heard many myths to explain the origin of the name

[1] *The St Dionis Backchurch Churchyard Act, 1965.*

of that famous tavern and, in its later days a notable posting-house, 'La Belle Sauvage'. A number of stories have been told, which introduce characters as diverse as Isabel Savage, the pretty landlady of the Middle Ages, and Pocahontas, that 'belle sauvage' whom Captain John Smith brought from America to die of London fogs. All have failed to present a convincing case for even one 'explanation'.

Like many another London name, 'La Belle Sauvage' is derived from a name current in Roman times – in this case the linked names of a Celtic and a Roman divinity.

Before we leave Belin-Sabazios, noting that his temple – our Roman Londoners preferred the word *fanum* to *templum*, by the way – stood by the river-bank, on the west side of the Forum Boarium (Cattle Market), we must call attention to the fact that he not only appears to have had another temple – or perhaps only a subsidiary shrine – on the Thames itself, but also had a connection with the most revered of all London divinities, Artemis, the Bear Goddess.

For Sabbis (or Sabb's) Dock and Key – made one of the Legal Quays by an Act of Elizabeth I in 1559 – led west out of Little Bear Key; whilst Sabb's Dock was also known by the name of Little Bear Stairs. The site is now occupied by that almost perfect eighteenth-century building, the Customs House.

The cult of Artemis, the Bear Goddess, will not be discussed here, but left until later. The influence of this divinity in London was so widespread and so enduring that, in a degenerate form, it lasted until nearly the end of the nineteenth-century. Because of the cult's importance in the religious life of Roman and post-Roman London, it will be given a chapter to itself.

A little further along the Thames, between Sabb's Key and Old London Bridge was the riverside temple of that ferocious oriental deity who has been described as the 'most un-Roman of all Rome's Gods' – Cybele (or Kybebe), the Great Mother, *Magna Mater deorum Idaea.*

It was in 205 B.C. that Rome, desperately anxious to end the already twelve-year-old campaign against Hannibal, consulted the Sibylline Books. The Books replied with the – to Romans – unwelcome advice that Hannibal could be defeated only if 'the Idaean Mother were brought from Pessinus', a Phrygian city.

Accordingly, Cybele, the Idaean Mother, together with her self-castrating lover, Attis, were brought to Rome, and there installed with a priesthood so odd in their behaviour and so repugnant to Roman ideals of 'good order and military discipline', that Romans were forbidden to join the ranks of the Galli, as the priests of Cybele were called.

The Galli castrated themselves, dedicated the separated genital organs to the goddess, and then – provided that they survived this brutal and dangerous mayhem – continued to serve the goddess, but dressed henceforward only as women.

When the Galli – their name survives in Galley Stairs, near to the church of St Magnus Martyr in which, almost unchanged, survives the name of their goddess, the *Magna Mater* – went abroad in procession, they danced and capered and frothed, and worked themselves into such a state of hysteria that they gashed themselves with the knives that they carried. 'Blood and sex' fairly sums up the atmosphere of that dark cult of Cybele – the blood including the *taurobolium*, a shower-bath of blood from a living bull, and the sex including ritual self-castration, a pair of forceps by which this sacrifice was effected having been found in the Thames almost within a stone's throw – we had nearly said 'almost within a forceps' throw' – of the Temple of the Great Mother, on the eastern side of the northern approach to London Bridge. (This was not, in all probability, a stone bridge but a wooden affair: the typical *pons sublicius* of Roman military architecture.)

That there was a bridge over the Thames in Roman times we know from historical accounts, but were there no historical record of the fact we should still be able to assert that a London Bridge had existed in Roman times. The evidence comes from the old name for the northern approach to the bridge: Oystergate. The first part of this name is plainly the only slightly corrupted Latin word for 'gate, entrance, approach', etc.: *ostium*. If there had been no bridge, why should there have been an *ostium*?

Mars Gradivus, as we have seen, had his college of Leaping Priests – the *Salii Palatini* – on that slight eminence that we now call Tower Hill. From the survival of the word *palatini*, in modern 'Barking', it is not unreasonable to suppose that, when

London was Roman, Tower Hill bore the name *Collis Palatinus* – so that London, like Rome, had its Palatine Hill, and, in all probability, other hills named after Rome's other six.

But Mars was worshipped elsewhere in London than hard by Tower Hill, 'the Palatine Mount'.

Mars was not always a God of War; in some of his aspects, as they are revealed by the prayers to Mars which have survived, he is clearly an agricultural deity, suitable to a people who, originally all farmers, never forgot their rustic origins.

That Mars, in his 'aspect' of fertility god, was worshipped in London, the history of All Hallows the Great, in Upper Thames Street, amply shows. 'All Hallows', is, of course, *aula Saliorum*, 'The Hall of the Salii – the Leaping Priests of Mars' – as 'the Great' (earlier 'Le Grand') is simply *Gradivi*, 'of (Mars) Gradivus'.

But there was another name for this church which indicates that, amongst the temples of Mars in London, it enjoyed a superior rank. In confirming the gift of this church to the monks of Tewkesbury, the charter of Gilbert, Bishop of London, refers to it as the church 'Omnia Sanctorum in London, quae dicitur Semannesire' – 'All Saints, which is called Semannesire' – and a charter of Henry I, 1100–7, refers to it as 'ecclesia in Londonia quae vocatur Semannescyrce'. When Harben says that 'it is not unlikely that the name "Semannescyrce" would be given to All Hallows the Great, situated as it was near to the great port of Dowgate, and therefore easy of access to the seamen trading there', we realize that he has not associated the church of All Hallows the Great with Mars, nor Mars with those ancient divinities, the 'Semones'.

A (to us) mysterious religious brotherhood, the *Fratres Arvales*, included a chant, the *carmen arvale*, in their ritual. It was an ancient hymn to Mars; so ancient that, when recorded in A.D. 218, it had, 'handed down through successive generations of religious functionaries . . . become mere gibberish to those who pronounced it[1]'.

The English text of this hymn, interpreted by E. Norden, makes clear beyond any doubt the originally agricultural aspect of Mars.

[1] L. R. Palmer, *The Latin Language*.

107

Within the *cancellarius vicus*, stood, until the time when London ceased to be completely Roman, a Temple of Mars Gradivus, in which – perhaps here alone of all the temples of Mars in London – a college of the Arval Brothers had its establishment.

Go down to London River, and walk west along Upper Thames Street until you come to All Hallows Lane, which runs along (and makes the eastern boundary of) Cannon Street Station.

Here, in the days until 1893, stood All Hallows the Great (it was moved from the north to the south side of Upper Thames Street in 1876). I went, recently, to the place where the church had stood, and looked up at the great grey walls of the railway station. Here, where the world was quiet, I could imagine myself standing, not within a modern City street, but in a narrow way of Roman London, outside the Temple of Mars Gradivus, through the open doors of which came the 'Gregorian' chanting of the ancient *carmen arvale*:

enos Lases iuuate,
enos Lases iuuate,
enos Lases iuuate.

neue luae rue Marma, sins incurrere in pleores,
neue lue rue Marmar, sins incurrere in pleoris,
neue lue rue Marmar, sers incurrere in pleoris.

satur furere Mars, limen sali, sta berber,
satur fu, fere Mars, limen sali, sta berber,
satur fu, fere Mars, limen sali, sta berber.

semunis alternei, aduocapit conctos,
semunis alternei, aduocapit conctos,
simunis alternei, aduocapit conctos.

enos Marmor iuuato,
enos Marmor iuuato,
enos Mamor iuuato.
triumpe, triumpe, triumpe! Triumpe, triumpe!

In English:

Hail ye Lares – aid us, pray! (*thrice*)
Let no evil touch our people! (*thrice*)
Be Thou appeased, wild Mars – leap Thou upon the boundary-mark, and there remain! (*thrice*)
Call ye, in their rightful order, all the Semones! (*thrice*)
Hail, Mars! – aid us, pray! (*thrice*)
Glory, glory, glory! Glory, glory!

So they sang at the temple which stood at the corner of Upper Thames Street and All Hallows Lane; and the temple, as the name surviving into the late Middle Ages testifies, must have been well known as that of the 'Semones', no less than it was well known as that of Mars Gradivus. This can mean only that this was the temple of Mars in which the Arval Brothers had their *collegium*.

'The Semones', says L. R. Palmer, in his indispensable *The Latin Language*, 'are a group of gods of whom little is known, but Norden suggests that they are divine potencies, executive agents, as it were, for the supreme gods: "The Semones, manifestations of powers which preserve the people, will co-operate." ' That these 'divine potencies', the Semones, were intimately associated with the Temple of Mars Gradivus in Upper Thames Street, the name 'Semanes-cherche' (thirteenth century) inarguably testifies.

Mars himself, of course, may have been one of the *Semones*, for the name is derived from the same root (Indo-European: *sa*, 'to sow') which has given both *semen*, 'seed' (i.e. that which is sown) and *satus*, 'son, daughter, offspring, standing crops, etc.' *Semo*, the singular of *Semones*, simply means 'The Sower', a very proper name for a divinity with basically agricultural associations. Indeed, though the beginning of the third stanza of the Arval Song has been rendered (e.g. by Norden) 'Be Thou appeased!', *satur fu, fere Mars!* might just as plausibly mean 'Be the living harvest, Actively-Bringing (the Fruits of the Earth) Mars! (*See under* 'Mars' in Appendix II.)

Sometimes Mars had a 'form' which denied to women any approach to him; such a 'form' was that of Mars Silvanus –

though here, as his name indicates, he is a god of woods and meadows and tillage.

However, there was a day, the Kalends of March, which, ushering in both the New Year – Roman style – and Mars's own month, gave women the opportunity to approach this most 'husbandly' (fighter and husbandman) of all the gods.

This was the Feast of Married Women, the *Matronalia*, a name to which we shall return shortly. On March 14th came another feast-day in honour of Mars: the horse-festival or *Equirria*, celebrated by horse-racing on the *Campus Martius*, the 'Field of Mars'. In Rome, this open ground reserved to the Martian festivals was sited on the north of the older part of the city; and – perhaps in conscious imitation of Roman precedents? – the open ground reserved for the same purpose in Londinium was also to be found to the north-west of the 'federated' city of London: Smithfield and St Bartholomew's – specifically, the former being more closely identified with judicial execution; the latter (as the name implies) being associated with the festivals of Mars.

St Bartholomew's Hospital, as most people have heard, was founded by the royal jester, Rahere, in thanksgiving for his having been saved from death by malaria – caught whilst on a visit to Rome. However, the Rahere foundation of the thirteenth century is built on the remains of a Roman structure, still in remarkably good preservation. Without casting too much doubt on the story of how Rahere founded his hospital, I may still call attention to the intrusion of the name 'Rome' into the story, and suggest that the memory of Rome, shall we say, was not far distant from the mind of him who first composed the legend of Rahere and St Bartholomew's Hospital.

I have often been astonished at what my search for the Roman originals of our London names has revealed; I do not think that I was ever more astonished in finding what lay behind the name 'St Bartholomew'.

'St Bartholomew' is a saint whose name – like his fame – is widely scattered throughout western Christendom; but, so far as London is concerned, his name traces directly back, without any doubt, to the great Martian Feast of Married Women – and the present St Bartholomew's Hospital is clearly the occupant of the site on which, when Rome ruled London, the Matronalia was celebrated.

Of course, 'St Bartholomew's' is a very corrupt form of 'Matronalia', but, briefly, the derivation goes like this:

(AD) MATRONALIAM > (A') MATRONALIAM > (A') BATRONALIAF
> BARTONALIAF > BARTONALIAW > BARTOMALIAW
> BARTOLAMIAW > BARTHOLOMEW

The Matronalia was celebrated outside the walls both of the Cripplegate Fort and of the 'final' Londinium into which 'Cripplegate', like all the other London forts, was eventually merged. That is to say, when the Wall embraced all the forts from which London had developed, the open ground on which the Matronalia was celebrated was still outside the city limits.

This places the site of the Matronalia somewhat to the west of Cripplegate and almost due north of St Paul's – the origin and significance of whose name we shall examine later.

The Matronalia, too, was celebrated to the north of the burial-ground, the *elysii campi* (Alsies Lane or Elsyngs Hospital) that we have already noticed, and whose memory is preserved in the name of the church in Newgate Street: St Sepulchre-without-Newgate.

But Mars was worshipped within the city, apart from the rites performed at his College of Leaping Priests – 'All Hallows' – on London's Palatine Hill.

Gracechurch Street, formerly known as 'Grass-church Street' or 'Gracious Street', is obviously a corruption of *Gradivus* – that title of Mars of which H. J. Rose remarks, 'the meaning of which was already lost in classical antiquity', but which, nevertheless, plainly means 'the Progressive'. Grace-church Street represents the *cardo* which – certainly in the later stages of the 'federated' Londinium – ran from London Bridge to Bishopsgate ('Porta Bissulca' – the 'two-furrowed' or 'two-way' gate), and passed through the Forum Civile centred upon what are now the crossroads of Gracechurch Street and Leadenhall Street.

In case the derivation of 'Gracechurch' (otherwise 'Grass' or 'Gracious') from 'Gradivus' should seem too fanciful or too daring, let me point out three attested derivations:

III

Latin *graphium* becomes Old Welsh *grephion* (therefore initial GR- is preserved)

Latin *radius* becomes Old Welsh *reith* or *reid* (therefore the A becomes the diphthong EI)

Latin *sedes* becomes Old Welsh *swyð* (therefore the dental sonant, 'd', may become the sonant fricative, 'ð' which passes easily into 's'.

We may, accordingly, reconstruct the development of *Gradivus* into 'Gracious' thus:

Gradivus > Greið > Greis (*Cf.* 'Lindsey' from *Lindum*)

– and so to 'Grass' and 'Gracious' – the latter being a confusion between an original 'Grass Street' and 'Grass-church Street' (that is, 'the Church of Grass or Gradivus').

What is now Gracechurch Street was that part of the *cardo*[1] which connected the southern entrance of the Forum Civile – the forum 'where government was conducted', as distinct from the Forum Boarium, 'where they sell cattle' – with the *ostium pontis sublicii*, the so-called 'Oystergate-by-London-Bridge' of later days.

As I have already stated, it is my belief that there was another complex of imperial and municipal governmental buildings, including the remand-prison, where roughly the Guildhall is today; but it is clear that many of London's most important administrative offices, as well as many temples of importance, lay within the close vicinity of the Forum Civile, part of which lies beneath the modern Leadenhall Market.

Let us look for a moment at an English suffix, that we shall meet often in the names of London's religious establishments: that is, the suffix '-church'. Like the suffix '–gate', it is a gloss, added at a time when Latin (or what passed in London for Latin) was still in use, but at a time, too, when the body of non-Latin-speaking immigrants had already grown so large that a gloss – an explanatory word – was felt necessary to be added to some common Latin word.

---

[1] Whose name survives here, and in other parts of London, in that of the Cardinall Hatte (i.e. [vicus] cardinalatus) tavern and/or alley.

The phenomenon is well known throughout England, where a common example of words from different languages being juxtaposed for mutual explanation is the name 'Woodcote' – favourite of suburban road-namers! – where English 'wood' means the same as British *coed*, and both words, meaning the same thing, explain each other. ('Wood' in such names as 'Wood Street' means something very different: *Vadum*, 'bridge'; but in the name 'Woodcote' the first part has the ordinary English meaning, that is, Latin *silva*.)

Just so does the suffixed English word '-church' explain the word to which it has been added, in the name 'Fenchurch', which (as a tablet on the wall of Fenchurch Buildings, Fenchurch Street, testifies, was spelt 'Fanchurch' until about the end of the eighteenth century). The name should properly be spelt thus 'Fan'(church)', for the first part has nothing to do with the mythmaking etymologists' 'fen, marsh, swamp', but is simply Latin *fanum*, 'shrine, temple', which, as is usual with Latin words imported into Old Welsh, has lost its ending, as *fan'* - just as Latin *pondus* becomes Old Welsh *pwnn*; Latin *sol'dus* becomes Old Welsh *swllt*; Latin *colpus* becomes Old Welsh *cwlf*; and so on.

'Fenchurch', then, does *not* mean 'the Church in the Fen' – in any case, one is on the high ground above the river at Fenchurch Street, and the land cannot have been marshy even before the Romans came to drain the City area. (Evidence for extensive drainage comes in the name 'Cloak Lane'; *cloaca* = the great drain of Tarquinian Rome, and so applied to all extensive drainage systems.) 'Fenchurch', indeed, could well be even more analytically spelt out thus: '*Fan(um)*, i.e. "church"'. As soon as I realized the meaning of Fen-church, I found myself asking: 'To which *fanum* does the name refer?'

Now there are three churches in modern Fenchurch Street – or at least their memories, for all three have now gone: one vanished in the Great Fire of 1666; one was demolished in 1878; and the third, though surviving until 1926, was pulled down to make way for a block of offices. Of these, only one included the name 'Fenchurch (Fanchurch)' in its title: 'St Gabriel Fanchurch', burnt down in 1666. I wondered whether or not it was this oddly 'dedicated' church which had given its

113

H

name to modern Fenchurch Street? I soon found that this was, indeed, the case – but I was astonished to find what lay at the back of that name, 'Gabriel'.

Before we go back to the origins of 'Gabriel', let us take a look at another church, only a few yards from 'St Gabriel Fanchurch', for the character of this other church helped me to determine the direction that my researches into the beginnings of 'St Gabriel's' ought to take.

At the corner of Lime Street (from *limes*, 'a fortified boundary line') and Fenchurch Street, stood, until 1878, the church of St Dionis Backchurch, which, as we have already seen, records the names, in Greek and Latin, of the god Bacchus, regularly modified by the attested rules of Welsh phonology – i.e. 'Dionysus' has become 'Dionis', and Bacchus has become 'Bach', the explanatory English word 'church' being added.

Taken in conjunction with the evidence – that we shall examine later – of a high concentration of legionary establishments in the neighbourhood, there is nothing astonishing in proving that there was a temple of Dionysus-Bacchus in the vicinity of the Forum Civile, nor that 'St Gabriel' should turn out to be objects of worship in high favour with legionary troops recruited in the East.

For 'Gabriel' is none other than an adjective *cabirialis*, formed from the plural noun *cabiri* – the Cabiri, the demon-gods of Samothrace, imported to fulfil the peculiar religious needs of garrison troops who, as the Empire drew towards its end, tended to come from further and further afield.

The church of St Leonard Milk, situate at the corner of the side street on the left hand, next in order as one goes down the *cardo* towards the bridge, need not detain us here; for behind the name of the Christian saint, 'St Leonard Milk', lurks not even a Samothracian demon-god, but a legionary *castellum*, specially sited to guard the approaches to the *fiscus*, the Imperial Treasury, whose name survives in those of Old Fish Street and Fish Street Hill.

This is an excellent example of how corrupt Latin words, their origin forgotten, were mistaken for Old English words, and adopted as such. *Fiscus*, 'treasury', would have been adopted into London Brittonic (or Old Welsh, if you prefer) as *ffyscu*, which would have become *ffysc'* in certain conditions.

By the time that the East Saxons and other immigrants had made their peace with the Lord of London and had been admitted, in treaty-friendship, to the City, the name of the street, Via Fiscalis, would have been so altered in pronunciation as to sound, to Saxon ears, like their word for 'fish' – *fysc*.

From that time on, the name, *ffysc* (from *fiscus*) developed as though it had been the Old English word *fysc*, 'fish', which is why, today, we say 'Old Fish Street', and not, perhaps, 'Old Fisk Street'.

The connection between Old Fish Street and the staple commodity sold therein and in the neighbouring streets is purely fortuitous. Fish is landed at Billingsgate simply because Billingsgate is on the river side. And to trace the name of Old Fish Street back to a Roman fish-market by the Thames is to ignore the special laws of Old London phonology. Latin *pisces*, 'fish', would not, in any circumstances, have developed into *ffysc*; I know of no case where Old Welsh has not retained, unaltered, Latin initial P. It is clear that our modern name, 'Old Fish Street', derives, not from Old English *fysc*, 'fish', but from Latin *fiscus*, 'treasury'.

It would be a mistake to assume that all the churches of London were originally 'pagan' temples. They were not. Some were government offices, others legionary guard-houses or barracks, one at least appears to have been a slave-market, whilst it is hard to resist the conclusion that one – St Pancras – whether as the saint to whom a church is dedicated or (without the prefixed 'St') as a narrow City thoroughfare, 'Pancras Lane', marks the former site of nothing holier than the place where Londoners could witness the *pancratium*, a complete gymnastic contest, which included both wrestling and boxing.

In this chapter, though, we are concerned with recovering the names of the gods of Roman London, and it is with their temples that our present interest lies.

There was an ancient Italic god, Semo Sancus Dius Fidius, who was often 'equated' with the Greek Heracles, Latinized as 'Hercules'. Semo Sancus Dius Fidius was a vegetation deity so venerable that he belonged to the very origins of the Italic

115

peoples, and though H. J. Rose, in his valuable *Ancient Roman Religion*, does not remark on the fact, 'Semo' was also the name for 'dolphin', in the more mystical aspect of that strange sea-mammal, whose odd characteristics fascinated the men of the ancient world, as they do the men of ours.

It rather looks as though Semo Sancus Dius Fidius had his temple well outside the City, though still within the *pomoerium*. The splendid Flitcroft Church of St Giles-in-the-Fields, at Seven Dials, is almost certainly the successor, at several removes, to a fane of Semo Sancus Dius Fidius, placed apart from the City, amongst the wooded groves of 'St Giles'.

As to the modern names, 'St Giles-in-the-Fields', and 'Seven Dials' – the crossroads on which the Shaftesbury Hotel now stands – one may easily see in them echoes of the name of Semo Sancus Dius Fidius. From 'Dius Fidius', came an adjectival phrase *Dialis Fidialis* – and *Dialis* has become 'Giles', whilst *Fidialis* has become 'Fields'.

'Seven' – which is almost invariably pronounced 'sem' by Cockneys – is thus seen to be 'Semo', and the name 'Seven Dials', that some 'educated' person of the past spelt out 'correctly', should properly be 'Sem Dials' – the place of Semo Dius.

That there was no mere isolated temple of Semo Sancus at 'St Giles', but a settlement, big enough to have a military post attached, is proved by the existence of a Little St Andrew's Street near Seven Dials. For, as we have seen, the name 'St Andrew' is merely the Latin *antro*, 'at the military lock-up'.

There is another 'St Giles', and thus another temple of Semo Sancus Dius Fidius, and though it is nearer to the City than is Seven Dials, it is still built outside the walls. This is the very old foundation of St Giles Cripplegate – where 'Oliver Williams *alias* Cromwell' married the Lady Elizabeth Bourchier, as may be seen in the church's marriage-register. The earliest mention that I can find is in a grant by Aelmund to the canons of St Paul's 'of his church of St Giles, *built outside the walls*'. The grant is of the time of Henry I, but the name 'St Giles' is evidence of a much older foundation of Semo Sancus Dius Fidius. This particular temple was built on the bank of the Town Ditch; and it would be interesting to know which ancient taboo prevented a temple of Semo Sancus's being built within the City limits.

Roman religion, so deeply and intimately affecting the Roman people, could not have been otherwise than an affair of the Roman State. And this State religion, like everything else in the world of Rome, was organized with typical Roman efficiency. To the rulers of Rome, it was a matter of supreme importance that the 'wrong' gods be kept out of the running of the Empire, for the *numen* of hostile or even merely unsympathetic divinities could wreak untold harm upon Rome. Most of the gods who had passed the test, as it were, of 'permissibility', were thereafter the direct concern of the State, though – just as certain communist or socialist economies license an unimportant degree of capitalism (one-man shops and peasants' market-stalls in Russia, for instance) – some 'non-governmental' religions were tolerated. These were usually, though not exclusively, managed by *collegia* – societies of believers – which had their origin in the fact that either the god to be worshipped was of too foreign, 'un-Roman', a character to be admitted to the permitted Roman Pantheon without some direct order from the Sibyls, or that the worshippers were of a depressed class – slaves, petty artisans, common labourers – who had united into a burial club, and had provided themselves with a religion not worthy to be accorded State patronage, only State recognition.

But for those gods who had earned the approval of Rome, there was an impressively large and correspondingly active civil service, which managed the religious 'schedules' of the Empire – looked after the temples, regulated the stipend of each 'beneficed clergyman', saw to it that the festivals were celebrated at the proper times and in decent order, and generally guarded the interests of the gods, in the sure and certain expectation that the gods would do as much for Rome.

At the summit of this imposing religious bureaucracy reigned the Supreme Pontiff (*pontifex maximus*) and his Board of Pontiffs (*collegium pontificum*). Originally there had been but three pontiffs, serving the three great Protectors of Rome, Jupiter, Mars and Quirinus – but as imported gods began to be set up alongside of the older gods, more pontiffs were needed

to 'service' the newcomers, and so the Board of Pontiffs grew
from its original three members to six, nine, fifteen and finally
sixteen. All but one pontiff had also a *flamen*, and of these
flamines there were fifteen. There were the six (originally four)
Vestal Virgins, who lived in the Regia, and whose duty it was
to tend the eternal fire of the Eternal City. Finally, outranked
only by the Supreme Pontiff, was the King of the Sacred Rites
(*rex sacrorum*), an official who had retained the priestly function
of the king when kingship had been abolished in Rome.

There is an opportunity here to rid ourselves of a too-often-
repeated fable concerning the origin of the word, *pontifex*,
English 'pontiff'. Every Latin dictionary gives the derivation
of the word as though from *pons* and *facs*, and every literary
comment on the name is but a variant of the following passage[1]:

'. . . the *pontifices* or bridge-builders, whose name is commonly
Anglicized into "pontiffs". Their original business must have
been to appease the river when it was necessary to throw a
bridge over it, thus putting it and its god in the magically
inferior position of being under the feet of those who walked
across.'

Sometimes this 'explanation' is varied in accounting for the
name of the *pontifex* by assuming that it was he who either made
or blessed or guarded (or all three!) the bridge which permitted entrance to the pile-built lake-dwellings or stockaded
terramara dwellings of the primitive Italians.

But all assume, with the dictionary, that *pontifex* is composed
of the Latin words for 'bridge' and 'maker'.

The true explanation of the name rids us of all need for
fanciful theories and unprovable hypotheses. The first part of
the word, *ponti-*, has nothing to do with 'bridge'. It is simply the
old Italic word for 'power, strength, might, *mana*', retained in
Greek both with and without the infixed nasal: πόσις, πότνια.
Religious conservatism amongst the Romans preserved the old
pronunciation with the N. *Ponti-*, then, is merely a metathesized
form of πότνια, *potnia*, 'power', and *ponti-fex* (that is, *potni-fex*)
does not mean 'bridge-builder', but – which seems far more
credible – 'power-wielder, power-master, magic-maker'. Just

[1] *Ancient Roman Religion*, H. J. Rose.

the title, in fact, that we should expect to see borne by the chief *shaman* of a primitive people!

With a calendar so strictly regulated on purely religious lines, and with the State itself (both personalized in the identity of the emperor and, more abstractly, in the reverence for Rome) actively competing with the gods for the worship of the people, it may hardly be a matter for wonder that the ordinary Roman felt some difficulty in distinguishing between the religious and civil functions of the state. We have seen how a wish, made on the Ides of March, that one should live throughout the year – *annare perennareque* – in health and wealth, was personalized into a 'goddess', Anna Perenna, whose 'reality' so developed that she had a grove officially set aside for her worship (which involved drinking too much wine at a picnic on the banks of the Tibur).

Another personification of one of the aspects of the year was Annona, who seems clearly to have become confused with Anna Perenna in the average Roman's religion-ridden mind.

Annona, as the name implies, was originally no more than 'the year's produce, the annual yield'. From that original, simple meaning, *annona* came to mean 'the market price of grain', and then – by way of a phrase *annonae horreum*, 'a storehouse for grain against fluctuations in price' – the word came to mean, first, the dole of grain to all needy Roman citizens, and then – as the duties of the *officina annonae* became more numerous – what we may call only 'the Welfare State'. The development of the word's meaning reached its final stage when Annona was personified as 'the Goddess Who Orders the Bounty of the State', and archaeologists were not astonished to uncover at Ostia the ruins of a temple dedicated to Annona Augusta. We shall now shew that this personification – and deification – of the State's administrative function took place in London as well as in Ostia: two busy ports whose public opinion might be held to reflect the everyday sentiments of the ordinary Roman citizen.

The identification of the various churches of St Ann(e) with the various London offices of the *praefectus annonae* was among the earliest of my identifications, and has already been mentioned on page 67.

The locations of London's 'St Ann(e)s' support the correctness of the identification, for each 'St Ann(e)' is placed where we should expect to find an office of the *Annona*.

Here are the surviving 'dedications' to St Ann(e):

1. St Anne (St Anne & St Agnes). On the north side of Gresham Street, once St Anne's Lane. This church was also known as 'St Anne-in-the-Willowes' and 'St Anne-near (*or* de)-Aldredsgate'. (But – see page 68 – this 'St Anne' may possibly be a 'bonded warehouse' for tin.)

2. St Ann Blackfriars, burnt down 1666. On the east side of Church Entry, north of Glasshouse Yard, in Farringdon Ward Without.

3. St Anne-on-the-Tower-Hill-and-Abbey-of-Whit-Monkys (i.e. 'White Monks'). This was attached to the Cistercian Abbey of the Graces – and 'Graces' here is the same word as is found in 'Gracious' or 'Grasschurch' or 'Gracechurch Street'. It is yet another survival of the name of Mars *Gradivus* – with the Cistercian monks inheriting the site formerly occupied by the *collegium* of Mars's Leaping Priests.

4. Chapel of St Anne, erected by John de Grantham near the church of St Antholin – spelt both 'Antonin' and 'St Antolini' (1353).

5. In the will of John de Camton (Grantham?) 1353, he makes a bequest to the Fraternity of St Anne in the chapel annexed to the fraternity church of St Antolini (*sic*).

   Elsewhere this chapel is referred to as 'the Chapel of St Anne and St John Baptist'. If this is in error for 'St Anne and St John Zachary' – as seems probable – we have here the interesting and significant association of 'St Anne', *Annona*, with 'St John Zachary', *saccararius*, 'accountant, paymaster, cashier,' etc. – our modern word 'exchequer'. If this is really the chapel of St John Zachary and not that of St John Baptist, we are justified in thinking that we have here the successor to the building in which the accounts of the *praefectus annonae* were kept.

6. St Ann's Alley. North out of St Ann(e)'s Lane, and east to

Noble Street, between St Anne's Church and churchyard. This is probably no more than the use of the same name as that of the church, and need not imply another office of the *annona*. Stow calls it 'Pope End Lane', which may, like the numerous other London alleys having the syllable 'pop-' in their names, recall a *popina* or cook-shop which once did business on or near the site.

7. Another de Grantham bequest points to a curious development in the administration of Roman London. A bequest by William de Grantham (*see* the other de Grantham bequests, above) is recorded for the year 1350–1 (*Ct.H.W.I.648*); the beneficiary being the Fraternity of St Anne in the church of St Michael Cornhill. A record of 5 Henry IV – over fifty years later – shows that this Fraternity of St Anne is still in existence, established in the church of St Michael Cornhill. This must be a separate Fraternity of St Anne from that established in St Antholin – the dates confirm this. But 'St Michael', as we shall see, is almost certainly Latin *macellum*, 'shambles, meat-market, provision-market'; the derivation of '*Michael*' from *macellum* being thus:

Latin *macellum* > British *macel* > Old Welsh *megyl* > Middle English *myghel* (sometimes *miles*) > Modern English *Michael*.

We have here, then, the office of the *annona* attached to a certified meat-market – was the *annona* of Cornhill specifically that dealing with the issue of free meat? One recalls Horace's *annona in macello carior, barathrum macelli* – 'Provisions are far more costly in the market – in that abyss of the butchers' stalls'! Still, it looks as though what is now Leadenhall Market either extended halfway down what is now Cornhill, or that (as seems more probable) modern Leadenhall Street and Cornhill were given over entirely to retail trading. That this was so is made more likely by the fact that the street next to 'St Michael Cornhill' is Birchin Lane, and that, most plainly, is Via Mercenaria[1] (M changing to B because it falls between two vowels), 'Street of Commerce'.

As one of London's slave-markets lay at the bottom of Cornhill, it looks as though Cornhill – the Via Principalis of

[1] Or *mercennaria*. But one must assume a form in London with only one N.

the 'sub-London' centred about the crossroads at St Peter Cornhill (*praetorium ad cornulam*) – was devoted to retail trade, as, indeed, it was until only a relatively short time ago. The preponderance of 'office' (i.e. insurance, banking, etc.) buildings in the City of London is a phenomenon of recent happening.

We have, then, one possible and six certain offices of the *praefectus annonae*, if we have interpreted the evidence of the 'St Anne' dedications correctly. But if we see where these 'St Annes' lie, we cannot but believe that they do, in truth, represent the sites of the original offices of the *annona*, the government organization which regulated the food supplies of the Empire's towns and cities.

For one clearly sees that the 'St Annes' – the offices of the Annona – are divided logically amongst the 'forts', the 'sub-Londons', which make up the composite City. There is a 'St Anne' at each of the 'forts', as thus:

CRIPPLEGATE FORT: St Anne & St Agnes ('St-Anne-in-the-Willowes')

RIVER FORT ('Blackfriars'): St Anne Blackfriars

'TOWER OF LONDON' FORT: St Anne-on-Tower-Hill

CHEAPSIDE: (2nd stage of Cripplegate Fort expansion) Chapel of St Anne in St Antholin

FORUM CIVILE (at top of 'Cornhill'): Fraternity of St Anne in St Michael Cornhill

There could hardly be more convincing evidence that, in its origins, London was a collection of five or six smaller Londons, each provided with its requisite government offices.

From the finding of a head of Serapis in the ruins of the Walbrook *Mithraeum*, we know that this strangest of all gods was amongst those worshipped in London. Strange, because this god was the deliberate creation of the first Ptolemy, who commissioned a leading Greek sculptor, Bryaxis, to design and execute a statue of the imaginary god, upon which Ptolemy built the splendid Serapaeum at Alexandria to house it. In spite of – or, perhaps, because of – these unusual origins, the god Serapis was accepted as a genuine deity, and was given fervently sincere worship. There is, indeed, no accounting for the impulses which drove the people of the Roman Empire to bestow their religious favours.

Yet, if unusual gods were the fashion in Romania, there was much to be urged in support of the cult of Antinoüs in Britain.

Antinoüs was a Bithynian and the pretty catamite of the brilliant Emperor Hadrian, who, with Augustus and Trajan, was one of the three greatest men who wore the purple.

In a pet, familiar to all who have ever had the misfortune to assist at a homosexual lovers' quarrel, Antinoüs jumped from the ship which was carrying him and his imperial lover up the Nile. Hadrian, of course, was stricken with grief, but even in his sorrow he could not have foreseen what would happen.

'The sequel was indeed strange. Among the emotionally charged communities of the east, Antinoüs was at once, and with evidently authentic fervour, worshipped as a saviour deity incarnate. Accepted as a god at Delphi and Olympia, he was identified with Dionysus, and at Hadrian's new city in Egypt, Antinoöpolis, men worshipped him as Osiris himself. Dramatic rites were invented to incorporate a Mystery play, the Passion of Antinoüs, at which ceremonial dances or moving images annually represented the pathos of his sorrowful, youthful death, and the glory and ecstasy of his resurrection.'[1]

But granted the normality of such a religion in the world of Rome, one would have expected this religion to have gained many adherents in Britain, where Hadrian's Wall stands to this day as evidence of only one of the benefits that the able Emperor conferred upon his most northerly province.

Judging by the immensity of the head which has been dredged up from the Thames, the statue of Hadrian in London was of a size to make one wonder if, indeed, there were not also a cult of Hadrian himself? But certain it is that his deified catamite was worshipped in Londinium: the Hospital and Church 'dedicated' to what later was written 'St Anthony' proves that.

The earliest reference to the survival of the name, Antinoüs,

[1] Michael Grant, *The World of Rome.*

is in a manuscript belonging to the Dean and Chapter of St Paul's, *c.* A.D. 1119, where there is a note 'de Sancto Antonino'.

The Hospital of St Anthony (*sc.* Antinoüs) was on the north side of Threadneedle Street. In 1254, King Henry III granted the site to the Brotherhood of St Anthony of Vienna, to be a cell of their house. But in 1414, following the passing of the Alien Priories Act,[1] the Hospital reverted to the Crown, the church of St Benet Fink (whose name will be explained later) being appropriated to the Hospital for the benefit of the free school.

The fact that stray pigs – 'St Anthony's pigs' – were held to be the perquisite of St Anthony's Hospital associates perhaps the worship of Antinoüs with that of Demeter, the Pig Goddess, to whose powerful *numen* Cicero bears testimony in his *Contra Verrem.*

Passing St James's Church, in Piccadilly recently, I saw that the rector had invited members of other branches of the One, Catholic and Apostolic Church to preach there. I forget all the names, but I recall that of 'General' Coutts, of the Salvation Army, and Mr Kenneth Slack, of the City Temple. This tolerance, which seems to mark the last days of Christianity, was also a characteristic of the last days of paganism, where every temple gave hospitality to the gods of another cult. Thus, it would not be astonishing to find that Demeter and Antinoüs shared the same temple, any more than it is astonishing that – as it happened – the temple of Mithras found room for statues of Dionysus, Serapis, Nodens and others.

Bellona, Goddess of War, was the sister of Mars, God of War; and this 'family relationship' may account for the proximity of buildings or places named after each. The priests of Mars Gradivus – the *Salii* – appear to have had their principal *collegium* on a hill which was named after Bellona – the *palatum Bellonarium*, 'Barkingside', but as the name 'All Hallows' shows, there were temples of Mars in every one of the five or six 'Londons'.

On the other hand, as we have already noticed, the presence

---

[1] For those to whom the Reformation invokes only the images of Luther and Henry VIII, a study of the anti-Roman legislation of previous centuries is to be recommended.

of a statue of Bona Dea in the remains of the Walbrook Mithraeum implies considerably more than that this goddess was a 'guest star' of the Mithraists – even though the willingness of Mithraism to take in other gods is well known. In Walbrook, there is a small court, Bond Court, whose name is so obviously derived from that Bona Dea (Bon' Dea > Bon' D' > Bond) whose sculptured head was found in the nearby Walbrook Mithraeum that we can hardly resist the conclusion that she, too, had a temple in Walbrook, relics from the remains of which were doubtless those bought by Roach Smith in 1878.

The difficulty that some people have, even today, in pronouncing the name, Antinoüs, may account for the startling variations that the name of the church 'dedicated' to him shows through recorded history:

'De Sancto Antonino' (Sanctus Antoninus)	c. 1119
St Antonin	1119
St Antolin	13 Edw. I.
St Antony	1350
St Auntelin	14 Edw. III
St Tauntelyne	7 Ric. II
St Antony Boge rowe (Budge Row)	7 Hen. IV
St Antonin de Watlyngstrete	1402
St Antonin de Walbrook	1403
St Antonin in Watlyngstrete	1443
St Antelyne in Bogerowe	1500–21
St Antolyns	(Arnold Chr. p. 77)
St Antelyne in Bogerowe	(Arnold Chr. p. 247)
Seynt Ancelyne	Fabyan p. 296)

All of which point unmistakably back to an earlier form *Antinonum* (*for* Antinoüm).

St Anthony's Hospital no longer exists, but a church of St Antholin still stands at the corner of Bow Lane – unwitting memorial to a long-dead emperor's wayward affection.

Echoes of the name of Apollo – that Greek god to whom Augustus was (or pretended to be) so deeply attached – are heard both in Cain-and-Abel's Alley and (even more clearly) in the name of a mysterious society which appears in the London records of the late Middle Ages: the Honour of Bononiae – reputedly a merchants' professional body. Let us take the former name first: Cain-and-Abel's Alley.

'Abel' derives most obviously from 'Apollo', whilst 'Cain' (or, more precisely, 'Cain-an'') derives from one of the best known titles of Apollo: 'shining, glowing dazzling, resplendent'. Apollo was also known as Apollo, Physician and Healer (*Apollo Medice, Apollo Paean*), but it was as the Bright, Shining One – Phoebus, the Sun-God, in his Latin guise – that Apollo was best worshipped and revered: Candens Phoebus . . . Candens Apollo . . . Cain-an' – Abel.

'Bononia' is the later name for the French town that we call Boulogne. In Caesar's day, it was known as Gessoriacum. It may well be doubted that the medieval London trade-society known as 'The Honour of Bononia' had much to do with either the Latin or French seaport. I think that here we have a bit of 'educated' correction, by someone who knew that modern 'Boulogne' had originally been Latin 'Bononia'.

But here the word had never been 'Bononia'. It had never originated in the Latin 'Bononia', but in the Latin form of the Greek name, Apollo. Instead of 'The Honour of Bononiae', the title of this mysterious society should have been something like 'The Honour of Boulogne', or, better still, 'the Honour of Bullen' – for to that had the name of Apollo developed by the fourteenth century. The origin of 'Boulogne' – in this specific connection, of course – is in the nominative/accusative case of the name *Apollo*, i.e. *Apollinem*, for in Late Latin the accusative form of the noun served for both nominative and accusative. The development is clear to see:

Apollinem > '*Pollinem* > '*Pollin* . . . > *Bullen*

and it is from the family's having had some connection with property whose name recalled that of Apollo, Physician and Healer, that Sir Thomas Bullen, father of the unlucky Anne Boleyn, bore his own patronymic.

What was 'The Honour of Bononiae'? Was it connected with

the cult of Apollo merely by a link of name – that is, from having occupied a building which, once, had been known as *ad Apollinem*, 'next-door to the Temple of Apollo'? Or was it a consciously pagan cult, surviving (as the Church was unhappily aware that so many were surviving) well into modern times? The answer belongs elsewhere than in this book; what seems certain is that several London names – names which, from being purely topographical, became family names – derive clearly from the cult of that Apollo whose religious importance was such that, in Rome, he rivalled great Jupiter himself. In London, Apollo could hardly have been much less significant.

Greatest of all the pagan temples of old London was that of Jupiter Dolichenus, whose site is to be found east of the present New Bridge Street (which marks the course of the buried Fleet River). Jupiter Dolichenus was one of those divine novelties that Rome imported with her ever-growing dependence on the exotic, both in recruits for her armies and in gods for her Pantheon. Jupiter Dolichenus was an 'aspect' of Jupiter as imported from Doliche, in Asia Minor, and had first been introduced into Rome by legionaries returning from service in what we later legionaries of a newer (but just as vanished) empire have learned to call 'the Middle East'.

Like Mithras and Cybele, Jupiter Dolichenus was an eastern god both in his origin and in his ritual, and the temples of Jupiter Lapis, Jupiter Liber, Jupiter Stator or any of the other older and more 'respectably' Roman Jupiters, would not do for this newest of all the Father-God's 'aspects'. In Londinium, as I have said, his was the most splendid temple of all, part, it seems certain, of the vast building complex which centred about the huge 'raft of concrete' discovered recently when demolishing bomb-ruined property south of St Paul's.

The name of the temple of Jupiter Dolichenus survives in that of a small passageway, Do Little Lane, which ran south from Carter Lane (*quartarius*, 'fourth-part', quarter' – i.e. of the City) to Knightrider Street, in Castle Baynard (*balnearia*, 'baths') Ward.

How modern, 'explanatory' Do Little Lane was derived from Dolichenus is easily seen:

Doe Litle Lane   1584
Dolittellane   1359
Dolytellane   1349
Dolytelane   1314–15

These forms point to an original *Dolit-* or *Dolich-* – the interchangeability of т and к (сн) being a common phenomenon throughout the European languages. Do Little Lane, then, seems to record the site – or the vicinity – of the Temple of Jupiter Dolichenus, just as the Ward in which Do Little Lane is situated records the splendid baths which were adjacent to, or perhaps a part of, the temple.

As I said earlier, the present Castle Baynard Ward, preserving the names of the *praetorium* (St Peter's), the baths (*balnearia*) and the *castellum* (Castle Baynard) in which both were sited, marks the site of a riverside 'fort' which – if we accept the evidence of the name 'Carter Lane', was regarded in the 'federated' London of later imperial times, as a distinct 'quarter' of the City.

Before we go on to consider what appears to have been the other temple in London, there is one persistent question which must be answered: 'Even if one admitted the claim that the majority of the older London names are derived from Latin words, why must these Latin words date from the centuries of the Roman rule of London? In the centuries following Roman rule – and most particularly in the centuries between the Norman invasion and the Commonwealth – the records of the City and its internal and external correspondence were maintained almost consistently in Latin. May it not be this Latin – and *not* the Latin of imperial times – which lies at the origin of such London words and names that you have shewn to be derived from Latin?'

As this is not only a fair, but also a likely-to-be-often-heard, objection, it is essential to answer it instantly, fully and finally.

The certain proof that London names are derived from imperial, and not from mediæval, Latin is the fact that Roman Latin-origined London names are to be found in old documents side-by-side with their mediæval Latin equivalents.

For instance, the mediæval Latinist translated the name,

'St Michael-over-against-the-Market' (the church mentioned in the 1181 Inquisition of London Churches as 'St Michael of the Shambles' and leased at a rent of 30s.) as *S.Michael juxta Macellum*. As we have seen, the Latin word *macellum*, 'butcher's stall, meat-market, provision-market, shambles', already existed in London under the form 'Myghel' (later 'Michael'). Yet the mediæval London clerk, penning the records of the City in his far-from-classical Latin, shows no awareness that *macellum* and 'Myghel' were one and the same word. So that, when a mediæval scribe comes to write of 'the Fraternity of St Anne in St Michael Cornhill', he Latinized the name of the church as 'St Michael de Cornhulla', and not 'Ecclesia Macelli apud Cornhullam'. In short, the Latin origin of London names had passed completely from the average London memory, even though Latin, of a sort, was then being consistently written and, to a large extent, spoken.

Nor was this ignorance of the Latin origin of London's names confined to home-bred writers. In *The Miracles of St Edmund the King* (*Miraculi Beati Edmundi Regis*), written about 1070, Hermannus says that London was entered '*a via que anglice dicitur "ealsegate"* ', 'by the entrance which in English is called "Alegate" '. It is clear that the writer is completely unaware that at least the first part of 'Alegate' (the word was not wrongly spelled 'Aldgate' until nearly at the end of the fifteenth century) is pure Latin, and that the origin of this first part is the Latin adjective, *alta(m)* = 'high, tall, lofty'.

The other (to me, convincing) example of a once-Latin name whose Latinity had come to be forgotten by Londoners habitually using Latin is that of St Vedast, commonly reported to be a miracle-working bishop of sixth-century Arras, better known to the French and the Belgians as St Vaast.

There may well have been a St Vaast – or even a real St Vedast – but the church in Foster Lane (itself a variation of the word from which 'St Vedast' is derived) has nothing to do with the saint of Arras.

Old documents shew that 'Foster' and 'Vedast' are the same word, the church of St Vedast once being more commonly known as 'St Fauster's', or even as plain 'Fosters'. The latter is much nearer to the original form than is 'St Vedast', as I shall

I

show. The most significant form of the name is found in that of an adjoining alley: Vastes Alley. In a document of 1352, the church is called as of 'SS Vedast and Amandus'.

I have suggested, in an earlier book of mine,[1] that originally the building in which this Christian church was later established was either a place where the *fasti* were displayed or connected in some other way with the *fasti* – which were days on which courts could be held or judgements pronounced. That our modern custom of displaying official notices of legal sessions on church doors, inside the porch or on the outside notice-board, is very ancient, we know. If, as seems probable, the name 'St Vedast' relates to such a custom, we may say that the custom goes back to the London of the Romans.

That a calendar of the *fasti*, 'court-days', was displayed in public places (particularly in the *fora*), we know from such a remark as that *Cn. Flavius fastos circa forum in albo proposuit*, 'Gnaeus Flavius set up a list of the court-days all around the Forum'. It is clear, then, that 'Vedast' or, better still, 'Vedasti', is a simple metathesis of *die fasti*, '(on) the court-day'.

Knowledge of the fact that the district around St Paul's, and at the west end of Cheapside, had been originally the Forum Boarium, the Cattle Market, is shown by the use of the phrase, *Warda Fori*, 'Ward of the Forum', in medieval London documents. The writers of such phrases were, presumably, well acquainted with the word *fasti*, from their reading of classical authors; yet, so completely had the Latin origin of London words and names been forgotten, that no one saw in such a name as 'Vedast' or 'Foster' the phrase *die fasti*. It cannot, I think, be argued that the Latin origin of our London names is medieval Latin: these names have their origins in much earlier times.

This brings us to a point noticed elsewhere: the 'blending' of Latin and Old English in such names as 'Oystergate', where the first part is plainly Latin *ostium*, 'a gate', and the second part gives what appears to be an English equivalent – 'gate'.

However, I tentatively suggest that even 'gate' – at least, in some words – may not be Old English at all, but as Latin as the word to which this 'gate' is found attached.

In our search for the face of lost Londinium, we meet saints

[1] *London Growing, op. cit.*

who were once pagan gods, and saints who were merely the government departments of *municipium* or province or empire. But at St Paul's we meet with a saint who has the most improbable origin of all. Every piece of evidence that we can gather from other than etymological sources confirms that, in the St Paul's district, within the Aldersgate-Newgate-Ludgate angle of the City wall, another forum – the Forum Boarium, or Cattle Market – was sited. What is more, this forum – or perhaps an open space near it – was the traditional meeting-point of the citizens of London. Originally outside the wall of the City, as the existence of a burial ground (*elysii campi*) just north of St Paul's proves, the open space in which the citizens gathered kept its character until the very end of the Middle Ages. It was here that 'the Viscounts (Sheriffs) and Citizens of the Londons' acclaimed Henry III as King of England – the last time that an English monarch had been elected in the old Teutonic fashion, by open acclamation of the citizens. But, long after King Henry, the citizens of London continued to elect their magistrates in this literally open way, and that a long tradition of government-by-citizens'-acclamation lay behind the election of Henry III is proved by the name 'St Paul's'.

No matter that the present cathedral is dedicated to St Paul, whose Roman sword, they say, appears in the City arms – the fact is that the name, 'St Paul's' is merely the corrupted Latin phrase, *Senatus Populusque* (*Londiniarum* or *Londinienses*): 'The Senate and the People of the Londons'. The name 'St Paul's' in fact, records the fact that it was here, on the western of London's two hills, that the first popular government of the City was established.

Once we have established the fact that St Paul's has its origin in a centre both of market-trading and of municipal government, many things which came later are made clear.

We can now understand why the outraged citizens of London expelled 'Bishop' Mellitus, who wished to build a cathedral where St Paul's now stands. (The story is that he did – which makes the action of the Londoners even more understandable!)

What Mellitus wished to do was to take over the site – or, perhaps only part of it – which, for hundreds of years had been used by the Londoners as their Forum Boarium, as well as their

Guildhall. I do not suppose that Mellitus instantly converted all the existing Roman establishments into churches – the barracks of the *gregarii* into 'St Gregory-by-St Paul's'; the college of the Fetiales[1] into 'St Faith's'; the *campus sanctus Augustinus* ('open space reserved for the use of the City of London') into 'St Augustine' – but that he intended to lay a boldly ecclesiastical hand upon the property of the Londoners seems certain; and the Londoners, with more spirit then than they have today, kicked the parvenu 'prelate' out.

However, Mellitus, or one of his more subtle successors, did succeed in converting at least a part of the Forum Boarium to a Christian religious use, and the first of London's St Paul's cathedrals rose alongside the places where men ruled London, sold cattle, exhibited the official notices and lent money.

But in taking over a part of this busy commercial and governmental precinct for the uses of his church, Mellitus did not succeed in taking the lot – and what was left to the people of London explains the exceedingly curious uses to which the mediæval Cathedral of St Paul's was put. It also explains why those curious uses were tolerated by even the most intolerant public opinion.

St Paul's was, in fact, never a church in the total sense of the word; that is, it was always a church *and something else*. And even up to the end of the mediæval St Paul's, when the Great Fire of 1666 finished its long history, the 'something else' always seemed more important to London than its purely ecclesiastical uses.

St Paul's was, despite its official rank of cathedral, merely the old Forum Boarium covered over, as markets are covered today in various parts of England. No matter that, as Weever points out, bills were stuck up to prevent the grossest abuses. 'At every door of this church was anciently this verse depicted, and in my time it might perfectly be read at the great south door: *Hic locus sacer est, hic nulli mingere fas est*' (This is a holy place, here no one should permit himself to make water).

'There were also within the sacred edifice', says Sampson,

---

[1] Fetiales were originally members of a Roman College of priests, who sanctioned treaties and demanded satisfaction from an enemy before a formal declaration of war.

'tobacco, book, and sempstress' shops; there was a pillar at which serving-men stood for hire, and another place where lawyers had their regular stands, like merchants on "Change".' At the period when Dekker wrote his curious *Gull's Horn-Book* (1609), and for many years after, the Cathedral was the lounging place for all idlers and hunters after news, as well as of men of almost every profession, cheats, usurers, and knights of the post. The Cathedral was likewise a seat of traffic and negotiation, even pimps and procuresses had their stations there; and the font itself, if credit may be given to a black-letter tract on the *Detestable Use of Dice-play*, printed early in Elizabeth's reign, was made '*a place for the advance and payment of loans, and the sealing of indentures and obligations for the security of the moneys borrowed*' (my italics).

In other words, as I could find many more contemporary quotations to prove, the bankers of Roman London – the *danistae* and *babylones* who had once done business in the two *collybi* south of the Forum Boarium were succeeded by bankers who did their business on roughly the same pitch, but within the great building which had extended itself, over the centuries, to include most of the Forum Boarium. The usurers and their clients cannot have objected to the development: a wet day in Norman London would have been a wet day indeed, and banking business must have been far more comfortably done under the groined roof of Gothic St Paul's.

Nothing, I think, better exemplifies the unbroken continuity of London custom than that St Paul's – 'Old St Paul's' – should have been, not a church, but little more than a covered market: the old Forum Boarium, with a stone roof to cover its busy affairs.

Long after the Roman Empire had ceased to be even the *de jure* ruler of Britain, the area about the Cattle Market, from which, it is clear, the municipal government of London was carried on, was held to be peculiarly the property of London and its people. The Senate of London continued to meet here, even though, after the Saxons had moved in, the Latin word *senatus* was replaced by the Saxon word *folkmot*.

This *folkmot*, or gathering of the citizens in a judicial capacity, was bitterly fought by both King and Church; yet the Folkmot

133

of London continued to meet for centuries after open war had been declared on the institution by newer authorities.

Depending on the differences between King and Church, the citizens of London would appeal to the King against some high-handed action of the Church. For instance, in the 14th year of his reign, Edward II, a notorious loose-liver whose perversions were condemned by Church and barons alike, could receive a complaint from the citizens that the Dean and Chapter of St Paul's had enclosed the land on which the Folkmot was held, 'to the deteriment of the citizens'. In this case, however, the Church seems to have won, and the Folkmot disappears from history.

Yet to appreciate how the ancient prestige – and indeed the ancient purpose – of the 'St Paul's' area had been maintained into late mediæval times, we have only to go back to the reign of Henry III (who owed his crown to the citizens of London), and read there how it was admitted that the citizens had the right to enter the bell-tower of St Paul's to convene the Folkmot. And in an extract from the Cotton MSS relating to Folkmoots and Mootbells, it is said that the Folkmoot (or Folkmot) ought to be held once a year, 'viz., in capite Kalendarium Maii'. In the *Liber Albus*, I, 118–9, provision is made for the holding of Folkmots three times a year, that is to say, at Midsummer, Michaelmas and Christmas, and, what is even more striking, the *Liber Albus* actually compares the mediæval institution of the Folkmot with the Roman *plebiscita* – which, indeed, it was. (The *Liber Albus* or *Liber Custumarum* is a mediæval record of London laws and customs, contained in the so-called *Munimenta Gildhallae Londinensis*, 'Documentary Records of the London Guildhall'.)

One subtly important fact is that it is only on very formal occasions, and then almost always in formal Church references to the institution that the Cathedral is referred to as '*St* Paul's'. A subconscious public memory of its august but profane origins caused Londoners to refer to it invariably as 'Paul's'. Fabian calls it: 'the churchyarde at Powlys', and this style was retained until after the restoration of Charles II. There is, indeed, something very striking in the way in which the citizens of London battled to keep this land their own, and to defend it against the constant encroachment of the Dean and Chapter.

That the Dean and Chapter, in spite of their strong position, as nominees of an ecclesiastical dictatorship, still felt unsure of themselves in laying claim to this very public area of London, seems to be indicated by the fact that, in the 31st year of Edward I, there is a reference to a *Capella Episcopis juxta Sanctum Paulum*, 'the Chapel of the Bishop alongside of St Paul's'. According to acceptable evidence, there appear to have been two chapels, and both, despite the usual meaning of *juxta* as 'alongside of', were *beneath* St Paul's. That one was known as 'St Mary' may well indicate its origin as a *statio* of a market weights-and-measures official: *statio sacomarii*, from which most (if not all) of London's 'St Marys' seem to have descended.

But even after the Church – or, perhaps, only the Dean and Chapter – had successfully alienated the public ground of the former Roman Cattle Market from the ownership of the citizens, the citizens, as I have noted elsewhere in this book, did not feel themselves utterly excluded from what had now become 'St Paul's'. As you have read on page 133, the Cattle Market merely moved inside 'St Paul's', and for all the re-proaches, thunderings, ordinances and prohibitions of Dean and Chapter, Old St Paul's, at least, was treated, to the end of its days, rather as a covered arcade than as a House of God.

An incautious glance at a newspaper the other day shewed me one of the cathedral's clerics parachuting down from an upper loft, whilst the cameramen got busy beneath; and on another page was the picture of a mini-skirted young woman playing a guitar within St Paul's. I didn't trouble to read the caption below the photograph, but I couldn't help reflecting that St Paul's, if it isn't returning to its old dignity as a cattle-market, is at least abandoning any pretence to a religious use.

We shall see later that there is another 'saint' connected with this area whose origins are equally improbable – but here we must leave the general consideration of the gods of Roman London to concentrate our attention on one who seems to have been, in a very special sense, the Londoners' own deity: Artemis, the Bear Goddess – a statue of whom was discovered not far from St Paul's, and whose memory has haunted the western hill until our own times.

Chapter VI

The Cult of Artemis, The Bear Goddess — London's Patron Deity

What the mediæval church well understood was that it enjoyed no monopoly of conformity; it realized that there were other faiths to which many reputedly devout Christians owed a secret and (to the Church) dangerous allegiance, and it was in connection with the widespread worship of one of the oldest of these subterranean faiths that I was in correspondence with the late Dr Margaret Murray just before she died.

Of all the Roman cults which were established in London during the government of the Imperium, that of Artemis appears to have had the greatest appeal to Londoners; and of all the ancient faiths which *ought* to have disappeared with the coming of Christianity, that of Artemis, the Bear Goddess, survived longest. Perhaps not all the numerous 'Browns' of the present day owe their familiar surname to their ancestors' dedication to Artemis, but there can be no doubt that *one* of the origins of the name 'Brown' was connected with the cult of the Bear Goddess. The Bear Gardens which survived until the eighteenth century are merely the English counterpart of the 'sacred' Bear Pit of Berne, the City of the Bear – the City of Artemis.

'Great is Diana of the Ephesians . . .'. But as great, possibly, was Diana – or Artemis – of the Londoners.

My first clue to the existence of a widespread cult of Artemis in Roman London came when I began to consider the curious name that the church of St Martin Vintry bore in mediæval times. 'Baermanncyrce' (early twelfth century) or 'Baremannes-churche' (mid-thirteenth century). Before we go on to consider exactly what 'Bear Man's church' means, we may notice that the references to the church are distinctly odd: '*Sancti Martini ubi vina venditur*', 'St Martin where the wines are sold'; '*St Martin of Baremanneschurch apud coquinas venetrie*', 'St Martin/ Bear Man's church, near the cookshops of the Vintry'. Plainly, this is an unusual sort of church, to merit such unusual descriptions.

But what do *Baermanncyrce* or *Baremanneschurche* mean?

We may dismiss all the many previous suggestions, including that of Harben whose *Dictionary of London* says: 'The name "Baremannchurch" is derived from the O.E. "baerman" = carrier, porter, persons in this neighbourhood being largely employed in the wine trade. This seems to have been the earliest distinguishing appellation of the church, and it may have been erected in the first instance for the use of those employed in the great wine trade of the neighbourhood.'

As I have pointed out elsewhere, there must have been carriers or porters employed, not only in the wine trade, but in every other trade of mediæval London – and, in fact, 'Baremanne' or (the earlier and more correct) 'Baermanne' does not derive from the Old English word for 'porter', but from the Teutonic word for 'bear' (that is, Latin *ursus*, the animal).

A pause here to consider the name for the animal that we, and the other Teutonic-speakers call a 'bear', and that the Greeks in later times and the Celts always called by names having the root, *arc-* or *orc-*.

The bear has always been regarded, by primitive peoples, with feelings of awe, and so far as the remains of Neanderthal man are concerned, we have evidence that the worship of the bear is the oldest of all Man's religions – at least, so far as the testimony of sacred objects is of value. So strong was this feeling that the bear (like the dolphin) was a numinous, an otherworldly, creature, that its 'true' name was never spoken, and it was always spoken of (and with proper reverence) by a 'respectful' nick-name. In Russia, its name is *medvezh*, 'honey eater'; for the ancient Slavs would no more have risked pronouncing its 'true' name than would the ancient Teutonic peoples, who called it by the word which has become our 'bear': 'the Brown One'.

How Artemis, the Greek Moon Goddess, inherited the mantle

of the far more ancient Bear Goddess, this is no place to discuss; but that the connection was strong in the Greek mind is proved by the ceremony of Artemis Braunonia.

Let me quote a brief passage from the enchanting biography of that great Hellenist, the late Jane Harrison, *Reminiscences of a Student's Life* (London: Hogarth Press, 1925):

'The first time I went to Athens, I had the luck to make a small archaeological discovery. I was turning over the fragments in the Acropolis Museum, then little more than a lumber-room. In a rubbish pile in the corner, to my great happiness, I lighted on *the small stone figure of a bear*.[1] The furry hind paw was sticking out, and caught my eye. I immediately had her – it was manifestly a she-bear – brought out and honourably placed. *She must have been set up originally in the precinct of Artemis Braunonia.*[1] Within this precinct, year by year, went on the *arkteia*, or bear-service. No well-born Athenian would marry a girl unless she had accomplished her bear-service, unless she was, in a word, *confirmed*[1] to Artemis.'

I suggest that the old church, later known as that of 'St Martin Vintry', must have been named 'Bear Man's church' because of the statue or statues of the Great She-bear with which the original building, surviving into the Saxon occupation of Roman London, must have been decorated. We recall that, if there was a 'Bear Woman' – the Goddess Artemis, into whose cult that of the Roman Diana was absorbed – there was also a famous 'Bear Man', apparently the polemarch of Britain, and notable in the days when Roman rule was now being taken up by the independent British: Artorius, 'King Arthur', 'The Bear of Britain'.

The land on which St Martin Vintry stood – for it was not rebuilt after the Great Fire of 1666 – lay between Maiden Lane and Queen Street. The latter, made after the Great Fire, need not detain us here, though its name may still have ancient echoes; but Maiden Lane becomes even more significant when we see that it once bore either another or a parallel name:

[1] My italics.

Kyrune, Kyrones, Kirone, Kyron, Kyroun, Kiroun and Kerion Lane.

Stow says that 'it was named of one Kerion, sometime dwelling there' – and, in a way, Stow is right. The One who dwelt there, in her bear-guarded shrine, was Koré the Maiden, a popular appellation for Artemis, Goddess of the Moon and of Maidenhood, as this appellation has been popular, later, for Mary, the Virgin Mother of Jesus. In the name, Kiroun or Kyron, we have a Greek word, hardly altered: κορῶν, 'of the Maidens', doubtless the remnant of some such phrase as ἀγορά κορῶν, *agora korōn*, 'the Place of the Maidens'. Nothing could be more positive evidence that here, in 'St Martin Vintry', we have what was once the Temple of Artemis, the Bear Goddess.

What, then, of the name 'St Martin'? (Or, better still, 'St Martin's'.) I suggest that this is no more than the slightly altered name of the Moon and Bear Goddess: Artemis.

St Martin Vintry has gone, but a beautiful proof of its original connection with Artemis-Diana, the Divine Huntress, survives in the shape of that ancient City Livery Company, the Vintners, whose hall stands near where the vanished church of St Martin Vintry stood until 1666. The proof? This: 'wine dealer' in Latin is *vinarius*, a word which, we may fairly state, never developed into *vintner*. But a Latin word which would have (and indeed, in my opinion, *has*) developed into *vintner* is *venator* (or its feminine form, *venatrix*) – and this is a word of extreme significance in this context, for it means 'hunter' (or, as a feminine, 'huntress').

In other – and revealing – words, the ancient livery company which has its hall near the site of vanished St Martin Vintry is not the Company of Vintners, 'wine dealers', but the Company of *Venators*, 'huntsmen' – a college, in its origin, of priests dedicated to the service of Artemis, the Divine Huntress. The Vintners Company is the still surviving (and, incidentally, still wealthy and powerful) college of priests associated with the worship of Artemis, the Bear Goddess.

Of the vast antiquity of the Vintners Company there can be no doubt, but there is a peculiarity of this livery company which proves that antiquity: the curious 'crowns' worn, on solemn occasions, by its principal functionaries.

If you find yourself in the British Museum, go to the splendidly redesigned Roman Room, and there seek out three 'crowns' or fillets worn by the officiating priest in ceremonies now forgotten. These 'crowns' are identical with those worn today by the Prime Warden and other officials of the Vintners Company – fillets whose design, sanctified by ancient tradition, has never been permitted to change in close on two thousand years of use.

Artemis the Bear Goddess kept her worshippers far into the later Middle Ages. In 1197, W. Brune and his wife Rosia founded a 'spital', under the name of 'Domus Dei and (sic) Beatae Mariae extra Bishopsgate' – 'The House of God and of Blessed Mary outside Bishopsgate'. The dedication was all properly orthodox, but, after having glanced at the donor's significant name, 'Brune', observe where he chose to plant his new hospital: in the parish of St Botolph without Bishopsgate in the Ward of Bishopsgate Without, *extending from Berwards* (*i.e. Bearward's*) *Lane*, south to the parish of St Leonard Shoreditch on the north, and from the King's Street west (Bishopsgate Street?) to the Bishop of London's field called Lollesworth east. The connection between the name of the 'pious' donors of the 'spital' – Brune – and the place at which the new foundation began – Bearward's Lane – is more than mere coincidence could possibly account for. It is evident – and it was almost certainly evident to his tolerant contemporaries – that W. Brune was a worshipper, perhaps even a priest, of Artemis, the Bear Goddess, at the very time that Richard Cœur-de-Lion was away in Palestine, trying to take back the Holy Lands from the Saracen. But if Margaret Murray is to be believed, all the early Norman kings were Christian only in a highly technical sense.

It is possible that a more modern name for Bearward's Lane is Artillery Lane, and here again we have echoes of the Bear Goddess. For 'Artillery' could well be derived from *Artemisium*, 'the Temple of Artemis', though the derivation, admittedly, is certainly not direct.

If the several dedications to 'St Martin' in London do not all refer to an original cult of Artemis – for one or two may well owe their origin to a temple of Mars, *fanum Martis* – there is one

'St Martin's' which hints strongly at a connection with the Bear Goddess.

This is the strangely named St Martin Orgar, which stood on the east side of St Martin's Lane, in Candlewick Ward – that is, within the 'reserved area' called by the Romans the *cancellarius vicus*. St Martin Orgar was burnt down in 1666, and not rebuilt.

The curious pendant name 'Orgar' puzzled those who had forgotten its original significance, and this name appears variously in ancient documents as 'Algar', 'Orgor', 'Ordgarium' 'Horgar', 'Orgon', 'Ongar' and – not so fantastically as it may seem – 'Morgan'; for though 'Orgar' had originally no con- nection with 'Morgan', the latter could well stand as a Celtic description of Artemis: *mor gan*, 'the Sea-born'.

Of all the variant forms quoted above, a thirteenth-century form 'Ordgarium' ('Scī martini ordgarii', 1285) comes nearest to the original, which can only have been some such word as *Arctorium* (for *Arcturium*), 'the Place of the Bear-keeper'.

But to return to the clearly identified temple of Artemis – St Martin Vintry – and the lane, Maiden Lane or Kyrune Lane, which bounded, as it were, the northern limits of the Artemisian 'Bear Man's church'. In this lane in the reign of Henry VIII, stood the capital messuage called 'Skales Inne', and two other messuages which need not concern us here. But 'Skales' is of significance, and shews how often the original Latin word survived almost unchanged.

This messuage, 'Skales', took its name from a flight of *steps* – Late Latin, *scalas* – which led from a Thames-side wharf to the river. These were no ordinary steps, but those that, from ancient tradition, the Lord Mayor took when he was about to go by boat from London to the King at Westminster.

Obviously, behind this choice of particular steps, lay a reason having its origin in a time long before there was a king at Westminster – but not, perhaps, before a time when there was a shrine of Artemis at whatever the Romans called that western suburb of Londinium. The fact that the name, *scalas*, of the steps had hardly altered in fifteen hundred years shows with what veneration this part of the City was regarded, for only in the conservative attitudes of Law and Religion is such un- changing survival possible to words.

But as the religion of Artemis the Bear Goddess slowly and reluctantly gave place to the cult of another maiden, the bear which had been worshipped long before ever Artemis had risen from the sea, continued to be reverenced in London.

The Latin names for the jobs – *arcturus*, perhaps, or *arctophylax* – had given place to *Berebyndere* (Bearbinder – 1341) and *Berewarde* (Bearward – 13 Edw. I): names which, though not wholly English in origin, are nevertheless no longer Latin.

Taking the 'Orgar' of St Martin Orgar to be *arctorius*, 'bear-keeper' (later times used the Latin *ursarius*), we have at least four London names which indicate that the keeping of bears, first practised as part of the cult of Artemis, continued until long after London speech had changed from Celtic or Latin to English.

Bearbinder Lane extended from the Stocks Market, site of the present Mansion House, east to St Swithin's Lane and Lombard Street. There were two Bereward Lanes, one on the east side of Bishopsgate, extending to Hogge (later Petticoat) Lane, the other in Tower Street, in the parish of All Hallows Barking, that we have already identified as a temple of Mars.

These four names mark the sites of places where the sacred bears and/or their keepers maintained permanent establishments; but there are many other 'Bear' names in London to testify to the wide dispersion of the Artemisian cult. The Bear Gardens of Southwark survived until the last century, but the many messuages, taverns, courts, alleys, yards and quays called 'Bear' must mean that the cult was an open not less than a widespread one.

Perhaps, as seems likely, the powerful Church of the later Middle Ages could afford to be tolerant of a cult that it felt it had no longer to fear – and the London faithful were allowed to keep their bears as 'mascots', just as the the good Christians of Berne were permitted to keep theirs.

It seems possible that this Bear Cult may explain a name which has puzzled better etymologists than Harben: The King's Artirce, in Lime Street, described by Stow as a mansion house of the King's. A document of 1474 describes it as 'the kynges artery in Lymestrete', and all that Harben has to offer in explanation of this curious word is this:

'It does not seem possible to arrive at any satisfactory explanation or derivation of this word unless it is a contracted form of the word "artelries" = "artillery", and was a storehouse for arms. The word "artelleries" occurs in this sense in Chaucer's "Tale of Melibeus" and "artery" might be a contraction, originally written thus: "arteries". The form "artry" is given in N.E.D., s.v. "artillery".'

The chief argument against this theory is that nowhere is there evidence that 'the King's Artery (or Artirce)' was ever a storehouse for arms – at least in post-Roman times. There is, however, an explanation of the word 'artery' or 'artirce' which will satisfy the strictest etymological rules, and tell us exactly what the original building housed.

'Artery' or 'Artirce' are, in fact, nothing but the corrupted forms of an original *arcturium*, 'the Place where the Bears are Kept'. We have already assigned four other 'bear-depots' to other quarters of the federated City: in 'the King's Artery' we have found the headquarters of the cult of Artemis in the district around the very important Forum Civile. If any of the *Legati* or *Vicarii* – the governors-general – were devotees of Artemis, it would have been at this temple of the Bear Goddess that they would have paid their vows. The later association with 'The kings and queens' (so Strype) testifies to an origin of more than usual importance. This may well have been, and almost certainly was, an Artemisium of the first rank. I have pointed out elsewhere the possible origin of the legend of King Lucius in the supposed presence, somewhere near the Forum Civile, of a temple of Artemis. In the 'Artirce' of Lime Street, we evidently have this supposed temple.

That St Martin le Grand was originally a temple of Artemis is proved by the presence, in the district, of two highly significant names: Maiden Lane and Carey Lane, the latter of which had the forms 'Kyron' (1306), 'Kyroun' (1361), etc., in earlier times, this more ancient name being identical, in fact, with the alternative (Greek) name of that Maiden Lane that we encountered close by St Martin Vintry.

It is evident that, in St Martin le Grand, we have the Temple of Artemis belonging to the 'Cripplegate Fort', and, judging from the importance attached to this site, even long after the Reformation had 'dissolved' the great monastic foundation, this temple of Artemis in the north-west of Londinium must have been one of the most important – if not, surely, *the* most important – of all the fanes of the Bear Goddess.

In the case of St Martin Vintry, the significantly-named lane to the north is called either Maiden Lane or Kyrone Lane; but in the case of St Martin le Grand, there seems to be both a Maiden Lane *and* a Kyrone Lane. There is an alternative name for the former which is curious enough: Englenelane (1282), Inggelelane (1310–11), Ingelane (1320), etc., all of which seem to echo the Greek word for 'woman', γύνη, as Kyrone Lane echoes the Greek word for 'girl, maiden'.

The same haunting echo of this Greek word for 'woman' occurs in the name of the supposed founder of the 'Collegiate Church of Secular Canons in the Ward of Aldersgate': Ingelricus, and his brother, who rebuilt and endowed an earlier foundation.

This new foundation, confirmed by royal charter of William I in 1067 – that is, immediately after William's assuming the crown of England – enjoyed from the first the most remarkable privileges, such as sanctuary, exemption from ecclesiastical and civil jurisdiction. 'The adjoining lands', says Harben, 'included in the foundation shared in these special and peculiar privileges, so that in later times and even after the dissolution of the monasteries, the area remained a privileged one, and constituted the precinct known as the Liberty of St Martin le Grand.' The privileges were, indeed, peculiar: nearly three hundred years after Henry VIII abolished the religious foundation, the Liberty was ringing its Curfew Bell to order the citizens to keep within doors; it had its own court, bailiff and prison, and not until the year of Waterloo, 1815, did Parliament do away with that right of sanctuary which made it, so they were complaining *in the time of Henry V,* 'a resort of felons and traitors'.

Now such privileges, which had the effect of rendering the Liberty independent of both royal and ecclesiastical discipline – creating, in short, an independent 'enclave' within the city-state of London – can have had their origin, and found their justification, only in an extraordinary sanctity that this place had acquired over a long period of time.

Even in the Middle Ages, it was not supposed that 'Ingelricus and his brother' had actually founded St Martin le Grand: what they had done was to extort from the new and still vulnerable king a confirmation of the Liberty's existing privileges, and in Tanner's remark that the collegiate church 'may have been founded by Victred or Wythred, King of Kent, *c.* 700', could survive a distorted remembrance of 'St Martin's' original purpose. For whether or not there was a 'Victred', his name is a sufficiently arresting one, being, in short, nothing but a slightly altered Latin name, *Victrix.*

What does this mean? Well, let us examine the significance of the name *Victrix* in this connection.

Up to the time of the Great Fire, there existed a small church on the west side of Foster Lane, called St Leonard. It is described by Stow as a small parish church 'for them of St Martins le graund', and the map shews that it lay directly to the east of the important north–south street known as St Martin's Lane or St Martin's Street, and which was entered from Cheapside through St Martin's Gate.

There is no doubt what 'Leonard' means: we have seen that it is simply the Latin word *legionarius*, 'legionary', and indicates that the church stood upon the site of a former military guard-house. And this fact – for fact it is – brings us to a fascinating speculation with regard to that name, Victred or Wythred, that is, Latin *Victrix.*

After the rising of Queen Boadicea (Boudicca), Rome had descended on Britain with no fewer than four legions: the Army of the Rhine sent three, Legio II, Legio XIV and Legio XX; the Army of the Danube sent the unlucky Legio IX, destined to be wiped out by the Brigantes in circumstances which have never been explained.

Roman legions, like modern British regiments, had their nicknames, and, whereas the British Army sports such nicknames as Pontius Pilate's Bodyguard, The Cherrypickers, The Greys, The Blues, and The Buffs, so the Roman Legions bore, as a mark of honourable distinction, not dissimilar types of nickname.

But it is with the nicknames of two legions stationed in Britain that we are concerned here: Legions XIV and XX, the

145

K

nickname of the first being *Gemina Martia Victrix*, that of the second being *Valeria Victrix*. Legio XX Valeria Victrix, arriving in Britain in A.D. 61, stayed in the island until the very end of Roman rule, *possibly more than four hundred years*. I feel that, in the traditional association of 'King Victred' (*Victrix*) with the foundation of St Martin le Grand, we have a memory that the legionary post adjoining the great temple of Artemis had been garrisoned by a legion with the nickname 'Victrix', and as the wild boar badge of Legio XX Valeria Victrix has been found in London, perhaps we may justly assume that it was with men of this 'invincible' legion that the fort which later became St Leonard Foster Lane was garrisoned.

It may strain the credulity of some of my readers that I should have sought an explanation of the name 'Kyrone' in the Greek word, κορών, korōn, 'of the Maidens'. A word here on the use of Greek in Roman London, then, ought not to be out of place.

In his truly excellent work, *Roman London*, Gordon Home points out, in talking of the funeral monuments which have survived from Londinium, that 'out of some twenty-seven inscriptions that may be classified as sepulchral, three are in Greek characters, and otherwise shew a certain amount of evidence that the persons commemorated came from the Hellenistic portion of the Roman Empire, while one or two other memorials bear Greek names. *In other words, one in eight or nine of the inscriptions of Londinium refers to Greeks, and this fact reveals in some degree how far these pioneers of banking and trading were represented in the capital of Roman Britain*'.[1]

Artemis was a purely Greek goddess, even though 'equated' with the Roman Diana, whose worship Artemis largely supplanted. But not altogether, and by one of those freaks of survival the name 'Diana' survived unchanged, whilst that of her more powerful Greek 'aspect' became so corrupted into 'Martin's' that all memory of the original name of Artemis's temples had gone long before the coming of the Normans.

It is almost certainly an altar from the great Cripplegate Artemisium – not yet located – which was found, 15 feet

[1] My italics.

beneath the surface, in Foster Lane. This altar, some 2½ Roman feet in height, had been built into the foundations of Goldsmiths Hall when the old livery hall was rebuilt in 1809. Here is a striking example of how traditional archaeology needs to confirm and be confirmed by the New Archaeology: the finding of an altar to Diana in Foster Lane supports the theory that 'St Martin le Grand' was once a temple of Artemis, but the etymological explanation of the name, 'St Martin le Grand', makes it certain that the altar of Diana belongs to another part of London, and has not strayed there from some other quarter. For 'St Martin le Grand' must be 'Mars Gradivus.'

Diana, as I said above, kept her name unaltered as Rome's paganism gave place to Rome's Christianity in London. If Londoners – most of them, at any rate – forgot that they had worshipped Artemis, they went on recalling how they had worshipped her under her more Roman name of Diana.

In the next chapter but one, 'The Defences of Londinium', I shall have occasion to refer to the district about St Paul's, but here it will interest us because of its association with Diana.

The tradition that a temple of Diana stood where St Pauls' Cathedral now stands originated, it is said, in the reign of Henry III, the last king to be elected by the open acclamation of the citizens and sheriffs of London. I think that the tradition must be far older, but here let us record the fact that, in the Cathedral archives, under date 1220, a messuage on the south side of the Cathedral is described as *domum qui fuit Diane*, 'a building which once was Diana's'.

This 'domum' was, in fact, a number of tenements on Paul's Wharf, next to Doctors' Commons, and were known under the collective name of *camera Dianae*, 'The Vault of Diana'. In mentioning that there was a Canon of St Paul's, 1220–2, named Osbert de Camera, Harben forsakes his usual habit of suggesting that the man gave his name to the place. Here he is content to assume, correctly, that Osbert de Camera took his name from the *camera Dianae* that presumably he or his forbears inhabited. There is something almost disturbingly strange about this vault which so impudently bore the name of a pagan goddess. In the archives of St Paul's, it is described as an inn belonging to the Dean and Chapter, called 'Camera Dianae alias Segrave in the parish of St Benedict (i.e. St Benet's) versus Paul's Wharf'. Strype says that it communicated by means of a subterranean passage with Baynard's Castle.

This reference, in the official description, to the name of the *camera* or vault as 'Diana's or Segrave', is puzzling if we accept 'Segrave' as the name of an old English family.

If, however, we remember that *segregavi* in Latin means 'I set apart', the alternative name becomes easily understood.

But possibly the most curious aspect of this survival of Diana's name into the era of monopolistic Christendom is that strange ritual, persisting until the middle of the eighteenth century, in which the Dean and Chapter of St Paul's, in vestments embroidered with antlers, moved in procession through the cathedral, carrying on their heads the antlered skulls of deer – the animal sacred to Diana.

Says Gordon Home, 'The worship of Diana does not appear to have been very popular in Britain, for apart from the shrine in Londinium [*i.e. the shrine that he supposes was associated with the statue found in Foster Lane*], only one other locality, namely Newstead, near Melrose, has so far revealed any association with this goddess. It is possible that, like Isis, she was worshipped mainly by foreign elements, perhaps from central Italy or the Hellenic lands, where her cult was anciently very widespread.'

This passage shews the deficiencies of traditional archaeology, where, if no visible evidence be turned up by the spade, an *argumentum ex silentio* is almost forced upon the historian. Whereas, with the New Archaeology, we can, as we have seen, positively affirm the widespread nature of the cult of Artemis in London and throughout Britain (where the quantity of churches 'dedicated' to 'St Martin' testify to temples of either Mars or Artemis), even though not a vestige of the Artemisian cult were turned up by the spade.

It is, one may say, a far cry from the solemn rites of Artemis, celebrated at possibly as many as four London temples, to the penny-gaff homeliness and squalor of the Southwark and Hockley-in-the-Hole bear-baiting. It was at the latter that the principal attraction was the prizefight *between women* ('each woman should hold half-a-crown in each hand, and the first woman that drops the money to lose the battle') – to such degeneration had the *arkteia* of Artemis Braunonia come by the end of the eighteenth century. But at the Bear Garden at Hockley-in-the-Hole, where, as the management stated, 'commodious seats are provided for the Ladies to separate them from the Mob', the bears were not forgotten.

The posters announced the following:

'A Mad Bull dressed up with fireworks is to be turned loose . . . likewise a Dog dressed up with fireworks; also a Bear to be turned loose. N.B. a Cat to be tied to the Bull's tail.'

It is the small word 'also' which shews how the bear of Artemis has come to take second place to the dog – he taking second place to a bull. But, translating 'fireworks' as 'fire', we see that the sacrifice of the bear was still something for Londoners to see two centuries ago.

In a less disagreeable fashion, the worship of the bear continued until this century – as the curious addiction of men to bear's grease. Here is a late eighteenth century advertisement from the *Daily Universal Register*:

'H. LITTLE, Perfumer, No. 1 Portugal Street, Lincoln's Inn Fields, acquaints the Public, that he has killed a remarkable fine RUSSIAN BEAR, the fat of which is matured by time to a proper state. He begs leave to solicit their attention to this Animal, which, for its fatness and size, is a real curiosity. He is now selling the fat, cut from the Animal, in boxes at 2s 6d and 5s each, or rendered down in pots, from One Shilling to One Guinea.'

The sale of bear's grease continued until the present century – and may still continue, for all I know.

If 'baiting a bear with fireworks' and setting two hefty 'heroines' to smack each other silly at a pound the fistfight seem a far cry from the solemn dedication of young girls to the Bear Goddess, the cult of the teddy-bear may seem even further. Yet teddy is as much a part of the chain of descent from Sea-born Artemis as was the bear's grease of 1740 or the bear-baiting of 1800.

The Sales Manager of Chad Valley Games told me, when I

was visiting his factory at Harborne, outside Birmingham, that his firm maintains a special department for the repair of old teddy-bears, kept by their owners until those owners are long past middle age.

It is surely not too fanciful to claim to trace the unbroken link, backwards in time, through teddy-bears and bear's grease and bear-baiting to a cult which, once, was perhaps the most powerful of all in its hold on London minds and London hearts: the cult of Artemis the Bear Goddess.

And now the New Archaeology has told us where the several temples of the Bear Goddess stood.

Chapter VII
Hotels, Picture Galleries, Restaurants and Baths

Strangers – particularly travellers – were, under Rome, the objects of close governmental attention. Travellers were no more free to come and go in the Empire of Rome than they are today in the Empire of Soviet Russia.

But, just as Russia supervises the comings and goings of strangers, to the point of providing them with proper lodging, so did every Roman town and city provide accommodation of standard quality and fixed prices for all who had legitimate reason to enter through the *limites* of the town.

Unlike the Russians, though, the Romans kept their travellers' hotels – 'hostels' if you like – *outside* the city limits, putting the living stranger on a social par with the Roman dead: both to be kept as far as possible away from the town.

These government-maintained Roman travellers' hotels were what we should call today most 'utilitarian': no frills, but no fancy prices either; and with the service strictly controlled by the Roman's essentially bureaucratic mind. In each *mansio*, accommodation for master, servant and horse was provided, and it was not to pamper the traveller that the *mansio* was usually sited – rather as with the hutments of a prisoner-of-war camp – so that it could be seen from the 'gun platform' of a City gate.

A certain site of one such *mansio* is Mansell Street, which runs south out of Aldgate High Street, at No. 45, to Tower Bridge Approach, but which, in former times, was far less extensive that at present, and was that part immediately adjacent to the City gate now known as Aldgate (*alta porta*).

The location of Mansell Street, just outside the eastern gate of federalized Londinium, answers perfectly to the requirements of a *via mansionalis*, 'Hotel Street'.

That this was not the only Hotel Street in Londinium may justly be doubted, and another *mansio* may be recalled in the names of Mason's Court, which lies partly in Bishopsgate Ward Without and partly outside the City boundary.

But if traces of the hotels of Londinium are few, evidence for the city's restaurants, taverns and cook-shops are more than merely plentiful, and, in passing, make it clear that for many a London tavern an unbroken link may be claimed between, say, a modern White Lion and a Roman taberna with the name *vitea legionaria*, 'Where the soldiers drink'.

As we drove through the gathering dusk of a winter's evening towards Palmer's Green, the neon sign stood out boldly against the shadowed building that it adorned. It said:

COCK INN

Suppers   Dancing

'Never mind about the neon,' I said, 'but that sign has been there a long time – and the name a great deal longer. Even the pronunciation has hardly altered since Roman days: *coquina – coquin*' – Cock Inn, from *coquina*, a cook-shop.'

There are many, many Cock Inns throughout Britain, and all derive from the old word for cook-shop. There was another – a Sabine – variant on that word, that the Romans adopted: *popina*, which is the origin of the Etonians' 'Pop'.

Popina, like *coquina*, has given London many a name, but in the case of *popina* the names are mostly of alleys and courts. What is amusing to consider is that, when the significance of *popina* has been forgotten 'above', popular usage maintains both its employment and meaning. To give an example, there is a well-known public-house in an alley off Fleet Street. It is called the Red Lion, and it is situated in Poppin's Court. In the fancifully-romantic late Victorian manner, a plaque records that this building bore, in mediæval times, the sign of the popinjay.

If it did, then it had no business to do so. What the Roman Londoner called this little alley was *ad popinam*, 'where the cook-shop is'; and 'Poppins' – *not* 'The Red Lion' – is what the thirsty journalist calls it to this day.

Popina, as one might have expected, has left its mark on

London names. The Italians have always been a race of small, fiercely independent businessmen, and in no branch of industry are the famed Italian qualities put to better use than in the conduct of small cook-shops. It was the Italian who must have brought the cook-shop – the *popina* – to London. (And, by the way, one derivation of this useful word is exceedingly curious, even in the curious history of words. The expression '[to] pop in' simply means 'to poppin' = to visit a cook-shop.)

Let us see where some of these Roman A.B.C.'s and Joe Lyonses and Express Dairies were.

Pope End Lane (in which St Anne-in-the-Willowes stood); Popes' Alley, 'situate by "le Stokkes", in parish of St Christopher' (by the present Bank of England); Pope's Head Alley, Broad Street; Pope's Head Alley, Cornhill; Pope's Head Court, Bell Yard, Fleet Street (where the Red Headed League began its infa ous operations), are some of them. In Pope's Head Alley, Cornhill, was a tavern – Stow describes it as a stone house having the royal arms on it – whose successor lasted until a little before the last war; so that there was a *popina* there from Roman times until about 1930.

Some more *popinae*:

Pope's Yard, Minories; Popynjay Aley, 'a tenement so-called without Crepylgate, 9. Henry VII'; Poppin's Court (which has been called Poppings, Poppinge, Popinjoy, Poppinger, Popingey, Papinger, Popyngey and many other names since the Romans called it *popina*!) and Popys Alley, on the south side of Thames Street.

The grouping is significant, as we shall see when we come to consider the survivals of that other form of *popina*: i.e. *coquina*.

Coquina, which also means 'cook-shop, eating-house, restaurant', etc., and was pronounced *coquin'* on the lips of Roman Londoners, has given London names even more numerous than those having *popina* for origin.

Here are some of the names indicating the site of a former *coquina* or cook-shop:

The Cock, in Aldersgate Street, Fleet Street, Jewry Street, Thames Street, Wood Street and 'adjoining the church of St

Bartholomew-by-the-Exchange' (i.e. by the Bank of England). Cock Alley in London Wall, Fleet Street, Jewry Street, Ludgate Hill, Ludgate Street, St Martin's-le-Grand, Moor Lane, Redcross Street, East Smithfield, and Wormwood Street.

There are also such variants as Cock Court (nine in all); Cock-and-Bottle Court; Cock-and-Crown Court (Aldersgate Street); Cock shill, Cock-and-Hoop Court, Cock-and-Hoop Yard, Cock-and-Lion Court, Cock-and-Py Court, and so on – far too numerous to give in full here. Altogether, there are more than fifty names with the word 'cock' as an element.

There is a London name, *Coptick*, obviously derived from *coquina*. Adjoining Poppin's Court, Fleet Street, was Coptick Court, and here we have the unusual phenomenon of the survival of alternating pronunciations: some calling the Fleet Street cook-house a *popina* (it was a rustic pronunciation, anyway) and some (perhaps the more self-consciously 'educated') calling it *coquina*. Just the same evidence for a non-standard London pronunciation is found in Botolph and Bolt, both derived from *mul(c)ta*, a 'customs house'.

I am of the opinion that, in addition to the various Cocks, Coppins, etc., derived from *coquina*, we must grant that the several Cook's Courts, Cook's Head Squares, etc., have a similar origin. And so, I believe, have the various tenements bearing such names as Coach and Horses Inn, Coach and Horses Yard, etc.

Later, I shall deal with this word 'Horse', but here let me point out that there is a variant on 'Cook's' – Coaks's buildings in Portsoken Ward – which links 'Cook' directly with 'Coach'. 'Horse' is simply Latin *horrea*,[1] a word used more often (as here) in the plural than in the singular, and meaning 'storehouse, barn, granary, magazine, cellar'.

'Coach and Horses' simply means, then, *coquina et horrea*, 'provender for man and beast'.

The names of modern pubs are significant in showing how very old the institution of the tavern is – the word tavern itself, *taberna*, is Latin – and how the original names have persisted through so many invasions and social revolutions.

---

[1] Pronounced 'horzea' by the Celtic Londoner.

'The Ram', for instance. Latin *ramus* means 'a branch, bough' (French, *rameau*) and is, in fact, the 'bush' which was once hung outside every tavern, to indicate that new wine was on sale. As the proverb has it, 'Good wine needs no bush'.

At the Leadenhall/Cornhill cross-roads, in the days when a legionary post was stationed there to guard the governor and other notables who frequented the buildings of the Forum Civile, there was a tavern specially patronized – if not exclusively reserved to – the legionaries.

Its original name survives in that of White Lion Court, a small yard on the left of Cornhill as one goes east, just before one comes to Bishopsgate. (The court is worth seeing, because it contains a banking-house doing business in a wonderfully preserved seventeenth century mansion, refronted some time in the beginning of the last century.)

Now the word *legio* (*legionem*), 'legion', becomes 'leon' in places as distant from each other as Wales and Spain, where, in both countries *castra legionum*, 'citadel of the legions', has become (in the case of Spain) Leon and (in the case of Wales) Caerleon. So the 'Lion' of White Lion Court means the same thing: 'of the legion(s)'.

In the seventeenth century, there was a tavern in this court, called by the significant name of 'The Great Ramping Lion'.

We see here all the elements which go to provide evidence that in Roman times there was a tavern here, frequented by the legionaries stationed in Leadenhall (*legionariorum aula*): *viteus*, 'of wine'; *ramus*, 'a branch, bush', and *legio*(*nem*), 'a legion'. So White Ramping Lion simply means *casa vitea ramosa legionum*, 'the legions' wine lodge'.

We may confidently accept that all pub-names which begin with 'White' – White Lion, White Hart (*hortus*, a garden), etc. – contain at least one Latin word, *viteus*, 'to do with wine'. The same applies to any pub-name with 'Ram' as a constituent part.

The frequency of such pub-names as 'Three Cups', 'Three Kings', etc., caught my attention, and I feel that we may find their origin in the Latin *triclinium*, 'dining-room, supper-room, eating-room'. This would have given, in London Britonnic, a sound somewhat like 'trī'kin', which, in after times, would have been interpreted as 'Three Kings'. By analogy, the various other pub-names beginning with the word 'three' have been coined.

Little of Roman London's art has survived, and what there is testifies to very divergent standards of taste. However, enough is left that we may say confidently that, at its most prosperous period – say between A.D. 100 and A.D. 250 – the luxury of London rivalled that of all but the most famous cities of the Empire. A provincial city whose basilica was over 500 feet long would not have lacked for even the smallest of the luxuries in which the best-equipped Roman cities specialized. There are certainly traces in London names – if not in the soil of London itself – of some luxuries which once, no doubt, were common-places in the life of the average Roman Londoner.

Pincock Alley, for instance, positively affirms the existence of a *pinacotheca*, 'art-gallery, museum of paintings'.

Pincock Alley (the name also appears as 'Pintottes' and 'Pentecost') is east out of Giltspur Street, by Newgate, where there is also a Pincock Lane, though I feel that both names refer to only one *pinacotheca*.

But, at the opposite corner of the federated city, in St Katherine's precincts, by the Tower of London, there is another name highly suggestive of a former *pinacotheca*: Pigot's Rents, alternatively spelt Piccard's Rents. Other *pinacothecae* are testified by the names, Pickax Alley, east out of Mark Lane, north of Hart Street – and, by the way, another name for the 'Pincock' of the Newgate area was Pickaxe Street ('Pyckthatche' in the time of Elizabeth I) – Pike's Corner, in the Tower Liberties, but which may be the same as 'Pigot's (or Piccard's) Rents;' and Pilkyngton's Place, in Aldersgate, if it be not the same as 'Pincock Lane' and 'Pincock Alley'. (This name also appears in the records as 'Pelican Court.) Pink's Alley, west out of Fetter Lane marks the site of yet another *pinacotheca*, as do the several Peacock Courts and Peacock Alleys.

All this testimony supports the conclusion that there was certainly one important picture-gallery somewhere where St Bartholomew Hospital Out-patient Department is today; with the strong possibility that there was another in Mark Lane – *vicus mangonum*, 'Street of the Slave-dealers' – whose relation to the eastern defensive system of the City we shall consider shortly, and the near certainty that these was one in each of the smaller 'Londons' of federated Londinium.

There is another piece of testimony to support the supposition that the more important, or most important, of Londinium's *pinacothecae* lay to the north-west, near what modern archaeological theory inclines to believe the original of the Five Londons.

That is that there is good reason to assume the presence, in that neighbourhood, of the great baths, the *thermae*. There is a record, 31 Elizabeth I, 1583, of 'a messuage so-called in the parish of St Sepulchre', named Fermes House. Nothing more is known of this 'messuage', but its name is so clearly derived from *thermae* (Late Latin *thermas*) that we cannot doubt that the *thermae*, the great baths, of Londinium stood in the very north-west corner of the City, though whether outside or inside the walls, when they came to be built, it is hard to say.

A theory of Roach Smith, put forward a century ago, ought to be mentioned here. Smith believed that the arena of London stood where, roughly, Smithfield and the St Bartholomew area are sited today, and that the cutting back of the Wall at Newgate was in order to accommodate the arena – leaving it, of course, outside the Wall.

So far, I have found no names which could positively identify any building as an arena, but I call the reader's attention to, say, a good map of London in the sixteenth century, and see how – leading from Newgate Street – Snow Hill, Cow Lane and Little Britain form an immense and quite regular oval, as though their path was once plotted by a great oval space around which they had to run. Was this the arena, of which all trace has been lost, but of whose 'performers' many relics have survived?

When the gladiator Martialis died, his wife Antonia erected a marble tombstone to his memory, and, through all the accidents of the years, this stone has survived. You may see it in the Guildhall Museum. Other objects – notably a trident as used by the *retiarius* or 'net-thrower' – have been found to give solid testimony that London, like all the other great Roman cities, had its arena. If St Albans had one, why not London? But we have still to determine its position.

The certainty that there was a *pinacotheca*, a picture-gallery, in the Newgate area, and the strong probability that there was also one in or near Mark Lane, *vicus mangonum*, brings me back to the consideration of the difference between the two names for 'cook-shop', i.e. *popina* and *coquina*. Though both are scattered throughout 'the Londons', it will have been noticed that the name *coquina* (the more 'classic' Roman form) predominates in what we now call 'the City', whilst *popina* is more common on the outskirts of Londinium and outside the walls. This may mean that the aristocracy – or at least, the wealth – of London was concentrated then, as it is today, in the small area around the Mansion House and within that triangle formed by Cornhill, Threadneedle Street and Bishopsgate. Around the Basilica and the Forum Civile, the lawyers and government functionaries, self-consciously defensive of their Romanism in British-speaking Londinium, took care to use the 'correct' *coquina*, when speaking of the nearest restaurant, whilst, outside the charmed circle of government – round about the *other* forum at 'St Paul's' – the Forum Boarium, the Cattle-Market – men were happy to use the more homely Sabine form, and talk of good meals available at the *popina*.

If this theory of mine be valid, then the eating-house at Palmer's Green – the modern Cock Inn – catered for a clientèle drawn from the more 'refined' elements of London. Palmer's Green, in other words, was a Roman suburb of some tone.

'Public baths, an invariable adjunct to Roman cities,' says Gordon Home, in his invaluable *Roman London*, 'must have existed, and after the Great Fire of London what appeared to be the remains of one of these came to light. Places of amusement have left no trace, and yet there is no doubt at all that they existed in the city – to cite one piece of evidence, the memorial to a gladiator is sufficient to point to the prevalence in Londinium of the sanguinary displays that made a Roman holiday.'

We shall, despite the gloomy certainty of the remark that 'places of amusement have left no trace', endeavour to show where some were, whilst we can show where many of the baths of London were to be found: in the provision of baths, London, our evidence shows, was not behind any other city of the Empire.

The Latin words for public baths were *balineum, balneum* or *balneae*, a plural form which may be compared with our phrase, 'the public baths'. In addition, there was the word *balnearia*, 'baths'. All these words have left traces, in London names, of the former existence, in the City, of baths and bath-houses of varying size, from the great baths at Baynard Castle to such (probably) small baths at 'The Bayne', near Paul's Chain, which, because it had a tennis-court attached in the time of Elizabeth I, must have established its identity in Roman times as a place of amusement. There is also a Latin word, that the French have adopted: *piscina*, 'a swimming-pool or bathing-place'.

We shall come to London's *piscinæ* presently.

But let us get back to the baths of London.

Baynard's Castle, in the parish of St Andrew Wardrobe and St Bennet Paul's Wharf (two names to which we shall return presently), has the usual fanciful mythology behind it: 'The Castle was originally built by Baynard, a Nobleman who came over with William the Conqueror, and died in the reign of William Rufus.' So says Stow. Harben is not much less fanciful when he adds that 'possibly the Bainiard mentioned in Domesday Book as holding 3 hides of land in the Vill of St Peter, of the Abbot of Westminster' was the same man.

People were named after places, not – as Harben and others of his thinking maintain – places after people. If there was a Bainiard in the entourage of William the Conqueror, he was so named because his ancestors had settled about a *balnearium* or 'bath'.

Just so were the various Banyards, Baynards, Bells, Panyers and so on, in London, named after the baths which had formerly been open to a Roman London public.

Bearing in mind that our present (City of) London was once a fairly loosely federated collection of smaller Londons, and that each of these Londons had all that the modern estate-agent calls 'its proper amenities', we notice that we may assign at least one bath to each of the Londons postulated in my theory of London's origin.

Anyway, let us see how many of the original London baths have survived – by name, that is, and not, perhaps, by archaeological remains – until the present.

Note the regular distribution throughout the five (or six) Londons:

1. *Baynard's Castle* ('River Fort' – West).
2. *Barn Yard.* North out of Beech Lane, in Cripplegate Ward Without. Between the present Beech Street and Beech Lane, near the boundary of the Ward. (Cripplegate Fort.)
3. *Baron's Yard* ('North-east Fort' – 'Bissulca Porta' – Bishopsgate). At north-east corner of Broad Street Buildings, at No. 8 in Bishopsgate Ward Without.
4. *Bandy Leg Alley.* By Fleet Ditch, in Farringdon Ward Without. ('River Gate' north-west: 'Fleet Bridge'.)
5. *Bane's-court* ('Basilican Area West') – Mansion House/Guildhall). West out of Old Jewry; north of St Olave's Church.
6. *Pannyor* ('Dowgate Fort' – *cancellarius vicus*: the 'restricted area' at Cannon Street). A messuage so-called in the parish of St Michael (i.e. *'ad macellam'*) at Quenehithe, 4. Eliz. I (Lond. 1. p.m. 11.7).
7. *Pannyor* ('Newgate Fort' – in parish of St Michael at Querne. Again notice that 'St Michael' = *ad macellam*, 'by the Meat Market'), 1535–6. Earliest recorded mention: 'Signum le Panyer in Peternosterewe', 20 Edward IV. Now known as Panyer Alley, of which the sign still exists, attached to the 'utility' warehouses recently erected around St Paul's.
8. *Peahen Alley* and *Peahen Court* (Bishopsgate). West out of Bishopsgate.
9. *Bell Inn* ('London Bridge River Fort'). Old Fish Street Hill, on the west side, south of St Mary Mounthaw (*sacomarii ad munimentum*, 'the Customs House by the [River] Fortifications'[1]).
10. All the 'Bell Inns' – of which, perhaps the most famous is that of Fleet Street (still existing), where Sir Christopher Wren had his office-of-works when rebuilding St Bride's – must refer to earlier *balnea* or *balnearia*, 'baths'. There are ten

---

[1] Latin *munimentum* means 'a defence, fortification, entrenchment, rampart, bulwark, protection', etc., and here refers to the River Wall across which Philpot Lane crossed (Phil-pot = (*ad*) *molis pontem*, 'the Bridge [way] across the Mole'). It is interesting to note that, even as early as 1275, the meaning of 'Mounthaw' had become so forgotten that it was translated into (dog) Latin as *'de Monte Alto'*.

Bell Inns, one Bell Tavern, eight Bell Yards, and some twenty other place – Alleys, Courts, Wharves, etc. – into which the name 'Bell' enters.

Note, by the way, that one of these 'Bells' provides support for the theory that Baynard's Castle derives from an earlier *balnearia* (*castra*) (or *balnearium castellum*): Bell Yard, near Helmet Court, in Thames Street, in the parish of St Benet, Paul's Wharf, in Castle Baynard Ward. Here 'Bell' is obviously but a shortened form of that Latin word of which 'Baynard' is the fuller form – cf. 'tele' and 'television'.

The distribution of these 'Panyers', 'Baynards', 'Bells', and so on, scattered as they are throughout the entire area of 'Greater Londinium' (from Paul's Wharf in the south-west, to Newgate in the north-west; from Fleet Street in the extreme west, to Bishopsgate Ward Without in the extreme north-east) show how generously Roman London was provided with public baths. That there were also private bath-houses is confirmed by the finding of, for instance, bath-houses in Cheapside and Billingsgate; but that there were also 'open air swimming-baths' would seem to be indicated by the name of Pissing Alley, which became, 'more delicately', Little Friday Street (it ran west out of Basing Lane into Friday Street, in Bread Street Ward) before it was absorbed into Cannon Street at its western extension, 1853–4. Another 'Pissing Alley', in the Temple, became Goldsmiths Buildings, its present name.

But there is nothing 'indelicate' in the name Pissing Alley, which is merely the Latin word *piscina*, 'a public fish-pond', but later 'an open-air swimming bath'.

It was not only at *popinae* and *coquinae* that Londoners took their meals. Something of the same sort of mock-simplicity which causes restaurateurs to prefer 'Eats' or 'Meals'[1] to 'Tea-Rooms' or 'Refreshments' is observable in a Latin word which has given London at least one pub-name and at least one yard (in Cripplegate Ward) its name: *alimentum*, 'nourishment, sustenance, food'.

The word *alimentum*, 'Eats', would regularly become, first, *aliment*' and then *alivent*', in the mouths of British-speaking

---

[1] Cf. the chain of modern London restaurants, Peter Evans Eating Houses.

Londoners. The transition to 'Elephant', is easy to understand, and indeed there is a modern pub (replacing an ancient one) in Fenchurch Street which bears this name.

Elephant Yard, in Cripplegate, testifies to the fact that a humble – or mock-humble – snack-bar owner did business with the legionaries and citizens in north-west Londinium. And, surprising though the reader may find it, I believe that both the names 'St Alphage London Wall' (formerly 'St Elfego', 'Sce Alphegi sone day', etc.) and two of the three 'St Edmunds' are merely variants of *alimentum*,[1] as also are Allum Yard, Crutched Friars; Alms Alley, Petticoat Lane; Almnes Lane, in the parish of St Leonard de Estchep (1322) and – possibly, though not certainly – Elbow Lane (formerly Eldebowe Lane).

Latin *caupona* means 'retail shop, inn, tavern', and the London names, Cooper's Row, Cooper's Yard, Coppedhall, Copt Hall, Cowface and Cowper's Court, all derive from this Latin word for shop and/or tavern.

It is interesting to notice the location of these shops/taverns: all in parts of the City which, even today, are the busiest. The original shops/taverns from which the modern names, Cooper's Row etc., are derived must have been unusually large or otherwise distinguished. For there would have been numerous shops and taverns in Roman Londinium – too many, we may think, that all should have given their names to a court, alley or street. Those which did must surely have been something special in the way of trading establishments.

[1] The church of 'Edmund King and Martyr,' in Lombard Street, is an exception: the name is derived from *ad administrationem*, 'at the Council Offices.'

Chapter VIII
The Defences of Londinium Augusta

My theory of London's survival as a Roman city involves the supposition that London held out against the attacks of the Saxons during the period following the withdrawal of Rome from the government of Britain. This period, which may have been – though it probably was not – as long as a century-and-a-half, ended at the very close of the sixth century, when the king of the East Saxons entered London as a monarch in friendly treaty relations with the Lordship of London.

London, surviving behind its unbroken defences, was not cut off from contact with the outer world. Had that been so, it could not have held out for more than a few months. The river – far wider then than it is today – provided a means of communication with the greater world of Europe and Eastern Rome, whilst, to the south, a strip of land never taken by the Saxons stretched from London to the Channel coast, providing food and the means of continental commerce to the last great Roman city in Britain which retained its complete Latinity.

What were the defences on which London relied?

Here traditional archaeology has much to say, for much of Roman London's defensive system is still above ground and visible to the eye. But, for all the evidence above and below ground – carefully surveyed and most intelligently explained – traditional archaeology still finds itself with some unanswerable problems, such as the date at which London was ringed with a continuous wall. Nor is traditional archaeology aware that there were many more defences than those of which the traces remain. Our New Archaeology will not only answer many questions that traditional archaeology can not; our method

163

will track down the defences of which every material trace has disappeared.

To understand the pattern of Londinium's defences, it is essential first to understand the pattern of Londinium itself. Until my theory revealed that Roman London began as a collection of independent forts, linked by a wall only long after the establishment of the separate forts, it was not possible to comprehend what the Romans had done in the way of providing London with defences, for no previous historian could have known what it was that the Romans had to defend.

Again and again, in ignorance of the 'dissociated' pattern of early Londinium, archaeologists have been puzzled by finding the remains of massive walls *within* the wall of Londinium, and have tried vainly to give an explanation of such massive walls. It has been suggested – for want of a better suggestion – that the massive walls were the foundations of more than ordinarily tall buildings, and there is no doubt that such great buildings as the east, west and central basilicas would have needed the support of very solid foundations. But there are many cases where what has been unearthed was plainly a wall, and not the foundation of a building. What had the archaeologists to advance, in explanation of this? In truth, they had nothing to offer; and so long as they were wedded to – and misled by – the theory that Londinium had been a 'single unit' city, the unanswerable problem of the wall within Londinium was bound to crop up, time and time again.

Besides the evidence that I have given for a London finding its beginnings in a number of small 'citylets', there are some other facts that I might have laid before the reader. Let us take but two of these additional facts.

The church of St Martin Pomary was a temple of Mars or Artemis situated within the *pomoerium*, the cleared belt of land which circled every Roman settlement, no matter of what size. The word is derived from the Latin words *post moerus*, 'beyond the wall'. The *pomoerium* ran both inside and outside the wall; all building of any sort was forbidden to be erected on it – it was in fact the 'unrestricted field of fire' of the classical military strategy – and its limits were marked by stones, *cippi* or *termini*.

'St Martin Pomary', then, was originally *fanum Artemidis ad pomoerium*, 'the Temple of Artemis near the *pomoerium*'. But where was this *pomoerium*?

St Martin Pomary stood on the east side of Ironmonger Lane, and this is a long way indeed from the *pomoerium* of the great wall which later encircled the whole city of Londinium. If there was a *pomoerium* near Ironmonger Lane, then there must have been a smaller London within what we now think of as the full circuit of London Wall. This smaller London was the so-called Cripplegate Fort, and it was near to the *pomoerium* of this fort, on the south-eastern corner, that the original of St Martin Pomary was sited.

Now for a further proof. We have seen that, at every gate of the City there is, or was, a St Botolph's Church, and we have explained that name as one derived from the Latin *mulcta*, 'a customs-house'.

Now, if we were to find a 'St Botolph' *within* the City proper, we should be encountering just the same problem which the finding of massive walls *within* the City presents. And the solution would be the same.

But in the list of London parish churches given in Fabyan's *Chronicle*, 1520, is included a church of St Botolph in Bread Street Ward. The church has not been further identified, and it is impossible, as yet, to say exactly where within Bread Street Ward it was sited. But the upper limits of Bread Street Ward front the southern edge of Cheapside: the 'second phase' of the Cripplegate Fort's expansion, within the outer limits of London, would, one assumes, have brought it with its southern edge along Cheapside. The now-vanished St Botolph, in or near Cheapside, must have been the customs-gate for the expanded Cripplegate Fort. In any case, the name of 'St Botolph' shows that there was at least one gate within the city, which proves that London's original pattern was of the fragmented type that my theory demands. The Romans, then, had to devise defences for the five or six 'smaller Londons' – the forts which commanded the approaches to the Celtic *oppidum*. Each of these forts would have had its traditional Roman layout and protection: a wall with a deep, wide *fossa* on the outer face. The remains of the Cripplegate Fort make it clear that, in building these London forts, the Roman military engineers did not depart from traditional practice.

It was not until the building of the 3¼ miles of wall, encircling all the 'Londons', that serious defensive problems presented themselves. The five or six forts were linked by a wall of Kentish ragstone, with Roman brick bonding tiles, the average height of the wall being some 15 feet. The existing gates of the forts were incorporated into the Wall, and altogether some eight or nine gates must have pierced the Wall. If the other gates of Londinium were as imposing as Newgate, which has been accurately surveyed and of which the plans have been restored, the gates of the City must have been impressive indeed.

But the Wall now called for special defensive measures that the collection of London forts had not imposed on the Roman government.

The date at which London was first walled may possibly be given as around A.D. 119–20, when Hadrian arrived to check the very serious revolt of the Brigantes, and wipe out the disgrace of Legio IX's complete elimination.

Not, however, until the latter part of the third century were the bastions added. In their construction and in the manner in which they have – or, rather, have *not* – been accurately bonded to the existing wall, they show signs of having been erected in considerable haste, as though to meet a most pressing danger. Yet they served their purpose so well that it is almost certainly to the bastions, even more than to the walls themselves, that London owed its survival during the Dark Ages.

The bastions were 'gun platforms' provided for the new 'mechanized weapons' which gave Roman arms continued superiority when the actual quality of the fighting man no longer provided it. There were seventy-two bastions altogether: forty-four on the land side and twenty-eight controlling the river. They were sited so that each pair of bastions gave mutual covering fire, and with the vast ditch before the wall, with the cleared space of the *pomoerium* ahead, the javelin-, stone-ball- or firebrand-hurling artillery of the bastions could – and, indeed, did – effectively prevent the capture of Londinium by an enemy, however strong and determined.

With a wall now linking the outer corners of the separate forts which had made up Roman London, the inner walls of the forts were no longer felt to be necessary – it is likely that the stone from these demolished inner walls went to the making of the great City Wall. But – if our date of 119–20 is accurate for the building of the great Wall of London; and this seems a possible likely date – the Roman authorities did not entirely trust the Londoners to refrain from revolt. So, though the inner walls of the five or six forts were pulled down, the forts were still cut off from the rest of the city by the defensive ditches of the type called *lilium*, of which the name and location exist in the two surviving Lilypot Lanes – one Lilypot Lane representing the removed southern wall of the Cripplegate Fort, the other (a small alley now serving as the main passageway in an office-building at 100, Leadenhall Street), perhaps the western wall of the fort at Aldgate.

On the eastern side of the new 'federated' Londinium, there appears to have been a sort of 'military precinct' in addition to, and apart from, the inner *pomoerium* which would have been cleared, no matter what buildings had been erected. Inside the inner *pomoerium*, the Roman authorities constructed a 'military road', Via Militaris (now Billiter Street), reserved strictly to the military, and serving as a means by which troops could be rushed from one part of the new 'Big' London to another. This Via Militaris lay between the *limites* (Lime Street) of the habitable area and the eastern wall, and a little beyond it, to the east, was – as we have seen – the *sarcinarium* (Saracen's Head) for that part of the City, where the garrison troops could store their *sarcinae* or war-equipment. If we had not known that the Romans provided a pattern of outer defences, beyond the outer *pomoerium* (or, at least, at its edge), surviving names would tell us. The City, newly walled around its entire circumference, was protected within, by strongly fortified barracks; at the wall itself, by guardhouses – though not yet by bastions; by a deep *fossa* just beyond the Wall; and, at the edge of the *pomoerium*, by what must have been an elaborate system of ring-trenches, over which the roads into London passed, doubtless through fortified gate-houses.

The evidence . . . ? Well, for a beginning, take the names of

167

two East End churches: St Leonard Shoreditch and St Mary Matfellon (Whitechapel). The first church lies on the north-eastern road, leading out of Bishopsgate (the *bissulca*, or 'Two-way' Gate); the second lies on the road which runs due east, from Aldgate (*alta porta*), through Mile End to Caesaromago (Chelmsford) and Camulodunum (Colchester).

'St Leonard', which lies about a mile out of Bishopsgate, is, of course, a legionary post, as we have seen. The now mysterious 'nickname' of St Mary Whitechapel – Matfellon (the guesses produce 'facts' even more mysterious than the name!) is easily explained as the corruption of a Latin word, *in medio mille*, 'halfway along the mile' (i.e. the mile distance between Aldgate and Mile End, which marked the limit of the *pomoerium*).

It is possible, though improbable, that the origin of the church of St Mary Matfellon – halfway to Mile End – was not a military post, but some sort of customs-house, where some *sacomarii* (which would give 'St Mary' later) had their offices. But the fact that St Leonard Shoreditch implies an original military post must also argue that there was a military post of similar nature on all the roads leading out of London. The name 'St Mary' implies that there was a customs-house attached to the military post.

The habitable area of London, at least during times of peace, extended far beyond the wall, and since, with other Roman cities on the continent, the area walled represented only a part of the settled area, we may take it that Roman London certainly extended as far as what are now called the 'bars', those points beyond the walled area to which the jurisdiction of the City extends.

That the Roman defensive system extended as far as the 'bars', we have certain evidence in a name from the Holborn district, where Holborn Bars are probably the most famous of all the 'bars' of London.

Were traditional archaeology to offer no evidence that there were defensive ditches outside the walls of London, the name of Scroop's Inn, on the north side of Holborn Hill, would provide all the needed evidence.

This inn – 'an inn of Serjeants' – was granted to Sir Henry le

Scrope ('le' means 'dwelling alongside of, or near to') in the 18th year of Edward III's reign.

In this, as in all similar cases, Sir Henry was named after the place, and not the other way about – and an alternative name to 'Scrope' clearly shews that the name is a great deal older than the time of Edward III. Scrub's Court lay by Scroop's Inn, and 'Scroop', 'Scrope' and 'Scrub' are all hardly altered forms of Latin *scrobis*, 'a ditch, dyke, trench'. It is hardly likely that any small ditch would have been considered worthy of remark, so that here, in this *scrobis*, we must have *the ditch which marked the defended limit of the pomoerium*. And what was true of Holborn – the north-west of the City – must equally have been true of the other quarters.

Indeed, the occurrence of the same word at Castle Baynard, on the Thames, in an almost identical form, Scrupes Inn, shews that dykes were constructed as part of the outer defensive system all around the City.

As with Scroop's Inn at the north-west, so with Scrupes Inn on the south-west. 'Next to Paul's Wharf is a great Messuage called "Scrupes Inn", sometime belonging to the Scrupes in the 31 Hen. VI.' It was in Castle Baynard Ward, and indicates that the *castellum balnearium*, fortified though its name shows it to have been, had yet the additional protection of the deep ditch – the *scrobis*. One may imagine London, after it had been walled around, as an inhabited area isolated by a flat, carefully cleared outer ring, the *pomoerium*, on which no building stood, and which itself was edged, first by a deep ditch, and then by the whitened stones, the *cippi* or *termini*, which continued to be used long after Roman London had become English London, and whose descendants (of cast iron) still stand at very much the same places today.

The distribution of the close-on fifty 'Castles' – Castell Alley, Castle Court, Castle Lane, Cat's Hole, and all the other variations – shows plainly that, in walling Londinium, the Romans did not relax their tight hold upon the Celtic inhabitants: the numerous 'Castles' refer to former legionary barracks and other fortified buildings, and that the name 'Castle' has survived in such profusion shows, too, that the *castella* and *castra* not only did not vanish when the great wall went up, but survived until long after Britain had obtained her political independence of Rome. For, had the interior forts vanished with the building of the great wall, their memory would not have persisted. The survival of the name 'Castle' shows that the *castella* themselves persisted at least to the end of the imperial occupation – and for perhaps far longer.

This name 'Castle' seems to thicken about centres where, so says our theory, the Romans had fortified buildings within the city. No plainer piece of evidence can be produced in support of the New Archaeology than the significant groupings of the name 'Castle'. This makes Roman defensive strategy much clearer. At the beginning of London's walled period, the wall evidently was not expected to take the full brunt of any attack from without. The Romans could contemplate a break-through by the enemy, repulsed from within the City, by legionary soldiers based on the original five or six forts. Only with the introduction of 'mechanized weapons' such as the *ballista* or the *onager*, and the provision of the bastions from which to fire them, could the military authorities consider total defence in terms of their holding the wall unbreached.

This brings me to a fascinating question. Did the defences of Londinium, especially after the withdrawal of the legions, include some *special* weapon? Was it some notably superior armament which kept the Saxons at bay for a century and a half – time enough to permit them to become, if only slightly more civilized, then at any rate a great deal less ferociously antagonistic? Did London, in short, possess the secret of Greek Fire? If so, the river would have been completely under the control of the Lordship of London, and there is no need to explain London's survival by a London-to-Pevensey strip, giving access to the Channel and the Continent. Control of the Thames by some such 'miracle weapon' as Greek Fire would have kept the Saxons well away.

What evidence have we for the supposition that London had Greek Fire at its disposal? Greek Fire is a nitrogenous compound which bursts into flame when brought into contact with water. It was the secret weapon with which Constantinople kept the Turk at bay – and some of the less amiable Christians, too – for a thousand years. But why should London have been given its supply of this useful compound?

Well, some time in the beginning of the sixth century, Jordanes, the Byzantine historian of the Goths, referred to the Roman Empire as it existed in his day – he died A.D. 552. He refers to Britain as *still a part of the Roman Empire*; that is to say, a century and more after the rescript of Honorius, and well over fifty years after the Saxons, according to the *Anglo-Saxon Chronicle*, had decisively beaten the Londoners at Crecganford (Crayford, in Kent).

What can this mean? Mere sentimental boasting on the part of a court-historian? A bit of Byzantine jingoism, to compensate the ego of the Romans for the loss of their once world-empire? Perhaps not.

There are four places in London known by the curious name of 'Romeland', to which we may add that of 'Romayn's Rent', lands and tenements on the south side of the church of St Mary Aldermary, a building lying within 'Cripplegate Fort'.

All the 'Romelands', though not Romayn's Rents, lay on the Thames: in Queenhithe Ward, in Dowgate Ward, in Billingsgate Ward and in Tower Ward. They were large open spaces by the river, at once, seemingly, wharves and markets, and though the rectors of neighbouring parishes made repeated efforts to establish ownership of these spaces, the citizens of London had no difficulty in getting the authorities to confirm the commonalty's right to the lands.

A decree of Chancery, 37 Henry VIII, confirmed to the citizens the possession of the Romeland at Billingsgate, the decree expressly stating that markets had been held *time out of mind* on the Romelands at both Billingsgate and Queenhithe. What were these Romelands which were of so special a character that the right of the citizens to their use could not, apparently, be alienated even by powerful ecclesiastical greed?

A writer in *Archaeologia* XXXVI, Pt 2, 410–12, quoted by Harben, suggests that the rents of these lands were appropriated to the sea of Rome, and so were called 'Romelands', as Peter's Pence was called 'Rome-scot'. This is ingenious, but takes no account of the significant fact that the Church did *not* own the lands, and that attempts made to convert them to the

Church's use met with rebuff after rebuff. What, then, were the Romelands?

I suggest that they were lands ceded by treaty to Imperial Rome, and that they constituted 'extra-territorial' property on which Rome would have the right to station troops, house her ambassadorial and consular officials, maintain her duty free warehouses, or *horrea* (there was a Horshoe Court in Upper Thames Street and a Horseshoe Wharf nearby).

In other words, Rome, in giving Britain (but particularly London) independence, had contracted to maintain at least a 'token garrison' in London, which meant withdrawing such troops as remained in London to the extra-territorial 'Romelands', situated at each of the principal docks and – perhaps for purely sentimental reasons – in the first of the forts, Cripplegate, erected by the Romans to control London.

The analogy with British practice, as successive British governments have given independence to subject peoples, is so obvious that it need not be laboured here, and makes it plain that, in giving up the British Empire, British politicians, consciously or unconsciously, have been following Roman precedents.

It must be borne in mind that the rescript of Honorius did not give the British total independence, did not abandon Roman pretensions to the sovereignty over Britain. It was an Imperial decree, admitting a crisis in Roman affairs, which compelled Rome to transfer to the British the obligation of providing their own defence. In Rome itself, and even more so in Eastern Rome, Britain would have been regarded as still within the Empire, and if Rome held territory in London (and perhaps in other British cities), and maintained diplomatic representation and 'embassy guards', then Rome might well have agreed, by treaty, to help preserve at least London's independence by making Greek Fire available. The way in which Great Powers handle 'secret weapons' does not change much over the centuries.

Of the river defences of London, whether or not we concede the probable existence, in the arsenals of one of the Romelands,[1]

---

[1] 'Roman', Latin *Romanum*, became both *ruffeyn* and *rumein* in Old Welsh. Obviously, since we have the form 'Romeland', the London Celt pronounced *Romanum* as *rumein*, and not *ruffeyn*.

of stores of Greek Fire, we can speak now with authority.

In the first place, both traditional authority and our New Archaeology testify to the existence of a massive river-wall, the line of which is marked today by Thames Street. It ran from Blackfriars to the Tower, and seems to have been double – that is, two great walls running parallel. In addition, our New Archaeology, by its interpretation of the names Philpot Lane and St Mary Mounthaw Church (respectively *ad molis pontem*, 'bridge over the mole', and *sacomarium ad munimentum*, 'excise-office near the fortifications') indicates the presence of extensive embankments and of fortifications almost certainly allied with the embankment. Creed (Lane) refers to *cratis* 'hurdle defences'.

But there is evidence of further defensive measures along the Thames: I have mentioned Cat's Hole, a narrow court which ran from east of Little Tower Hill to St Katherine's New Court. This 'Cat's Hole', as I have explained earlier, is a mere corruption of *castellum*, and shews that there were fortified guard-houses along the river-wall.

It was one of the first notable successes of the New Archaeology that I was able to identify, in this oddly named 'Cat's Hole', a vanished *castellum* whose remains, however, have now been unearthed and are marked by a metal plate.

But the name 'Katherine' is significant, and especially so in connection with the river defences. The origin of the name is made clearer when we consider that the earlier form of the numerous 'Catherine Wheels' to be found in London – streets, alleys, courts, inns – was 'Cat and Wheel', and this plainly derives from Latin *catena* or *catella*, a chain. The river, then, was furnished with chain-bars to control the passage of ships; and these chain-bars, covered by the river *castella*, must have provided the citizens with a greatly appreciated security against the Saxon pirates who were then running wild throughout the seas and rivers of the civilized world.

Catella or *catena*, a chain, became 'Cat and Wheel', and eventually 'Catherine Wheel'. Wherever we find the name 'Catherine' or 'Catherine Wheel', we have the site of one of those chain-bars or chain-barriers with which the Roman authorities cut off parts of the river and parts of the City, so as to keep a tight control over pirates or citizens.

Napoleon III ordered Haussmann to sweep away the narrow, twisting streets and alleys of old Paris, and to give him broad, straight streets that a cannon might clear of a mob.

The Roman government of London had a different method of controlling its mob: chains which prevented the fluid transition of the rabble from one street to the next.

This system – simple and efficient – of internal municipal control was too good to be lost when the change from dependence on Rome to *de facto* independence took place. Control-by-chain became so basic an element of London city governance that it lasted until . . . well, it has lasted until to-day, though such expressions 'Poules-cheyne' (1444) indicates that this system had survived from Roman days. In this case, a chain was drawn across the carriage-way of the churchyard of St Paul's during public worship, and such chains were a commonplace of London life, until the toll gates (their lineal descendants) were abolished in 1856.

The names whose origins we have recovered by our method reveal the *richness* of London's defences. The Latin names, as we have noted, did not always yield the same word in late English. The forts along the River, for instance, could be called, by the Tower, 'Cat's Hole', but nearby the same Latin word, *castellum* or *castrum*, could appear in after times as 'Chester' – Chester Quay in Tower Ward, between Brewers Quay east and Galley Quay west.

The various 'Cheshire Cheeses' – a pub-name known to almost every American who has ever been to London – are not named, as has been stated, because a Cheshire nunnery had its town house in the vicinity, but because, in this part of London, they had a slightly different pronunciation, making *mulcta*, 'a customs-house', become Bolt (Court) instead of St Botolph, or Bothaw, and making 'Cheshire' rather than 'Chester' out of Latin *castrum*, a fort.

But, however the original Latin words may have been corrupted – and the corruptions assumed different forms according to the part of London in which the changes took place – we can recover, in almost every instance, the original Latin, and thus recover the defensive plan which made London inviolate during the years following the collapse of Roman authority in Britain.

Traditional archaeology helps us here, by confirming the existence of forts and walls, but the New Archaeology tells us far more. From the presence of Chesters and Cheshires and Castles and Cat's Holes we can place, upon our map of Londinium, the various forts and barracks and guard-houses with which Roman military genius, allied with an unrivalled urban authority, maintained the *pax Romana* in the capital of Britain.

Immediately within the walls or other encircling defences of any Roman quadrangular fort, ran a road, the *via sagularis* (from *sagulum*, a military cloak). This road enabled men and weapons to be brought up to any weak point in the defences; it was a road strictly reserved to the use of the military. The phrase *via sagularis* has become in modern London nomenclature 'Sugar Loaf' (-Alley, -Court or -Yard), of which fifteen (seventeen, if we include the two Sugar Baker's) examples survive. Their locations present us with a problem to be solved only by assuming that London-within-the-Wall has to-day a bigger area than it had at one time; in other words, that there was an intermediate stage in the defensive walling of London when the eastern limits of the citadel or nucleus were considerably to the west of the present eastern wall – only a little to the east, in fact, of Lime Street, whose derivation from *limes* (boundary) is thus made even more probable.

If we go back now to the Cripplegate Fort, we have three names there to support the findings of archaeology that this was indeed a fort. At the back of the *principia* of every Roman fort ran a road, slightly narrower than, and parallel with, the *via principalis* (Prince's Street, by the Bank of England, marks the site or proximity of one) which ran in front of the *principia*. This 'back street' was known as the *via quintana*, and is represented, in the Cripplegate Fort, by a small court, known variously as Winton Court or Vincent Court. That there was the usual *via sagularis* here is testified by the presence of a Sugarloaf Court and a Sugarloaf Alley. And that the north–south street in the Fort was known as the *cardo*, 'hinge', is evidenced by a messuage, in the parishes of St Vedast and St Matthew Friday Street named 'Le Cardenalshat'.

Now, if 'Sugarloaf' means *via sagularis* here, it means just the same elsewhere in London, and the locations of these other Sugarloaf alleys and courts and yards are most significant. They seem to shew, for instance, that the present Billiter Street (Via Militaris) coincided with a *via sagularis* running north and south to the east of the great Forum Civile at Leadenhall Street cross-roads, and this is a piece of mutually confirming evidence that we are on the right etymological track, since the meaning of *via militaris* and *via sagularis* is the same: military roads for the quick investiture of any threatened point in the outer defences.

But, at a point a little to the north of modern Fenchurch Street, where Billiter Street joins Leadenhall Street, the Via Sagularis turns sharply to the west, appearing to curve to join the Via Praetoria which must have run due north from the Leadenhall basilica and forum.

Was this Via Sagularis an *inner* defence, additional to the wall running between Bishopsgate (*porta bissulca*) and Aldgate (*alta porta*), and between Aldgate and the Tower (*turris*)? Or was it the first stage of a defensive system which eventually pushed the wall out to the east, as far as its present boundary? I think the latter the more probable, for the interesting reason that the plotting of the vanished wall, by means of a linking-up of the various Sugarloaf names, shews that the supposed Via Sagularis, running within this hypothetical inner wall, is roughly parallel with the eastern and southern limits of the later defences, though considerably within them. If we join the Sugarloaf Alley in Tower Ward with the Sugar Loaf Court in Garlick Hill (slightly to the west of present Queen Street) it will be seen that the Via Sagularis ran almost parallel with the Thames, but considerably to the north of the determined Roman foreshore. This would mean, if I read the evidence correctly, that this line of a supposed Via Sagularis represented the line of Londinium's southern boundary before the extensive reclamation of the foreshore, and the extension of the building-line, on massive substructures indicated by such names as Suffolk Lane (*suffultus*, 'under-pinned', 'raised up', etc.), Garlickhithe (*grallictus*, 'raised on *grallæ* – stilts or piles'), Belliney's Palace (*palatum*, 'vaulting, undercroft').

From a point to the west of Queen Street – that is, beyond

the Walbrook – this putative Via Sagularis turns sharp north to just below Cannon Street, moves 'half-left' (that is, north-west) to just below the verified Roman road of Newgate Street and runs apparently through the *cardo* – or, to be exact, slightly to the east of the *cardo* – of the Cripplegate Fort. If this evidence may be accepted at its face value, it can only mean that Londinium was 'enucleated', with a wall or other defence, *before* the building of the Cripplegate Fort – and that this is no improbability is perhaps testified by the fact that a cemetery existed late enough, to the west of this Via Sagularis, to have given its name to later generations (*elysii campi* = Elsyng Spital or Alsies Lane). If this evidence is to be trusted, then Gomme, Lethaby and Home are right in thinking that London – that is, Roman-fortified London – began rather in the east than in the west: rather around Dowgate and the Leadenhall basilica than around St Paul's. It is notable that the plotted western line of this supposed Via Sagularis skirts the eastern edge of my suggested Forum Boarium where St Paul's Cathedral now stands, leaving the Forum Boarium *outside* it.

One further point, before we leave the tantalizing specula-tions raised by this evidence of an inner Via Sagularis: at the north it appears to run parallel to the present wall-line, but at some distance *beyond the wall*; in other words, the present wall line, at the north of the City, was constructed *within* the line of an earlier Via Sagularis.

It is now clear, from the purely archaeological evidence, that London was not only ringed with a defensive *water-filled* moat of considerable width, save on its river front, but that the various forts, including the Cripplegate Fort and the Tower, had their own moat-system, providing each with completely 'autono-mous' defence.

That London was garrisoned by 'ordinary' as well as by Legionary troops – Caesar is always very careful to mark the difference – is proved by the fact that both have left their names as part of London's traditional nomenclature.

We have already seen how '*legionarius*' has been corrupted over the centuries into the first part of such names as Leaden-hall, Leden-pentitz (*legionaria appendix*, 'legionary additional barracks', in Holborn Street), Le Leden-porch (*legionaria porticus*, 'legionary covered-parade-ground') and two other Leden Porches, one in Holborn, the other in Smithfield. Lad Lane derives from some word originally connected with *legionem* – in any case, the presence of nearby Milk Street (*Vicus Militaris Stratus*, 'Paved Street of the Soldiers') confirms the 'legionary' origin of Lad Lane, an origin shared by all the 'Lions'.

Common soldiers, privates, were, in Latin, *gregarii milites* – *gregarii* for short. And it is after these London-based squaddies that the churches of St Gregory-by-St Paul's and St Gregory the Martyr near Estchepe, which seems to have vanished after its mention in 1349, are named.

Two other London names which mark the sites of former 'gregarian' barracks are Gregory Place, north out of Half Moon Passage (the half-moon was the sacred symbol of Artemis/Diana) on the east side of Bartholomew (*Matronalia*) Close, and Gregg's or Grigg's Court, in the Minories. As the latter was in the parish of St Mary Matfellon, Whitechapel, this supports the theory that detachments of Roman soldiers were on guard duty outside as well as inside the city proper.

We must be careful not to exaggerate the 'military invest-ment' of London by reading into the plentiful evidence of barracks, guard-houses, forts, etc., the fact of a total armed occupation of Celtic London.

The imperial Roman police system was conspicuously efficient, and the corps of *vigiles*, under the *praefectus vigilum*, carried out the various duties of both policemen and firemen. Organized – as most of the police forces of the world are to this day – on a para-military basis, their guard-houses, 'precinct stations' and barracks would have been indistinguishable from similar buildings in military tenancy. We shall obviously have to include police establishments amongst the 'military' buildings whose existence we have determined.

All the same, London must always, after that fearful sacking that Queen Boadicea gave it, have been a well-garrisoned and well-protected place. When it fell, at the end of the third century, it fell only politically, to usurping legates and em-perors. There is, of course, the mysterious evidence of a great fire of Londinium, occurring from just before Hadrian's building the great northern wall and the completion of London's first town-wall, say in the years between A.D. 100 and 130. The combustible nature of the contemporary buildings might well account for this large-scale conflagration, of which there is no surviving historical mention, but for which traditional archaeology has supplied the certain evidence. Yet suppose that the buried ashes mark an unrecorded invasion of as-yet-unwalled London – some daring attack by the insurgent Britons, closely connected with the still unexplained annihilation of Legion IX by the Brigantes?

Was it *this* which brought Hadrian hot-foot to save, not only Britain in general, but Londinium in particular? If so, it would have been clear that the old isolated fort system – the grouping of five or six fortified 'Londonlets' straddling the east and west hills – could not prevent the danger of the group's being infiltrated and one or more of the forts being taken. This would explain the thinking which counselled a 'federation' of the five or six Londons within one strong wall.

And, as we have seen, with the building of London's city-wall, the Roman military mind did not feel that Rome's soldier-masons could lay down their mattocks and trowels. With a strategic *pomoerium* within and without the wall, with military roads internally (for Billiter Street cannot have been the only *via militaris*) to move troops quickly from one part of the wall to another, with deep, wide external and internal water-filled ditches, and fortified military posts to guard the approaches to the city, whether by land or by river, London's defensive system must eventually have extended to the full fifteen miles radius of its *territorium* – the city's land on which it fed. This was why, when the great battle was fought between the Londoners and the Saxons, the Londoners met their foes at the very edge of the *territorium*: Crayford, on the banks of the River Cray, fifteen miles from London.

Chapter IX
Food and Finance in Londinium

'Food supplies in large quantities', says Gordon Home, in his *Roman London*, 'had to be brought in daily to the markets of Londinium, and, apart from oil and wine, it may be taken that at first nearly all requirements were produced within a short radius.'

These remarks are applicable to the perishables, such as butter, fish, fruit and so on (root vegetables were the discovery of a later age), but surviving London names make it clear that the authorities of Londinium relied, for provisioning the city, on numerous and evenly distributed warehouses and granaries. The Londoners were not Italians, but they relied on an 'Italianate' diet in which the principal ingredient was corn or some other farinaceous food, given flavour and variety by small additions of meat or fish.

All food supplies, whether under State or private control, were the business of the State – to be precise, of the *praefectus annonae*, the official whose function has been described elsewhere.

In Rome, it was on the fourth storey of the great building overlooking the Forum that the Public Assistance offices were located – the *stationes arcariorum Caesarianorum* – and here the *congiaria*, gifts of food or money, were distributed to the public. Rich men had also their hangers-on – the more the hangers-on, the more impressive the status of the rich man – and these, by a curious custom, received their daily dole of food or money. For these doles the clients would bring their own baskets, and the rate at which they were 'paid' had established itself, by Trajan's day, at 6¼ sesterces per client per day. It is unlikely that this foolish custom had not been imported into London, and so the rich men would need to draw upon the city's granaries or other warehouses to keep the always demanding 'clients' appeased.

In London, as has been pointed out, each separate quarter of the federated city had its own *statio annonae* – the various churches of 'St Anne' marking the vicinity of the local office of Public Assistance.

Fortunately, we can determine the site of the granaries and warehouses on which the *praefectus annonae* drew for his supplies: 'granary' in Latin is *granaria*; 'storehouse, barn, granary, magazine' is *horreum*. *Horreum* also meant 'shop'.

The first, *granaria*, has been corrupted into 'Green Arbour'. There are four Green Arbour Courts in London: one on a site now covered by Holborn Viaduct railway station; one off Lambeth Hill, in Castle Baynard Ward; one off Little Moorfields, in Cripplegate Ward; and the last off Seething Lane, in Tower Ward.

Here are four certain *granariae*, one in each of all but one of London's separate 'citylets'. And we may so mark them upon our street-map of Londinium.

However, there are nearly forty other names with the word 'Green' as a component, and it seems more than probable that these names were formed by analogy with 'Green Arbour'. It would be strange if none was derived from *granaria*. For the present, though, we shall leave them 'unassigned', until the exact meaning of such a name as 'Green Dragon Court', say, shall have been determined. (Probably from *tragus*, 'a fish'.)

I have stated earlier that Latin *horreum* (plural: *horrea*) 'storehouse, granary, barn, warehouse, retail shop', etc. yielded the word 'Horse' in such names as 'Horse Yard' and 'Horseshoe Alley'.

I mentioned that the London Celtic pronunciation of 'rr' between vowels in such words as *horreum* produced a sort of 'rz' sound. A friend to whom I explained my theory took leave to doubt the correctness of my arguments, but since I spoke to him I have discovered that it was not only the Celts who changed intervocalic 'rr' to 'rz', but the Italic peoples too. When we consider that Latin *hordeum*, 'barley', has become *orzo* in Italian, it will not be considered too fanciful on my part to take Latin *horreum*, 'storehouse, shop', as the probable original of English 'Horse' in such names as I have quoted above.

What makes the derivation even more acceptable is that at least two of these 'Horse' names are intimately associated with that of the 'Saracen's Head'. In other words, a store or shop, *horreum*, was adjacent to, or formed part of the same property as that occupied by, the 'Saracen's Head' – the *sarcinarium*, where the military deposited their war-equipment.

In passing, it seems certain that, following normal Late Latin practice, the singular form, *horreum*, would have been abandoned, and the plural form, *horrea*, adopted as a singular. This, in turn, would be provided with a new plural, *horreas* (not *horreae*), whose likeness to later 'Horse' is even more apparent.

If *horreum* meant both 'storehouse' and 'shop', how can we differ between the uses to which the word was put? I think that in several cases we can say definitely that *horreum* or *horreas* meant 'shop', 'shops', and not 'warehouse'.

For instance, Horseshoe Passage, in Farringdon Ward Within, led north-east out of Blow Bladder Street to St Martin's le Grand. We have already seen that 'Blow Bladder Street' means simply *via* (*saxea strata*) *propolaria*, '(paved) street of retail shops'.

If Horseshoe Passage was a turning off this street of retail shops, its *horreas* would, in all likelihood, be (perhaps more modest) retail shops, too.

Again, those 'Horse' names associated with the various 'St Dunstans' are likely to have been shops and not warehouses – or, at least, warehouses with shops attached. For we shall see later what 'St Dunstan' really means, and the connection with shops will be made clear.

Man cannot live by bread alone. He must have water, too, if he is to survive, and the problem of providing London with water was rather a big than a difficult one. There was water everywhere, and the likely reason why no aqueduct has been found is that none was built – the numerous streams and wells providing an illimitable source of water.

A well, in other countries, is something more than a mere source of water; it is also a meeting-place for the gossips – even the businessmen – of a town; and the names which have survived prove that London's wells, in this respect, did not differ from those of Siena or Seville or Sens.

Surviving or recoverable London names testify to the

existence of five public wells in Roman times, though there must have been many more.

Latin *puteus* (French *puits*) means 'well, pit, dungeon for slaves', and *puteal* was either an enclosure around a well, to prevent people's falling in or a similar enclosure around a sacred spot – a favourite place for men of affairs to meet.

Names having an obvious connection with either *puteus* or *puteal* are:

1.	*Pewter Dishe*	Parish of St Mildred Poultry
2.	*Pewter Platter-alley*	Creechurch Lane
3.	*Pewter Platter-alley*	Gracechurch Street
4.	*Pewter Pot*	'Messuage called Puter Pott in parish of S Mildred', 1529.
5.	*Pewter Pot Inn*	Leadenhall Street, in Aldgate Ward. Afterwards a famous coaching inn.

'Platter' is obviously Latin *platea*, 'a street'; and 'Pewter Platter' means 'the street where the open space round the well is'. 'Pot' here, as elsewhere, means original *pont(em)*, 'duck-board, planking, etc., over the well, or around it.' It is, however, clear that all the 'Pewters' – observe the solitary form 'puter' – mark the sites of public wells in Londinium.

The name 'Michael' – which sometimes appears as the alternative 'Miles' – indicates, as we have seen, the presence of a market in Roman times. That the consecration of a part of the City to one particular use continued throughout all the political and social changes which followed the departure of the Eagles is strikingly illustrated in the name of a church 'St Michael juxta Macellum' ['St Michael over against the Market'], which was the subject of twelfth-century agreement between the canons of St Paul and Roger the priest, by which the said Roger was granted this church at a yearly rent of 30 solide. In the same century, in 1181, the Inquisition of London Churches mentions this same church under the name of 'St Michael of the Shambles'.

Harben asks: 'Surely an error in transcript for "St Nicholas ad Macellas"?'

Not so. Here we have the original name, *macellum*, 'market', with its meaning quite forgotten, and transformed into

'Michael', united, in monkish Latin, with the original word, *macellum*. It is not a slip. It shows that the market, once called *macellum*, and now called 'Michael', was as flouring in 1181 as it was in, say, 381.

The various 'Michaels', then, record the presence of markets throughout Londinium – again the map shows that they were fairly evenly distributed, and that each of the original Londons had its own market.

But there are also indications that trades tended to separate – 'hive off' is the modern phrase – from the more general traffic in food or other products; and we can state with certainty where some of the specialized dealers in foodstuffs had their congregations of *horrea*.

There are two names, 'Scomer' in Houndsditch, and 'Skomer' in Birchin Lane, which testify that the Roman lords of London brought their eating habits with them. 'Scummer', a later spelling, gives the exact London pronunciation of Latin *scomber*, which means either a mackerel or a kind of tunny, a fish of which the Romans were inordinately fond.

As the London names 'Scomer', 'Skomer', and 'Scummer' eventually became 'Skimmer' and then 'Skinner', it is not unlikely that the Skinners Company, sixth in precedence of the twelve great Livery Companies, is so called, not because the Mistery of Skinners dealt originally in skins, as because they dealt in *scombri*, 'scummers', tunny fish brought in brine from the Mediterranean.

Fish was a favourite food of the Romans, and if our interpretation of 'scummer' is correct, and there was a fish-market in Birchin Lane, just to the west of the great Forum Civile which crowned Cornhill, then we have here exactly the same pattern as obtained in Imperial Rome itself.

We have seen how, in the tall building flanking the Forum, in Rome, the offices of the Public Assistance authority were installed on the fourth floor; on the fifth and topmost storey were to found the market fishponds. One set of these fishponds was supplied with fresh water by direct link with the Forum aqueduct, whilst another set was supplied with sea-water brought from the port of Ostia.

Piscina in Latin means both 'public bathing pool' and

'fishpond', and the two Pissing Alleys – the later Little Friday Street and Goldsmith's Buildings (Temple) – could have marked the site of former fishponds.

However, what is certain is that the pattern of Roman commercial practice was copied in every city and town of an Empire which stretched from the Indian Ocean to the Atlantic. If fish was sold in Rome's Forum, be sure that it was sold in or near London's.

Incidentally, that *scombri* were sold in what is now Houndsditch is interesting in showing that here, again, established custom maintained its hold on trading habits. Outside Aldgate, especially in the district of small alleys between Houndsditch and Petticoat Lane, fishmongers are still plentiful and active.

The question as to whether the great Livery Companies of London are descended from the trade-guilds, the *collegia*, of Roman London is one that I had hoped to be able to answer in this book, but which, on mature consideration, I propose to leave over until a later work. It is tempting to see, in the ancient Salters Company, the lineal descendant of a *collegium* of *Saltatorii*, the Dancing Priests. But I feel that there is strong evidence that the Skinners Company descends from the merchants of *scombri*. Not only does the word *scomber*, 'tunny', become 'skinner' in colloquial London pronunciation, but the livery company itself used to be called 'The Mistery of Pellipers or Skinners'.

'Pelliper' has been interpreted as a variant of the Latin word *pellio*, 'a furrier', from Latin *pellis*, 'a skin, hide'. But the rules of etymology will not allow this.

'Pelliper', in fact, is Latin *parochus* (Late Latin *parochum*) 'a purveyor, a supplier of necessaries to magistrates and other public officers'. Later, the word came to mean merely 'a supplier'. The phrase 'Pellipers and Skinners' was, in the original Latin, *parochi scombrorum*, 'suppliers of tunny fish'.

Excavations at No. 42, Lombard Street (Via Lambecta) in 1925 revealed foundations which suggested that the buildings which once stood on this site were similar in type to some found, in a far better state of preservation, at Ostia, the principal port of Rome. The space between the 'party walls' dividing the houses was 10 feet 6 inches. 'The shops or offices', says Gordon Home, 'that the ground plan seems to suggest fronted a passage

10 feet wide, on the south side of which ran a great wall 4 feet thick. These buildings appear to have occupied a position on the south side of the Great Forum (i.e. of Londinium).'

Remarking, in passing, that the 'great wall 4 feet thick' was a retaining wall behind which the river ran along Lombard Street, we have here part of a row of shops, *horrea*, of which both the memory and the name survive in that of the 'tenement called "Le Horsmylle" in Graschirchstrete in parish of St Peter upon Cornhulle'. This 'development' was the *horrea militares*.

The *horrea* of ancient Rome were, as Carcopino points out, 'differentiated by the name of the place they occupied or the name they had inherited from their first proprietor and retained even when they had passed into the hands of the Caesars: the *horrea Nervae* flanked the Via Latina; the *horrea Ummidiana* lay on the Aventine; the *horrea Agrippiniana* between the Clivius Victoriae and the Vicus Tuscus on the fringe of the Forum; others were grouped between the Aventine and the Tiber. Then there were the *horrea Seiana*, the *horrea Lolliana*, and the most important of all, the *horrea Galbae*, whose foundation went back to the end of the second century B.C. The *horrea Galbae* were enlarged under the Empire and possessed rows of *tabernae* ranged round three large intermediate courtyards which covered more than eight acres. In these *tabernae* were stocked not only wine and oil but all sorts of materials and provisions, at least if we are to judge by the inscriptions deciphered by the epigraphists indicating the merchants to whom these "granaries" gave shelter: in one place a woman fish-merchant (*piscatrix*), in another a merchant of marbles (*marmorarius*), farther off an outfitter with tunics and mantles for sale (*sagarius*).'

Identifying the various *horrea* and, in particular, the specialized trading quarters, of London is no easy task. I think, however, that we may identify and name one important set of shops-cum-warehouses, *horrea*, just outside the Fleet water-gate (Ludgate) but still within the City's *pomoerium*.

This is the site now known as Bridewell, and was almost certainly, in Roman times, the *horrea Braduales*, named after the man who probably ordered their construction: Marcus Appius Bradua,[1] Legate of Britain under Hadrian, and the British

[1] Bradwell Bay, Isle of Wight, site of roman villa, may be named after him.

Governor in whose term of office the total walling of London was, in all likelihood, begun.

We can state at least one part of London where the very specialized *fructuarii* – purveyors of fruit – used to congregate: in Froggesmerestrete in St Olave's Lane.

Here plied their trade the sellers of *fructus merus*, 'fruit – nothing *but!*' as was probably scrawled on the little boards that fruiterers, from time immemorial, have used to advertise their wares.

We do not know where the *domini navium*, the builders and managers of ships, had their offices and yards, though, as the shipping lines of the City are mostly to be found in Leadenhall Street, it is probable that we have here a tradition of occupancy continued from Roman times. We have, however, a tantalizingly brief fragment of a business memorandum, scratched on a wooden tablet which had once been coated with wax. This, with two other similar business memoranda, was found in Lothbury, still in the heart of London's commercial centre, and only a few yards from Leadenhall Street. The fragment relates to some sort of sale from a shop, and also to a grant of permission connected with the building of a ship and the manufacture of a rudder:

> . . . .
> . . . . . . *rem vendidisse*
> *ex taberna sua* . . . .
> . . . . *m navem faci*
> *endam et permissionem dedisse*
> . . . . *clavi faciendi*

There were fishmongers of a general sort – not the specialists who sold *scomber*, 'tunny'. These were the *piscatores*, and it is amusing to see what that simple word *piscator* has become in English nomenclature over the centuries.

Pig's Court (St Catherine's Court – probably near the preceding) and Pig's Quay (at the southern end of William Street, on the Thames) are but two of the names into which *piscator* (or *piscatores*) has developed.

We have already noticed the places of business of the innkeepers, the *caupones*, remembered in such London names as

Cooper's Court and the rest. We must now go back to the *saccararius*, the City Treasurer, and see something of the system which financed this smaller Rome of ours, so remote from the imperial mother city: London, the outpost of Roman culture at the western edge of the known world.

Within the all-embracing 'nanny-ness' of Rome, which saw everything and managed everything, there was yet room for individualism of the most aggressive type. Capitalism, in often its crudest forms, flourished, and Seneca, that tutor of Nero's whom the Early Church liked to claim as a Christian out of his time, was a mean and savagely griping usurer who contrived to get the Roman State to take the legions to collect what was owing to him by the feckless British princes.

I mention this disgreeable trait in the Roman system because there is evidence that the trade (profession?) of banker flourished in London: wherever one finds the name 'Dunstan', 'Dunstone' or 'Dunster' – with or without the prefixed 'St' – one has come across the site of a banker (moneylender, usurer – choose the word to suit your prejudice!) of Roman days: the Latin word is *danista*. '*Ad dan'stam*' was the phrase by which Roman Londoners said where they were going to get an overdraft. The 'proper' name for the banker's place of business was *statio danistae* – in Late Latin this would have become *stationem danistanis*, no far cry from 'St Dunstan'.

There are nine occurrences of 'Dunstan' (or 'Dunstone' or 'Dunster') in the London records, and it is almost certain proof that I have derived the name accurately from *danista*, 'a banker, moneylender, etc.', in noting, not only where these *danista*'s offices were sited, but also that the name 'Dunstan' is so often associated with the mediæval goldsmiths.

There was a *danista's* office in the following 'key places' of Roman London:

1. West out of Little Old Bailey – that is, within the Cripplegate Fort area, and handy for the Forum Boarium by St Paul's.
2. In Fleet Street, just by Bolt Court – that is, by the western customs-office. (St Dunstan's-court.)

3. In Fleet Street, by Temple Bar – that is, at the 'bar' where travellers entering and leaving the city would be halted by the guards.

This *danista's* office, now known as the church of St Dunstan in the West, deserves special mention, as shewing how tenacious London habits are. The name of the church indicates that banking has been done here since Roman times: today the Law Courts branch of the Bank of England still does business a few yards away. The Bank built this branch in the latter part of the last century, demolishing the ancient Cock Tavern (formerly the Cock and Bottle) to do so. The name of this ancient pub indicates that someone had been dispensing refreshments on this site for perhaps as many as seventeen centuries, and that it had been close to a 'bottle', i.e. *mulcta*, 'Customs house'. So here we have the Roman *coquina's* descendant, the Cock Tavern, crossing the road, to make way for a branch of the Bank of England, coming to the place where – as the name of nearby St Dunstan's indicates – they were doing banking business nearly two thousand years ago. Fleet Street, where Hoare's, Snow's, Twining's, Child's, Gosling's and many another old bank had its beginnings, has an ancient tradition of banking. Surely this tradition goes back, by the evidence of at least two 'Dunstans' in the street, to Roman days?

The other *danista's* offices were:

4. In Great Trinity Lane – that is, by the Thames in the vicinity of the great temple of Jupiter Dolichenus, in a place where enormous walls and wonderful fresco paintings have recently been discovered.

5. By the Tower – that is, where Thames shipping and the vicinity of the temple of Juno Moneta (now the Royal Mint) would necessitate the presence of a banking office.

6. In Cannon Street – that is, within the *cancellarius vicus*, 'restricted area', where the main shipping activities of Londinium were controlled.

7. In Eastcheap (church of St Dunstan in the East) – that is, to the east of, and near, not only the Forum Civile, but also the eastern Imperial Treasury (the *fiscus*, now Fish Street).

8. In the 'Goldsmithery', the 'Orfaveria', (mediæval name),

the Goldsmith's quarter, extending from Wood Street to Foster Lane and Old Change. There was a Fraternity of St Dunstan, very richly endowed.

9. On the Thames – Seint Dunstones Wat'-gate. That is, a banking office to finance shipping, discount sailor's pay-advances, underwrite cargoes, lend money for customs' dues etc.

But the *danistae* were not the only bankers doing business in London – there were the *babylones* too. The *babylo* seems to have been a banker of rather a grander sort, and probably thought of himself in Roman London much as a 'merchant banker' of today thinks of himself in relation to a merely ordinary banker.

The tip-top bankers, the *babylones*, did their business in the *vicus babylonum*, now the street called London Wall, in the parish of St Alphage, Cripplegate Ward Within. The name persisted to as late as the end of the fourteenth century, for in 1385–6 documents refer to it as 'Babeloyne'.

There is, however, an earlier indication of the survival of a name reminiscent of the *babylones*: there is a mention, 1197–1221, of the 'Ward of Alan Baalun'. 'Baalun' should be spelt 'Ba'alun', and is obviously a phonetic spelling of 'Babylon' as Londoners pronounced the word.

That the church of St Nicholas is mentioned in connection with Alan de Baalun makes it certain that this is the church of St Nicholas Cole Abbey; and 'Cole Abbey' here is simply Latin *collybi*: 'of banking business, moneylending, exchange, etc.', and those who have doubted my insistence that very little changes in London should pause and reflect on the fact that the church of St Nicholas Cole Abbey is – or was, before the building of Queen Victoria Street a hundred years ago – situated between Old Fish Street Hill (*fiscus*, 'the Imperial Treasury') and Old *Change* Hill. If the sceptical reader doubts that London businesses *always* do business 'at the old pitch', he or she should consider that *The Financial Times* have chosen for their office a building at 110, Cannon Street, in the churchyard of St Nicholas Cole Abbey – 'St Nicholas of the Banking Business'.

Note that the word *collybus*, 'banking business, money-changing', cannot date from the revived use of Latin in those mediæval times when all Europe, ecclesiastical and civil, was dominated by the Roman Church. Since, in a document of 1331, in Latin, it is called the church of 'St Nicholas Colabei', the original meaning of 'Colabei' – Cole Abbey, as we say today – must have been forgotten completely, which would not have been the case had the Latin name been given in post-Conquest days.

In referring to the church as 'St Nicholas *le* Coldabbay' (another variant of the corrupted spelling) a document of 52 Henry III makes it clear that St Nicholas stood *near* or *by* – not *on* – the Collybus, which, continuing its ancient use, must, after the meaning of its Latin name had been forgotten, have been renamed 'The Old Exchange', the name ('Old Change') that it preserves to this day.

The significance of this particular *collybus* is that it was close to the western *fiscus*, a name which, as with the eastern *fiscus*, has become 'Fish'. By London Bridge the eastern *fiscus* survives, as a name, under the style of Fish Street Hill, whilst the western *fiscus* retains its name under the style of Old Fish Street Hill.

Various ways of distinguishing between these two 'Fish' names (the original meaning of which had been quite forgotten long before the reign of Richard I, when 'West Fish Street' was Latinized as 'Westpiscaria') have been used over the centuries, and it is possible that the west/east distinction originated when the two buildings were still called *fisci*.

In Latin usage, the *fiscus* was the Imperial Treasury, the emperor's privy purse (as distinct from his private property); the *aerarium* was the public chest or treasury, and this 'civil' treasury was sub-divided into the *aerarium* (what we may call the 'Treasury'), the *aerarium sanctius*, a reserved fund, to be touched only in times of gravest need, and finally the *aerarium militare*, the military chest (our 'War Office vote'), which was under the control only of the *magister militum* or his staff.

In Rome – and it seems unlikely that the custom was not followed in London – the principal *fiscus*, the Treasury of the Roman people, was in the Temple of Saturn. The public archives and military standards were also, by custom, kept in the *fiscus*.

The use of the word 'old' to describe the western *fiscus* – 'Eldefihstrete,' 1305 – may be evidence that the western *fiscus* was established first, and since modern London archaeology tends to the belief that the 'first of the Londons' was the so-called Cripplegate Fort, it may be that the Baynard Castle Fort was the second of 'the Londons' to be built.

Once the north was protected by the Cripplegate Fort, it would have been reasonable to build another fortified Roman 'citylet' on the Thames, into which a more commercial element, centred about the Temple of Jupiter Dolichenus, the extensive baths and the *fiscus* would naturally develop.

The distinction between the functions of the *fiscus* and the *aerarium* disappeared in the later Empire, though, as is evident from the persistence of the names (*fiscus* = 'Fish', *aerarium* = Arounes Lane, slightly to the west of the *fiscus*, and a little to the north, perhaps, of the Castle Baynard *praetorium* whose name survives in that of the church of St Peter, Paul's Wharf) the distinction must have endured for many years – perhaps, even many centuries.

Before we return to the other *collybi* in London, let us note that 'St Nicholas'[1] seems to be derived from Latin *nexus* (adjective, *nexilis*, 'bound' or 'bound together'). *Nexus* had a strictly legal definition in Latin, and meant (amongst other things) – I quote here from Sir William Smith – 'the state or condition of a *nexus*, a personal obligation, a voluntary assign-ment of the person for debt, etc.' These meanings would very well fit a phrase of which the latter part was *collybi* 'of the money-exchange', and we may suppose that the original name of St Nicholas Cole Abbey was something like *statio nexilis collybi*, 'Office for Loans on Personal Security'. On the other side of Old Fish Street Hill was St Nicholas Olave (Olaui, Olof, Olaph, etc.). 'Olave' = *alius*, 'the other one', to dis-tinguish this *collybus* from the other nearer the *fiscus*.

The other London *collybi* of which the (corrupted) name has survived are: Cold Abbaye in Wendageynes Lane, held under the Fraternity of St Katherine in St Sepulchre, 1361 – in other words, within the area of the Cripplegate Fort; Coldharbour (Coldeherberghere, 1347) in Dowgate Ward, within, or on the edge of, the *cancellarius vicus*; another Coldharbour (Colher-

---

1 At this part of London, of course; elsewhere Nicholas < Nicaeus.

berd, 1534), this time within the Tower Fort; Le Colebrewous, Bread Street (Bradstreet), 1348–9; the churches of St Stephen Coleman, St Mary Colechurch and St Katherine Colman; and Colemanhawe, near Aldgate. That makes, with the two St Nicholases, some eight *collybi* whose names have survived.

With the nine *danistae* and evidence of a whole street of *babylones*, private banking practice may be said to have flourished in Londinium Augusta.

The essentially senior character of the *fiscus* to the west, 'Eldefihstrete', as well as its distinctly official nature, is clearly shown by the fact that its site is still, at the end of the Middle Ages, used as 'a branch of the Exchequer, for the receipt and disbursement of monies in the personal expenditure of the Sovereign'. If for 'Sovereign' we substitute the word 'Emperor', we have here an exact definition of the function of the Imperial *fiscus*. It is clear that the 'King's Wardrobe', as it came to be called, had inherited all the rights, privileges and functions of the former Imperial *fiscus*. The fact becomes even more evident when we consider that it was in the King's Wardrobe and not in Chancery that the King's letters were enrolled, and that in 1327 the chests kept there contained the City's books of account. Ogilby & Morgan's map, 1677, shows a large blank space, inscribed 'The King's Wardrobe was here'. The 'regal' character of the Castle Baynard Fort, where the sense of a vanished imperial presence seems to have affected later ages most strongly, is indicated by the presence of a Kyngesgate near the church of St Peter (the *praetorium*) and by the fact that the later name of Arounes Lane (Arounes = *aerarium*) was Kyngeslane.

The name of the modern church which preserves the memory of the King's Wardrobe, St Andrew by the Wardrobe, also recalls the *antrum*, the lock-up which must have been attached to the legionary post guarding the western *fiscus*, a supposition that a first mention of the thirteenth century makes very credible: 'S̄ci andree de Castello', c. 1244.

To the Romans who raised the Celtic *oppidum* of London to the rank and splendour of an imperial city of the first class, the two east and west hills that we now call Cornhill and St Paul's

N

were known as the 'horns' – *duo Londinii cornua* (or *cornula*):
'London's twin peaks', as we might say.

The name of the eastern 'horn' survives in the name 'Cornhill'; that of the western (St Paul's) in the name of a now vanished church which stood, until 1666, at the extreme western end of Cheapside, between Blow Bladder Street (Via Propolaria) north and Paternoster Row south.

In passing, we may note the correct derivation of the name 'Paternoster' which occurs not only here, in the Newgate area, but farther south, in Dowgate Ward, by the river, in the name of a church, St Michael (i.e. *macellum*, 'a market') Paternoster Royal.

There is an absurd legend which 'explains' that the monks of nearby St Martins used to tell their beads, beginning the prayers in Ave-Maria Lane, continuing them up Paternoster Row, and finishing them, appropriately, in Amen Court.

All the same, there is a connection between 'Paternoster' and 'Amen' as indeed there is between both and 'Ave-Maria'. But the connection does not concern either monks or their prayers.

As I have said elsewhere, 'Amen' is the only slightly altered form of the phrase *ad amnem*, 'by the stream'. 'Paternoster' is derived from two Latin words, *patiens*, 'navigable' (to boats), and *ostium*, a word that we have met before at Oystergate, and meaning any kind of entrance or exit. Here it specifically means *ostium fluminis*, 'mouth of the river'. The phrase *amnis navium patiens*, 'a stream navigable to ships', occurs in Livy, and we need have no doubt that, taken together, 'Amen' and 'Paternoster' refer to a stream and its practical navigability, and not to Christian devotions. What, then, in this context, can have been the origin of 'Ave-Maria'?

The answer is obvious: 'Ave-Maria' derives from *alvearia*, 'a place for *alvei* (or *alvea*)', 'boats, small ships'.

The name of the vanished church which preserves the name of the western 'horn' of London is 'St Michael le Querne', that is, *macella ad cornum*; indeed, the spelling 'Querne' is based on an erroneous supposition that the name was associated with 'corn' ('St Michael, where corn in sold,' 1258–9), and a spelling of 1297–8 is much more like the original: 'St Michael atte Corn', *macellum ad cornum*. But even when, in mediæval times, the use of Latin had again become a commonplace in compiling official documents, so that we read 'Par. S. Michis in capite fori de sopis ad portam cimiterrii' (1285) – 'Parish of St Michael in the front of the Forum . . . by the gate of the cemetery' – everyone has forgotten that 'Michael' is simply the old word *macellum*, 'market'. This, though the old Latin word *forum* has never been forgotten, either in its original pronunciation or in its original meaning. More than a thousand years after the Forum Boarium – the western, 'cattle' forum – had been built by the Romans, the Ward of Cheap was still called, in mediæval London records, 'Warda Fori' – the Ward of the Forum.

Since 'Paul's' – but even more convincingly, the older form 'Powlys' – is derived from the Latin *populus*, 'the citizens *considered as a political community*', the meaning that it retained in the phrase *populus jussit*, the term that Cicero uses for the formal voting of the Roman people, it is evident that it was in this part of Londinium, by the western Cattle Market, that the *cives Londinienses*, the citizens of London, recorded their votes, as they were to continue to do until the end of the Middle Ages.

The names 'St Vedast's', 'Foster Lane', 'Faster', etc., recall the fact that it was here, on the north side of the Forum Boarium, that the *fasti Londinienses*, a mixture of municipal calendar, official notice-board and Law List, were displayed. But the actual government of the City was not actually in the St Paul's area, but slightly to the north-east where, in the 'Cripplegate Fort', the name 'Oat Lane' recalls the municipal council of the City, the *ordo amplissimus* or *curialis*, which must have had its permanent offices here.

The imperial government of the City was, I feel more and more certain, centred about the area which now contains the Guildhall, and a piece of evidence, that I quite overlooked when writing the first draft of this book, has now happily presented itself to me as yet one more proof that London was governed from the *basilica* at Guildhall.

This additional proof resides in the name of a vanished thoroughfare with the odd name of Gropecuntelane. In explaining the origin of this name, I should like here to quote from *Street-Names of the City of London*, by Eilert Ekwall,[1] to take

---

[1] Oxford: Clarendon Press, 1954. Quoted by permission.

a convenient opportunity of showing, by an actual example of this scholar's etymological methods, how greatly his views differ from my own. Of course, once Herr Ekwall had accepted as fact the hardly supportable premise that all London's names began with the Saxons, he had, with that acceptance, condemned himself to find a Saxon or post-Saxon origin for every name. But let us see what he has to say about the origin of that oddly-sounding Gropecuntelane.

'*Gropecuntelane* is the lost name of a lane in St Pancras and St Mary Colechurch. As the two parishes are on opposite sides of Cheap, it is difficult to say how the lane can have touched both, unless one extended across Cheapside. The probability seems to be that the lane was north of Cheapside. The examples noted are:

Gropecontelane, 1279 . . . Groppecounte Lane 1276 . . . Gropecuntelane 1323 . . . Gropecountelane 1340. The name is an indecent one; Middle English *cunte* means "cunnus".'

Herr Ekwall then goes on to mention other streets having a similar name in Oxford, Wells (Somerset), Peterborough, Stebbing Ess, Chipping Barnet and York. In mentioning that 'the name is found in other towns', Herr Ekwall adds that it is found 'sometimes varying with the euphemism Grope Lane'.

This is all very misleading stuff! In the first place, 'Gropecunte' (more correctly 'Gropecounte') is no more indecent, as the name of a lane, than is 'Pissing'. The latter (see page 161) derives from Latin *piscina*, 'a fish-pond, bathing-pool', whilst the explanation of the former I am about to give.

Nor is Grope (or Grape) Lane a euphemism; it is merely a shorter version of Gropecuntelane. In London, 'Grope' also appears as 'Grub'; let us see now what both 'Gropecunte' and 'Grope (Grub)' really mean.

To take the first: 'Gropecounte' is derived from two Latin words, *gubernacula*, 'government', and *comitium*, 'a place of assembly'. As the modern English word 'count' (title of nobility) is derived from the Latin *comitem*, so, in London Latin, did *comitium* eventually become *counte* or *cunte*. Herr Ekwall's delicately shocked reference to 'cunnus' is quite uncalled for here. Our ancestors, in fact, were not half so smutty-minded or even coarse as some of our present-day commentators would have us believe. I do not propose here to trace the successive steps by which Latin *gubernacula* became English 'Grope-' but the first step in the change came with the form **grubernacula*, from which it is easy to see how *Grub* Street got its name.

The Latin phrase, then, which was the origin of the name 'Gropecounte' was – in the non-classical later idiom – *gubernaculae comitium*, turning soon into *grubernac' -comit'*, in the lazy mouths of the Cockneys of Roman London. From there to 'Gropecunte' ('Grapcunt' in York) is an obvious and inevitable phonetic development.

Incidentally, Herr Ekwall's remark 'as the two parishes [of St Pancras and St Mary Colechurch] are on opposite sides of Cheap, it is difficult to see how the lane can have touched both' may now be answered, by the findings of (I am happy to say) traditional archaeology.

It has, since Herr Ekwall published his book in 1954, been discovered that the Roman original of Cheapside ran some 50 to 75 feet more to the south, which would bring the southern end of Gropecountelane above the northern side of Roman Cheapside (Via Capidis). The problem, then, of deciding how the lane crossed Cheapside does not arise.

Before we leave this chapter, which has dealt with the food and finance of Londinium, we shall recall that the civil treasury of London – the *Augustinus thesaurus* – was much later moved to what must have been considered both a safer and a more central site in the north-east of the 'federated' city: a site indicated by its present name of Austin Friars.

The proximity of a church called St Peter le Poer – or *praetorium ad portam*, 'the *praetorium* by the Gate' – indicates that the Treasury had been moved to one of the original London 'citylets'. Perhaps it was felt that the treasury was in some danger from the direction of the river, and in any case the name *Augustinus thesaurus* (Austin Friars) must date from a period after Rome had conferred upon London the illustrious title of 'Augusta'. This seems to have been given to London at some time between A.D. 337 and 368, that is, following the death of

Constantine the Great and before the relief of London by Count Theodosius the Elder.

Now, having 'restored' the major aspect of Roman London by the New Archaeology, let us take a walk through the splendid city, from west to east, and look at London again through the eyes of its citizens and visitors as they lived some fifteen hundred years ago.

Chapter X
A Walk through Roman London

Suppose that it were a bright May day in London, a hundred years, say, after the day on which Sextus Julius Severus, whom we met in the first chapter of this book, arrived at London Bridge to take up his appointment as Imperial Legate.

Since then, the wall around London has been completed, the last revolt of the Brigantes has been crushed; their position as Roman Britain's 'Public Enemy Number One' being taken by the Caledonians. The turf wall between the Clyde and Forth, built under Titus Aurelius Antoninus I 'Pius' as a protection against these hairy, warlike and savage northerners, has proved ineffective in retaining them in their rugged fatherland. They have rushed over the turf wall, which has been abandoned – though only after the Caledonians have been soundly defeated by Marcellus, and sent howling back to their heather and oatcakes. Bad public relations in Rome have blurred the image of Divine Majesty, and the British, always restive under the Roman yoke, have elected the first of their 'do-it-yourself' Emperors, Albinus Augustus, who is 'acknowledged' by the co-Emperor, L. Septimius Severus I, until the latter has a chance to get at the usurper and kill him.

Severus I, now unchallenged Emperor, splits Britain into two provinces, Upper and Lower – London being in Lower Britain. The Legate, Lucius Virius Lupus, a weak man, tries the cowardly and dangerous way of buying off threatening enemies: he pays off the Caledonians, who take his money, and – nine years later – break through Hadrian's Wall. Severus and his sons go north, defeat the Caledonians, driving them back beyond the Wall, which is then strengthened. But the territory behind the Wall is abandoned.

With all these excursions and alarms to the north, London has remained at peace; no invader has come within shouting distance of the greatest city of Roman Britain. Growing richer and richer with a commerce that war never hinders and war always helps, London is now only a smaller Rome, with the same rule, the same laws, the same customs and – we may think – the same material ambitions. It is a lucky place: each citizen, we may assume, attributes this to the particular god or gods of his allegiance – but it is a fact that the terrible plague, the 'Yellow Death', which swept the Roman Empire from end to end in A.D. 165, hardly affected Britain. There have been scandals in Rome, as the Empire seems to have degenerated into something to be bought and sold by the Praetorian Guard; but Rome itself – the culture, standing and stability of Rome, considered apart from its venal politicians, its grasping tax-farmers and its mercenary soldiers (in both senses of the word) – has remained as it had ever been: unshakable, unshaken . . . eternal.

All that Rome had, London now has. And if London enjoys the material comforts of Rome in a lesser degree, this is a difference of quality and not of quantity. Not even after two centuries of Roman rule does the average Londoner doubt that all roads lead to Rome.

Still, from a Celtic *oppidum* of wattle-and-daub huts, with thatched roofs, London – chief settlement of the tribe of the Londinies – has grown this splendid city: a little provincial, still, perhaps; a little laggard in following the Roman fashions; a little narrow in its outlook and a little timid in its urban development . . . but still something not to be compared with the kraal-type settlement out of which it has grown.

Let us see now what it must have looked like to someone entering from the west, on a bright May morning in A.D. 230, when the Divine Emperor is Lucius Julius Aurelius Uranius Antoninus IX, and his Legate in Britain is Valerius Crescens Fulvianus.

The law of Julius Caesar, forbidding any wheeled traffic to move in the streets of Rome between dawn and dusk, had been extended by Marcus Aurelius to apply to all parts of the Empire.

Our traveller, coming into London from, say, Corinium (Cirencester), would have been able to take one of the slow, comfortable waggons of the type which went only with the coming of the automobile. This would have brought him along the great paved road, *via strata*, through Pontes (Staines) and Brentford to the fortified suburb of Westminster, the memory of whose *praetorium* survives in the name of its abbey church, 'St Peter'.

Our traveller – let us say that he is an apprentice cabinet-maker (*citrarius*) just out of his time – is coming to London to take up a position as journeyman for one of the big firms which service the villa-dwellers of what is now called Outer London.

He first becomes aware of London, not at Westminster, nor even at Charing Cross, where the impressive bulk of the Temple of Mars and of Dius Fidius stands at the corner of the long road leading to Tottenham (*tutamento*, 'where the defences are'). He travels in the slow old covered waggon – of which the tilt has been drawn back, so that the passengers can take the view – and looks out, marvelling, at the fine houses which line the Thames-side road, that today we call the Strand.

London, indeed, bursts on the view when the waggoner, checking the team of Kentish horses, shouts, 'We're there! Londinium! Everybody alight!'

The passengers, not footsore but cramped and aching with having sat so long on piles of canvas-wrapped bales of west-country wool, get down from the waggon on tottering legs. With 'Oohs!' and 'Ahs!' of mingled pain and pleasure, they try out their unused feet, and flex their half-numbed arms. All give the customary tip to the waggoner: the regular travellers no more than a *denarius*; the prudent ones, no more than a *victoriatus*. Let us assume that our young man, happy and excited to have arrived at last in London, and not at all sure of what one gave in such circumstances, cheers the waggoner's heart by dropping a couple of *denarii* in the man's willing hand.

The waggon had stopped at what is now Temple Bar – then a collection of houses on which the various signs indicated plainly enough a bath-house in Bell Yard, an eating-house, with the word COQUINA painted in vast letters on its façade, a *danista's* office, with MONEY LENT OR CHANGED written thereon, the *mulcta* or customs-house, and, of course, the white-painted *cippi* which marked the beginning of London's civil jurisdiction.

A gentle declivity led down to an arm of the Tamesa, and on the opposite slope, some hundred yards from the river's edge our traveller could see the twin towers, capped with orange-red tiles, of the City's western river-gate – Ludgate to us.

'Customs-office a little way down the street!' the waggoner shouted. 'Sorry I've got to put you folks off here, but Julian law is Julian law – and I dursen't move this here waggon another foot whilst there's a glimmer of daylight!'

He threw the reins to a waiting boy, and climbed down from the driver's seat, to make his way to the *coquina* which stayed on the same site (as the Cock Tavern) until 1883.

Our traveller – let us give him a name: Aulus Didius Lepidus (for though he was a pure-born Celt, his parents had adopted the fashion of a Roman-sounding name for their son) – had nothing but his tools to declare, but, nevertheless, he showed them to the customs-officer who was waiting at the barrier blocking Fleet Street at the *mulcta*.

Only a minute's delay, and he was passed on. On his right, as he came to the edge of the *Fretum* – the Fleet River – he was impressed by the size of the collection of shops and warehouses about which the crowds were thronging: especially by the *horrea Braduales* (Bridewell), the 'supermarket' named after a previous Governor of Britain.

The future employer of Aulus the cabinet-maker lived in a small house, with a shop on the ground floor, in the Via Lambecta that we now call Lombard Street. Aulus considered asking the way of a passer-by, but thought better of it; M. Burdonius Salutifer, his employer, had written, with full instructions, how to find the shop in the Via Lambecta, and Aulus decided to move into the City itself before confessing his ignorance of its complexity.

Aulus walked down Fleet Street to the edge of the Fleet, and handed a copper *as* – about a halfpenny – to the toll-keeper.

'Stranger?' the man asked, in a friendly way, but without evincing much interest, one way or the other.

'Yes,' said Aulus, 'I've come up from Corinium. I've got a

job in London. With Marcus Burdonius Salutifer, the master cabinet-maker. Do you know him?'

'No', said the toll-keeper.

'He lives in the Via Lambecta.'

'There are a lot of Via Lambectas. Anywhere where there's water – and there's a precious lot of water in this city, *I* can tell you! – is called Via Lambecta.'

'It's near the Forum Civile.'

'Oh, *that* Via Lambecta! Well, all you've got to do is to go straight on. Up the hill there, through the River Gate – the Porta ad Litum – and up to the Forum Boarium. Through that, straight on, along the Via Propolaria, and keep going until you come to the Slave Market – the Venalicium. You'll see a slight hill straight ahead, with the great Basilica at the top – can't miss it. Well, go there, and turn right, down the Via Gradiva, and then right again, where there's a row of shops. A street with a river running down the middle. That's the Via Lambecta you want. And you'll find your new master there.'

'Thank you very much,' said Aulus.

The bridge across the Fretum – a small river which had been converted by the *ordo* of Londinium into a defensive wet ditch – was small even by the standards of some that Aulus had seen in his very restricted travels. It was a bridge whose two halves could be raised and lowered on counterweights, to allow the passage of larger vessels. Smaller vessels could pass under the bridge by merely shipping their masts. As Aulus approached, the bridge was down.

Living in Roman Britain, the presence everywhere of soldiers and military installations did not strike our traveller as other than commonplace. There were sentry-boxes at each side of the bridge, and on both sides of the Fretum as well (Aulus was told, later in that day, that the river was called 'Fretum' – our 'Fleet' – because it was the principal estuary of the Thames).

He crossed the booming bridge – booming because of the multitude of pedestrians who were crossing, in both directions, as Aulus passed over.

There was something, he thought, a little curious about the arrangement of the City Wall. Immediately to his right, it came down to within a few feet of the river's eastern bank, and at the sharp right-angle so formed there was a defensive tower whose view commanded the broad expanse of the Tamesa, the Fretum in both directions and – straight ahead – over the roofs of the *horrea Braduales* and the customs-house and all the offices, shops and taverns of the Via Fretensis (Fleet Street).

The Wall then ran back to the River Gate, so that the street to the gate was bounded on the right hand side, as one went up the gentle hill, by the towering masonry of the wall.

However, on the left-hand side of the gate, the Wall ran north parallel with the gate, leaving a broad, flat expanse of drained land, on which only an obvious temple and some small buildings – a couple of taverns amongst them – stood in somewhat marked isolation. Temples outside the walls of a city, Aulus knew, belonged to cults not yet recognized by the Roman State as worthy of its citizens' allegiance. The broadmindedness of the Roman State in regard to religion was such that it never forbade any worship that it deemed to be congruous with the worship of the Divine Emperor; but though it might not forbid a religion, it did not, for all that, welcome all religions which sought congregations in a Roman city. Wondering to which god or goddess this particular 'banned' temple belonged, Aulus turned towards a tall, fair-haired man of middle age who was walking beside him.

'Excuse me,' said Aulus, in his polite countryman's fashion, 'but could you please tell me to whom that temple there is dedicated?'

'Countryman?' the other asked, using the ambiguous word, *paganus*. He saw that Aulus did not respond to the hidden meaning of the word, nodded as though to himself, and continued: 'Trade?'

'*Citrarius*. Just out of my time. From Corinium. On my way to meet my new employer. And you, sir?'

'*Portitor*. I am an official of the Portoria – the Customs House in the Suburra . . . the other side of the Tamesa, where there aren't so many ships and consequently there aren't so many cargoes to examine. I come from Gaul. But there's better money here, and no Alemanni itching for trouble just across the Rhine. Yes, now . . . that temple there? It's dedicated to Belin-Sabazios, imported with troops from the farthest east.'

'It's very handsome,' said Aulus, admiring the chaste yet impressive façade of the temple at the place that we now call 'Belle Sauvage'.

'It's new, that's why. I'm crossing the City myself – making for London Bridge. Can I direct you in any way?'

'I'm making for the Via Lambecta, by the Forum Civile . . .'.

'Then we *are* going the same way! Good! I'll take you. Never been to London before?'

'Never. It's very big, isn't it? And splendid . . .'.

'Yes. It's bigger now than even Lutetia of the Parisii, that I know well. And I'm told that the Forum Civile here – not this Forum up the hill here; that's the Forum Boarium, where all the shopping's done (well, at any rate, the greater part of it) – the Forum Civile, as I was saying, is supposed to be the biggest in the Empire, outside that of Rome itself. I don't how know true that is, but it's over five hundred feet wide – as far as the distance between this River Gate and the Fretum at our back there. You should *see* it! Well, you will, for I'll take you by it . . . it's only a little out of my way; no trouble at all, I assure you.'

They passed through the gate, again inspected by two guards of distinctly non-European appearance.

'Alans', Aulus's friend muttered. 'They come from a land far, far to the east, so they say, even beyond the land of the Scythians. There are many more of them in Gaul, where they are being settled in the region around the north-east promontory, where the Veneti dwell. I can't say that I like these Alans. They are savage and . . . I don't know: don't let's speak of such people. Are you not dusty and thirsty after your journey from Corinium . . .?'

'I am', said Aulus, diffidently. 'I was wondering if I could venture to ask you to take a poculum of wine with me?'

The customs-man laughed.

'The same thought crossed my own mind! Come,' he said, taking Aulus's arm in a comradely fashion, 'there's a tavern that I know well, where the wine is old and the water fresh – straight from its own well. See, on the left-hand side there, next door to the temple – it's the Temple of Artemis, by the way.'

The elder led the way to a small, plain-fronted two-storeyed building, across whose stucco façade was painted, in the familiar 'rustic' capitals, the one significant word, TRICLINIUM, 'eating-house'.

The *triclinium* – they were still drinking here in the nineteenth century, when the name had changed slightly to 'Three Kings' – had, as was usual with shops and offices modelled upon the Italian pattern, an open front under the single arch which spanned the entire building. The 'counter' of the tavern, which had wooden tables both on the pavement and inside the shop for those who wished to eat, was a stone slab, some five feet in length by three feet in depth, whose upper surface was pierced with a regular series of holes. In these holes were pottery *amphorae* filled with the various wines that this tavern-keeper, like all the other *thermopolae* of London, was offering for sale already mixed with water, for the Romans had a special term of contempt for the drinker who took his wine neat. Ingeniously arranged charcoal heating beneath the stone counter of this *thermopolium* – a tavern where warm drinks were a 'speciality of the house' – enabled the wines to be poured hot into the *pocula*.

There were some rough wooden stools vacant, and Aulus and the *portitor* seated themselves, as the latter gave his order to the barman. 'This is a bit better than walking up this dusty hill', he said. 'So you work – or you're going to work – in the Via Lambecta? You'll like it there. A branch of the Vallatum – that's what we call the other, rather larger, branch of the Tamesa – a branch of the Vallatum runs along the Via Lambecta, and it's cooler there in the hot weather.'

The serving-lad brought their *pocula*, and Aulus, lifting his bowl, toasted the other, '*Deo optimo maximo*', 'By Jupiter, Best and Greatest'. The *portitor* smiled an acknowledgment, but said nothing. Aulus wondered to which odd cult the man belonged, that he did not care to say the name of his god aloud. Still, in the prejudice-free Roman opinion of the times, such things were of small account, and Aulus dismissed the momentary uncertainty of his companion from his mind.

'What are the things worth seeing here?' he asked. 'They say that there is a fine stadium, not far from the Slave Market?'

'There is, my lad, there is! But the best sight, in my opinion, is not to be seen at the Stadium – though the contests are very good there, mark my words! – but at the Pancratium, which lies just at the back of the Stadium. You get everything for your money at the Pancratium – a complete contest, with boxing, wrestling . . . in fact, as I said, everything! It's first class.'

'Yes, I shall be sure to go', said Aulus. 'Is there an amphitheatre, too, in London?'

'Yes,' said the other, curtly. 'Just outside the wall, a little way beyond the north-eastern gate, the one they call the New Gate. The criminals are executed close at hand, and often they have a choice – if one can call it that – to die under the claws of the lions or the swords of the gladiators, rather than be racked or crucified *ad Patibulas* [Petty Gales] – there's more than one, by the way – or at one of the various *viae crucitalae* [Crooked Lanes] scattered so plentifully around the city.' He added abruptly, and, Aulus thought, a little diffidently, 'Don't ask me to describe the spectacles of the amphitheatre to you: it's not one of my pleasures. Come, drink up, and we'll have the other half before we set out again.' The order was given, the two fresh *pocula* placed before the chance-met friends, and again Aulus gave the customary toast to Jupiter, and again the other said nothing.

'It's very peaceful here,' said Aulus. 'There are soldiers, of course, but one gets the feeling that the people go about their business without fear of any invasion by the enemy.'

'We've had our scares,' said the portitor, 'but, fortunately, they came to nothing. The problem once was not far-off Caledonia, but fairly near-to-hand Brigantia. However, even the Brigantes are friendly now, though they have to enter London by their own wharf on the Tamesa, the *portus brigantinus* [Broken Wharf]. As for the Caledonians, the authorities tried buying them off, and *that* didn't work. So Severus *beat* them off, and that *has* worked. We've left them their side of the wall that Hadrian built, and they've agreed to let us keep *our* side. I don't understand high politics, but, as I said, it seems to work. At any rate, we're peaceful here, not too heavily taxed, and always with plenty to do and plenty to earn. You'll like it here. Wages are good, and prices not too high. Well, are we ready? Shall we push on?'

There was a small but friendly argument about who should pay. 'Toss you!' said Aulus. '*Navia aut capita* – heads or tails!'

207

'*Navia aut capita* it is!' cried the *portitor*, pulling out a *dupondius* and sending it spinning up into the bright air.

'Call!'

'Navia!'

'Navia it is!' said the *portitor*, clapping his hand over the coin, and adding some *asses* to the *dupondius*. 'Thanks for the good wine, landlord! Come, my friend, let's set out for the Via Lambecta.'

At the top of the hill the five-storeyed buildings of the Cattle Market – the Forum Boarium – stood, brilliant white in the May morning sunshine, roughly where St Paul's Cathedral stands today.

'We'll take a quick turn around the Market, and then go by the street which joins the other side of the Market to the Venalicium. We pass not only the shops that way, but the Stadium as well, and I can point out to you where the Pancratium lies at the back. You won't take it all in in one telling, but something will stick.'

'What do they call this hill we're walking up?' Aulus asked.

The customs-officer shook his head.

'I don't think it's got a name. If it has, *I* never heard of it. We all call it 'by the Cattle Market' – *foro boario* [Bowyer Row]. Of course, it's only the trading forum; the other one's the governing forum, where the Legate has his palace and the Magister Militum directs military matters.

'But', said the *portitor* thoughtfully, 'it's a bit different from that, really. There's a bit more in it than that, you might say. This bit of London here is more Londonish, if you get my meaning, than the part around the other Horn. . . .'

'The other Horn?'

'Yes. Rome, they say, is built on seven hills. London's built only on two. And they're called the Twin Horns – western Horn, where we are now, and eastern Horn, where the Governor in state. Actually, locals don't call them *cornua* [horns] but *cornula* [little horns]. Sometimes they call this hill a horn (*cornu*) but they say that the eastern hill is slightly lower than this, and they *never* call that anything but *cornulum* [Cornhill].'

The market was as busy as ever, with the *tabernae* of the licensed shopkeepers ranged around the three sides of the

Forum Boarium, and on every floor of the five-storeyed *horreum*. At the eastern end of the Forum a majestic façade showed a columned portico, in the pediment of which was a sculptured figure of Britannia, and on either side of the figure, the huge gilded letters S.P.Q.L. – *Senatus Populusque Londiniarum*, 'the Senate and the People of the Londons'.

'This used to be six separate little Londons', said the customs-officer, who, whatever his religious prejudices, seemed willing and able to act as Aulus's most voluble guide. 'Then, about a hundred years ago, they put a wall round the lot, and made it all into one big city. But the people still keep to their own little Londons, and each has its own set of temples, its own basilica, place of execution, and so on. Of course, the little Londons by the Tamesa have ports and wharves and things to do with river-trade as well. But all these little Londons stay remarkably independent, I can tell you. Even the cemetery, the *elysii campi* [Alsies Lane], which used to be outside the city wall until they built the great ring wall, is still here. It's against Roman urban law, you know as well as I do, to have burials inside the city; so they took the corpses away, and buried them outside, and left the cemetery, with the gravestones, inside. The people of the north-western fort did that. I tell you, they're very set in their ways, these older Londoners.'

'That's the fort over there?'

'Yes. They've kept the outer walls – they're part of the great city wall now. But the inner walls they've pulled down, and replaced them by a *lilium* – a ditch with spikes inside, that you have to cross by a small wooden bridge. Not worth seeing now, but you can visit it some other time. Well, here's the famous Cattle Market; there's the barracks for the common soldiers – the *gregarii* [St Gregory-by-St-Paul's] who are here to suppress any tumult in the market, and provide a guard for the magistrates.'

'They sit here?'

'In that basilica. The whole *ordo* – with all the *decuriones* in their formal robes. It's very impressive. There's the Temple of Diana – or Artemis, as the Greeks call her – and it's mostly Greeks you see going into her temple.

'Now come over here. That's the small basilica where the purely municipal government is carried out – on those pillars

O

there they . . . do you see those white-painted patches? . . . yes, well, on those white patches they write up the various notices, the *die fasti* [St Vedast's] – days on which the magistrates sit.

'Now look at these shops. You won't see anything finer in Rome, they tell me. Certainly there's nothing half so good in Lutetia of the Parisii. They're very proud of this street of shops in London, which is why they've called it "Via Propolaria" [Blow Bladder Street], "Street of the Retail Shops".

'There', said the customs-officer, pointing to an official-looking building on whose site St Peter Westcheap, at the corner of Wood Street, was later to arise, 'is the *praetorium* of the first little London, they say, to be built. The *cardo* leads to the first of the northern gates, the one they call *circ'lus*, because it's designed like a ring [Cripplegate].

'Now, over there', said the customs-officer, turning so that he was now pointing across the Forum Boarium, in the direction of what is now Castle Baynard and the river, 'are a whole mass of wonderful sights that you must see on your next day off – or if your master sends you to do a job in this direction.

'You see the tall pillar, on its own, with a statue on top? Well, that's the greatest temple of all in London, bar the temple of the Divinity of the Emperor, very near your Via Lambecta . . . in fact, only a few yards from it, on the south side. This huge temple of which you can see the standing pillar from here is the Temple of Jupiter Dolichenus. Between that and where we stand is the first of the imperial treasuries to be built, after the temporary financial arrangements when the Circlus Fort was all that Rome had in London.

'You can bet your boots that the *fiscus* (the Imperial Treasury) there – you can see the sentry parading on the flat part of the roof! – has attracted all the gents who like the chink of coin better than bees like nectar. Look over there: see the sign painted in those big letters over the shop? DANISTA – *Money Lent, Bills of Exchange Negotiated*. And this street which cuts at the back of the Forum and the basilica and barracks of the *gregarii* is the Via Collybicia, for there are so many *collybi*, all engaged in money changing business, that they've given their name to a whole street.

'Over there, on the other side of the collection of *collybi* all doing business around the Imperial Treasury, only you can't see it from here, is a street leading down to the Tamesa. At least, it begins as a street . . . and ends in a flight of stairs: very steep, very dangerous to those who have business there . . . the *scalae gemoniae* [St James's Garlickhithe].'

'*Gemoniae*? I don't quite understand.'

'Ah, I forgot that you haven't lived in London. Well, we have all the customs of Rome here, and I'm told that there's a hill in Rome called the Aventine, and that on this Aventine Hill is a flight of steep steps, and that they drag the bodies of executed criminals down these steps with hooks, so as to cast them into whatever river it is which flows through Rome.'

'And that's what they do here?'

'That's what they do here. There's a Place of Patibulas or a Street of Torture outside every one of the separate Londons, and there are no lack of these *gemoniae* to drag the corpses of criminals down.'

'Don't the corpses pollute the river?'

'Not for long,' said the customs-officer, with a sigh. 'The fishes soon make away with them – the salmon, the sturgeon, the pike, and all the rest. They grow fat on what the river gives them . . . and what men give the river. Well, let's turn to more pleasant thoughts. Do you see the masts and spars of the ships in the river – have you ever seen so busy a port?'

'Never!'

'I see your eye light up,' said the *portitor*, with a laugh, 'as you think to yourself, "Macte! there'll be some profitable work for an industrious joiner and carpenter in connection with such a fleet of ships", eh?'

'Or for a customs-officer, equally industrious', Aulus replied. 'Mehercle! you should not envy us carpenters!'

'What you want to try for,' said the other, 'is to get a regular job looking after the panelling and other joinery in one of the great basilicas. Here's one we're coming to, on our left. There – just at the end of that wide street turning off to the left. Here it is. Isn't it splendid? It deals with all the purely criminal cases, and on the left of the entrance, there, is the remand prison, where they hold prisoners awaiting trial – the *lautumiæ juridicae* [St Lawrence Jewry]'.

The two walkers were by now halfway down Cheapside, the western half of which formed the southern boundary of the Cripplegate Fort, now denuded of its interior walls, but still maintaining its ancient pattern, with its *praetorium* (St Peter Westcheap), its defensive *lilium* (Lilypot Lane), its now unused but still cared-for *mulcta* (St Botolph Cheapside) and its very own temple of Artemis (St Martin Pomary).

On the south side of the busy thoroughfare, where the church of St Mary le Bow now stands above a Roman crypt, the *statio* of the *sacomarii* of the Forum Boarium was open and doing a brisk business checking the weights of the goods bought and sold at the Market. The name 'St Mary le Bow' is only a corruption of *sacomarii ad (forum) boarium*, 'Weights-and-measures inspectors attached to the Cattle Market'.

'There are plenty of baths in London', said the customs-officer, pointing to a modest but elegantly decorated *balneum* on the opposite side of the road. In distant centuries, this bath-building was to be found (1956) under Nos 100–116, Cheapside, as foundations were being dug for the new Sun Life Assurance building. In modern terms, this bath, dating from the first century and rebuilt in the second, appears to have been abandoned in the third century, in what we have since learnt to call 'a time of national preoccupation'. But when the customs-officer and Aulus passed it by, it was well-painted, clean and obviously much frequented by the now highly Romanized Londoner. 'All this street', the customs-man went on, 'has water beneath it. But mostly the streams are led through conduits, and you don't see the water which makes this place so full of wells and baths and wash-houses.

'A bit beyond the Forum Boarium, where I showed you a few sights, the streams do come to the surface: it's just by the *porta occidentalis* [Newgate], and they call that part simply 'by the Stream' – *ad amnem* [Amen Corner and Amen Court].

'Now, *here's* something you'd have to go to Rome to match', said the other, pointing to a tall 'skyscraper' some eight storeys high, which occupied the entire block beyond the bath-house, going east.

'Land's not so valuable here as in Rome, so there's no need for these big *insulae* – these blocks of flats over shops. But this has proved very successful, for the capitalist who cleared the site and got permission from the *praefectus urbi* to put it up.'

The two men stopped to stare at the 'skyscraper' which, with its projecting balconies bright with potted plants and creepers of many shades of green, presented a beautiful as well as an impressive sight.

'What's it called, this big block of flats?' Aulus asked.

'The "Big Apartment Block", that's all, *insula magna* [Isenmongere – later Ironmonger – Lane].'

There were no wheeled vehicles, even though under the law of Julius Ceasar which had forbidden wheeled traffic in Rome during the hours of daylight, exceptions had been made for certain classes of vehicle, amongst them the waggons used by demolition contractors or builders. But there were none of these on the streets this day.

All the same, the noise was deafening. The hiss of the leather sandals on the ragstone-paved streets and raised sidewalks was astonishingly loud – so loud that Aulus found hearing difficult; found that he had to raise his voice in order to be heard by his companion. Then there were the cries of the hawkers and pedlars; the harsh, thrilling cry of a military trumpet, announcing the changing of the guard at the basilica up the street on the left; the chatter of voices raised in a dozen tongues – a bearded man banged into the customs-officer, and excused himself with a quick, involuntary Gaulish 'The Niskas save you, brother!' – at which the *portitor* smiled his forgiveness but again, as Aulus noticed, made no answer. The Via Capidis (Cheapside), as the Via Propolaria was called after it had passed the *sacomarium* of the Forum Boarium (St Mary le Bow) was lined on both sides with shops, their shutters up, and their owners, assistants and apprentices all bawling pleas for custom.

'Is it always as noisy as this?' Aulus asked, banishing from his mind the slight uneasiness that the custom-officer's refusal to reply to the blessing had inspired. 'One can't hear oneself think!'

'This is a quiet day,' his companion answered. 'You should hear it when, in addition to all you hear now, there are the soldiers marching by, with their band; the Salii leaping and screaming; and, perhaps, a crowd blocking up the road and footpath as they fight their way into the Stadium – which, by the way, is here!'

The two men stopped, so that the elder could point out the Stadium, its front modelled on that of the Colosseum in Rome: storeys of arcades rising to some six floors. Painted 'posters' on the walls of the Stadium offered programmes of the current and forthcoming attractions, and a dozen 'bookies' were bawling the odds for and against this and that favourite, as they took bets from the passers-by, and recorded them on their wax tablets.

'I was telling you of the Pancratium,' said the customs-officer. He pronounced the word as 'pancratsium', which was the way in which most people of the Empire said it. 'It lies just at the back here – back of the Stadium. I told you that I much preferred the all-in wrestling and all the other contests of the 'Pancratsium' [Pancrets Lane].[1]

'Over there, on your left – small building, with the little bear [Latin *ursula*] over the door, is a chapel of Artemis.'

'There seem to be more of her temples than of any other divinity', said Aulus.

'She is the favoured divinity of the Londoners', said the other. 'And next door, as we come to the plaza ahead of us, is one of the seven temples of Mithras [St Mildred Poultry].'

'Forgive me,' said Aulus, 'but you seem to speak that name with more respect than you have given to the names of other gods. Are you – again forgive my presumption – of that faith?'

'No,' said the customs-officer, after a long pause, 'I am not. But I respect the teachings of that faith, and I speak with respect both of Mithras and of those who worship him.'

'Yet you do not offer yourself as a member of the cult?'

'I belong to another cult', said his companion curtly, though without anger. 'I could not join that of Mithras.'

Aulus wished to ask the customs-officer to which cult the man *did* belong, but hadn't the courage. 'Perhaps he will tell me of his own accord', he reflected.

'Well,' said Aulus, 'this is a splendid plaza, to be sure! I dare say that there's nothing better in Rome than this!'

[1] Or 'Penkridge', 'Penritch', 'Pancridge', 'Pancras', etc. The last form is that now in use.

'So the Romans, even, say! This, one could call the centre of the new London – I say "new" because the London that we now see was made up of a number of smaller settlements.'

'What is the name of this plaza?'

'The Portico of the Stoics – the *porticus stoica* [the Stocks Market]. You find that an odd name? I see that you do. Well, the great Hadrian, who did much to beautify this city and to magnify its importance, gave it that name – as, indeed, he gave the portico itself to London.

'They say that this plaza, with its statues and arbours set amidst these handsome colonnades, with the walls painted with scenes copied, they say, from the finest in Rome or Pompeii, was commissioned by Hadrian from the architect to be as near as possible to the stoa – as the Greeks call a portico – the stoa, that is, in which the famous Greek philosopher Zeno taught his school of disciples. After the stoa in which Zeno's school of philosophy gathered, his system was called the Stoic system. And so this portico that you see is called the *porticus stoica*.'

'But why does the street which leads to this pleasant place have the name Via Capidis (Cheapside) – the Street of the Sacrifice?'

'Because', said the other, 'it comes *from* the altar in the Forum Boarium where sacrifices are made to the ancient numen of the cross-roads – the *compitum* [Wood Street Compter] just by the *praetorium* that I showed you. No street is named after this *porticus stoica*, but the markets attached are generally called the *macella stoica* [Stocks Market].

'On the left, ahead of us, and outside the *porticus stoica*, is one of the most splendid temples in the city. It is the Temple of Antinoüs [St Anthony's Hospital], where it is the custom to sacrifice swine to the memory of Hadrian's lover. It was the great Emperor himself who, even before he commanded that this plaza be built, ordered the splendid temple for his beloved friend.

'We have just come along what is now the *decumanus maximus* of the new city – we are coming now to the *cardo*, that they call here the Via Principalis [Princes Street]. As you see, it runs on both sides of the Vallatum, whose bridge we are now about to cross.'

215

The Vallatum (Wallbrook) was in that state of well-regulated efficiency that one might have expected after nearly two centuries of Roman rule. About 150 feet wide at its mouth, the small river was somewhat narrower at the bridge which spanned the water between the great plaza and the Via Capidis (Cheapside) – say, about 100 feet.

The bridge was of wood, but built very solidly and with elaborate bronze enrichments which took away any suggestion of flimsiness from the timber structure. The bow of the arch – it was a single-span bridge – rose high into the air, to allow for the passage of quite large vessels beneath; and, as usual, sentry-boxes were placed at each side of the bridge. On the right-hand side, as one approached the bridge from either direction, there was a large statue of gilded bronze, on a plinth of pink Kentish marble. The statue on the 'plaza' side was that of the Emperor Claudius, whose legions had conquered Britain in A.V.C. 796; that on the Via Capidis side was a striking likeness of the Emperor Nero, under whose authority the Imperial Legate P. Petronius Turpilianus had recommended the rebuilding of Londinium, destroyed by Queen Boadicea.

Small altars stood before each statue, and pious passers-by, putting a small coin into a bowl by the altar, threw a handful of incense on to some glowing charcoal that a small boy kept smouldering with a pair of bellows.

The Via Capidis ended, not exactly at the bridge, but at the Via Principalis which cut at right angles, both the Via Capidis and the bridge-approach. At the left-hand corner of the Via Capidis stood the small but handsome structure beneath which the temple of Mithras stood. This was the second of the Mithraic temples on the Vallatum; the other being some five hundred yards nearer the Thames. There were seven of these temples in London, catering for the seven steps of initiation that each aspirant to full 'Mithraism' had to take before becoming a fully initiated member of the cult.

On the right-hand side of the Via Capidis, at the corner, was a large temple, the Dianium [St John Walbrook] whose arcaded front, open to the street, was protected from the sun by wide shades of dyed canvas. Next-door to the Stadium, it drew a great deal of its custom from those who had just seen, or were waiting to see, the show, either at the Stadium (Stodies Inn) or at the Pancratium (Pancrets Lane) at the rear.

From the Via Capidis, one crossed the bridge into a large and level plaza, from which roads spread in all directions: on the left, the Via Principalis went due north to what is now Moorgate; on the right, the Via Vallata (Walbrook) continued the Via Principalis to the *vicus cancellarius* (Candlewick Ward) and the river.

Ahead, from the left and right angles of the plaza, went respectively the Via Trinundinalis (Threadneedle Street) so called because of the *trinundinae*, the monthly markets, which were held in the big square, and the Via Cornula (Cornhill), which continued the line of the Via Capidis (Cheapside) up the second of London's hills to the Praetorium (St Peter upon Cornhill) and the Forum Civile.

The big square, used as Aulus was to a town about a market-place, was the largest that he had seen, and for the first time he began to appreciate, not only what the customs-officer had had to say about London's size, but also the reasons for the pride that the man so obviously took in London's greatness.

The customs-officer laid a hand on Aulus's arm, halting him at the crown of the bridge.

'Pause a moment, and see the square from here', he urged. 'There is no market today, but when the stalls are erected and all the hucksters are shouting their wares, the eye is blinded with colour and tumult; the ear is literally deafened with noise. Now, whilst we pause for a space, let me point out to you some of the buildings around the square.

'There, to your right, is the famous Slave Market of London – the Venalicium [St Mary Wenlock or Woolnoth]. There are others, particularly one the other side of the Forum Civile in what is called the Via Mangonum [Mincing Lane]. But of all the places in London where they buy and sell human flesh, this is the most famous, the most successful and – naturally – the most frequented.

'Would you care to halt a while, and see what is on sale?'

The other did not wait for Aulus's consent, but strode off to the right, where slaves in iron-barred pens, and slaves on the auctioneer's block and slaves in the 'viewing compound' were all the subject of intense and professional scrutiny by dealers and prospective owners, amongst whom Aulus was not astonished to see a number of ladies, attended by their maids. As the customs-officer and Aulus came up to the row of iron cages, a tall, red-faced man, with shaggy yellow hair – an obvious Pict, even if he had not been tattooed all over the face and neck with flame-like patterns in blue pigment, shouted to them, in a despairing voice: 'Da . . . a . . . uisghe . . . ahwa . . . da . . .'.

'He is asking for water', said Aulus, gazing with pity on the man. 'His owner is starving him, so that he shall appear thinner – and so smaller. He will sell better, if he appears to be one cheaper to feed.'

The Pict, seeing that he had caught the interest of the pair, redoubled his pleas for *aqua* that he pronounced 'ahwa' – and, thinking that perhaps Aulus and his friend might not have understood his uncouth Pictish talk, he made pouring motions from an upheld hand.

'Yes, yes, my poor fellow,' said the customs-officer, 'I would willingly buy you a cup of water from the water-seller there; but what will it profit you if your master lash you brutally afterwards? Better to be thirsty than crippled by blows from an angry owner. And yet. . . .'

'One could buy him', murmured Aulus.

The other smiled, shaking his head.

'One does not buy a fine fellow like this with the money that you or I, my friend, command. No . . . but since it is a man chained up there, let us behave like men. Or, rather, since this is no affair of yours, let *me* behave like a man, and do for this poor man what I would have others do for me, were *I* behind those bars.' Purposefully he strode over to the water-seller, and bought a cupful of fresh water for an *as*. This he brought over the prisoner, and gave it to him, though not without making signs that the man should conceal the fact that he had been given a drink. The prisoner drank eagerly, and passed the cup back, without anyone's having seen the simple transaction.

Had Aulus been a Roman, he would have found it incomprehensible that his companion should have had sympathy for a prisoner-of-war. But as both he and the customs-officer were Celts, neither had to explain to the other that the sight of a fellow human being in distress aroused feelings of compassion.

Aulus and the customs-officer were speaking to each other in Latin – though it was Latin with considerable changes, owing to their own speech habits. The customs-man spoke Gaulish; Aulus's native tongue was a form of Celtic that we now call Welsh. The languages that the two men spoke, as from birth, sprang from a common stem, but the differences were already so great that they understood each other better when speaking the *koiné* of a Latin which had already become a sort of Catalan or Provençal.

Latin, as it ought to have been spoken, both could – and did, when occasion demanded – speak. But with the classic Latin that formal occasions demanded, they had not learnt the harsh Roman ways of thought. They could still feel pity for a stranger – even for an enemy.

The Pictish Celtic was so different from the Gaulish and British Celtic that it was with faint hope of being understood that the customs-officer said to the prisoner, in Gaulish.

'We have done what we could, friend. We dare do no more – for your sake, as well as for our own. But . . . may God preserve you!'

If the prisoner did not understand the words, he understood the sentiment with which they were uttered. He smiled and raised a hand in grateful acknowledgement of the *portitor's* act of charity.

'This place saddens me', said the customs-officer. 'Over there – (I merely point this out to you, you understand?) – is something that you may visit or not, as you wish. I never pass it by, but with a shudder. There is a *statio* of the chief of the *virginesvendonides* – the hucksters who deal only in virgins. This', he said with more feeling than Aulus had yet heard him express, 'is an evil place. One day – I pray – something better will replace these markets which deal in human bodies, regardless of the misery that human beings have to endure. But . . . here they are . . . and here, I suppose, they will remain for centuries to come.'

'I know what you are now', said Aulus. 'I have wondered,

219

as we passed the temples of this god and that. And now I know. You are a Christian.'

'Yes,' said the *portitor*. 'One of our saints once denied it, when challenged. I shall not deny it. I am a Christian.'

'You have nothing to fear from me', said Aulus. 'I am not a Christian, but I have no enmity for them. Why should you not be a Christian?'

'No reason', said the other, as one who should say there is excellent reason. 'But we are not popular.'

'That's true. They . . . they say that you will not pay the customary dues to the Divinity of the Emperor?'

'Our founder', said the *portitor*, with the air of one who wishes to end a conversation, 'bade us render to Caesar the things which were Caesar's due. We render to Caesar what is Caesar's. I think that no man could be expected to do more.'

'No', said Aulus, somewhat embarrassed by the serious tone that the conversation had taken. 'Which way do we go now?'

'We pass the markets here. The principal weighing and measuring is done in this particular market. Look at the stationes of the *sacomarii* and the *mensores*. It is here that the City's measures are kept, by which all weights and measures are checked. There, in that building, are kept the standard *unica*, the standard *modius*, the standard *amphora quadrantal*, the standard *actus*, and all the rest of them. Here, you might say, one gets the exact measures and weights at their most exact. You were asking . . .? Well, we cross the plaza, and go up the Via Cornula [Cornhill] to the Forum Civile, and then we turn to the right, both for your destination, and mine.'

They crossed the big square, which was paved with Kentish ragstone, arranged in decorative patterns. In the very centre of the square was an altar.

'That altar is the other reason, I suppose, why the western side of the *decumanus maximus*, the Via Capidis [Cheapside] – the Street of the Sacrifice – got its name. On this altar are sacrificed the animals to the tutelary divinities of the City. This is London's own altar. It is here that the Romans felt that the genius of the City should be honoured.'

The customs-officer paused, about where the war memorial to London's dead now stands, and pointed to the left.

'There is where they hold the Matronalia in this part of London. The women worship Mars in their own way at the Matronalia [St Bartholomew's] – and though there is one within the area of the Circlus [Cripplegate] Fort, there is no reason, it was felt, why Mars should not be worshipped by the women down here as well. Come, your master will be anxious about you. Let us go up the Via Cornula [Cornhill] and take you to your destination.'

They crossed the right-hand corner of the square, and entered the Via Cornula. The street was lined with shops on both sides, and half-way up on the right of the fairly steep incline of the Cornula, they came across the wide opening of a market, the *macellum cornulum* [St Michael Cornhill].

'We won't visit this market now', said Aulus's guide. 'Leave it for another time. But you could go through this market and reach your destination in the Via Lambecta [Lombard Street].

'What makes this particular market interesting is that they made a tributary of the Vallatum [Wallbrook], ran it along the Via Lambecta – *your* street – and then, at the back of the Via Lambecta (and at the back of this market, incidentally) con-structed a small basin, into which the smaller cargo ships and lighters could come. They discharge right on to the market's own quays – very convenient. You don't need to look now – if I'd known how the Via Lambecta is laid out, I'd say you'd be able to see the *portus corbitensis* [Corbett's Court] from your back window. This is another very busy part of London', he added. 'With the Forum Civile so near, you'd expect that, anyway. Next turning on the right's the Via Mercenaria [Birchin Lane] – 'Shopping-street'. Over there is a tavern that the legionaries like to use – their barracks are on the other side of the Forum. Yes, let's stop a moment – it's quite something, isn't it? They say that the architect who built this basilica came all the way from Rome to see that the builders followed his design.'

The Via Mercenaria [Birchin Lane] formed the western boundary of the biggest building that Aulus had ever seen; bigger not only than anything in his experience, but in his imaginings as well.

Correctly orientated on an east–west line, it stretched for

over 500 feet, from the corner of the Via Gradiva [Gracechurch Street] to half-way down the Via Cornula [Cornhill]. It was imposing as only Roman municipal architecture could contrive to be imposing: every element had been designed to impress even the least sensitive observer with the inescapable conviction that, in seeing this, he was seeing the eternal majesty of Rome.

They continued their walk up Cornhill, turning right at the crossroads to pass through the Basilica, and into the enormous Forum Civile, finding themselves then between the Praetorium [St Peter] on their right and the *legionaria aula* [Leadenhall – Hall of the Legions] on their left.

'More temples', said the *portitor*. 'And these are temples of the first class, *I* can tell you! So near the palace of the Governor-General. . . . They'd *have* to be top-notchers, wouldn't they? Left, the Temple of Artemis – Selene, they call her here: you see the half-moon over the gable? [Half-moon Tavern].

'Still on the left, the Temple of Dionysus-Bacchus [St Dionis Backchurch], and beyond that, up that street on the left, the Temple of the Cabiri – the *fanum Cabirialis* [St Gabriel Fanchurch]. Down there are the Imperial Treasury, legionary barracks and a lock-up, and . . . well, my boy, you can see it as well for yourself, now that you are, practically speaking, home. See, the Via Lambecta is on your right, there! *My* way lies over the Bridge, to the Suburra, where the big arena is . . . though that's not where I'm making for.'

The two men, one young, the other at middle age, stood in the centre of the Forum Civile, which, because of its austerely official function, permitted no market stalls within its walls. The *sub-basilicani* – as the loungers were called, because they hung around *under* the walls of the basilica – stared unemotionally at the two chance-met companions, thinking (those of the *sub-basilicani* who could bother to spare a thought): 'Another couple of rubber-necks from the sticks!'

Through an opening to the right, Aulus could see the busy Cornhill market – life and light and colour and a vast commercial energy: the fish-merchants (*piscatores*), pastrycook (*pastillarii*), the coster-mongers (*negotiatores leguminarii*), the ready-made tailors – the John Colliers or Montague Burtons of the day (*vestifici*) . . . all shouting their wares in an ordered chaos which hummed with sound and throbbed with colour.

A platoon of soldiers emerged from a corner of the Basilica, and moved, in the undeviating Roman fashion, across the great court: Aulus and his friend gave way. The men, light of skin yet swarthy, wore the regulation Roman soldier's uniform, yet varied this with blackish-grey goatskin caps of curious cut.

'Moors', said the tanner. 'They're importing a lot of them these days. They say they're bringing in a legion of Negroes soon. It may be just talk, but you never know. These Moors are funny fellows – I wouldn't like to be out on a dark night, and meet one of *them.*'

'And that's the famous London Bridge,' said Aulus, looking straight down Gracechurch Street (Via Gradiva) – 'the famous *pons sublicius* of which everyone talks. It certainly is impressive. The red and purple paint sets off the gilded railings and statues wonderfully. *What* a city these Romans have made of London!'

The other smiled.

'Are you not a Roman, then?' he gently chided the young man.

'I am a Roman citizen, yes', said Aulus, somewhat shortly. 'But before my family were Roman citizens, they were Silures. And you: are you not, first a Suessio, and *then* a Roman?'

'Do you mean that, should we cease to be Roman citizens, we shall still be Silures or Suessiones or Catuvellauni or Atrebates?'

'I mean nothing more', said Aulus, uncomfortably, 'than that we are descended from what gave us birth . . . and our being Roman cannot alter that fact. What, friend, are you asking?'

'Nothing that need trouble you', said the customs-officer, soothingly. 'Come, here are the shops of Via Lambecta, and there, if I mistake not, is the shop of your master, the cabinet-maker. The name above the shop reads BURDONIVS. Is that your master?'

'It is. It was kind of you to have brought me here. I am grateful. Your talk has been most interesting . . . and thank you for the wine, as well.'

'It was *navia aut capita.*'

'I know. Yet it was your money which bought it . . . so I thank you, just the same. My name is Aulus, by the way, if ever you should chance to be passing by this shop.'

The other paused a moment.

'How curious. . . . How *very* curious!'

'How so?'

'Aulus. The same as mine, with such a little bit taken away. Mine, friend Aulus, is Augulus. May I give you a blessing?'

'Of your god?' Aulus asked, a little stiffly, but unable to repel the kindly intention which, he saw, inspired the friendliness of Augulus. 'Well . . . yes . . . thanks.'

'*Sit pax vobiscum!*'

'Pax . . . peace. . . . Well, that's not such a bad blessing. Is that how you Christians wish each other well?'

'Each other . . . and you others as well. May peace be with you, my son!'

' "My son." You sound like a *flamen* of your cult. Are you?'

'A *flamen*? Yes, since you ask it, and I must tell the truth. I am a *flamen* of the Christians, and if you should ever think to visit us, our *cella*[1] is out by the New Gate. A small place, just by the edge of the *pomoerium*. Come and see us – you will be very welcome. And now I must be on my way.'

Aulus stood and watched the customs-officer, Augulus – Bishop of London – stride out, past the sentries, and past the temples of Mars Gradivus and Dionysus and Selene and of the Glory of the Divinity of the Emperor. Past the Imperial Fiscus, with the heavily fortified barracks of the legionary guard. Past the high Jove-and-Dragon column, and the great gilded statue of Hadrian. Past the customs-house on the bridge seatings, and then – Aulus felt that he could hear the firm tread of those hob-nailed boots shaking the Bridge with regular thumps.

Why Aulus watched until the figure of the customs-officer merged into the throng of passengers over the bridge, and was lost to sight, he did not know. There was simply the compulsion to watch . . . until watching shewed nothing against the busy traffic of the bridge.

---

[1] Later, after Christianity had become a no-longer-persecuted religion, the Christian Bishop of London had his 'palace' in the east end of Londinium: *Sedes Augustini Papae* ('Seat of the London Pope' – St Augustine Papey).

Then Aulus turned into Lombard Street, noting how clear the water was in the stream which ran along the street, and walked into the shop with BURDONIVS over the front.

'Aulus, Master, reporting for duty', he greeted the master.

'Greetings, Aulus!' said the master cabinet-maker. 'Wash if you wish, at the basin there; more tools are over there . . . see. A cypress cabinet is on order for the *legatus Augusti pro praetore*. Here are the drawings. Are you ready to begin work?'

'Ready, master,' said Aulus.

'Good! That's said real London fashion! I think we are going to get on well together, you and I, Aulus.'

'I sincerely hope so, master', said Aulus, opening the rush basket and fingering his shining new tools.

Appendix I

Some London church names and their Latin originals

There is, so far as I know, only one 'address' surviving from Roman London, but that one address is sufficient to provide us with a pattern on which, without doubt, most other London addresses were modelled.

On a jug, found in Southwark,[1] is written, in well-formed 'rustic' uncials, LONDINI AD FANVM ISIDIS – 'At London, near the Temple of Isis' – where the tavern was situated from which the jug came.

Yet even in this single surviving address, we may catch a valuable hint as to the character of those Londoners of perhaps as much as nineteen hundred years ago. Even the most self-conscious classical usage would not have found it necessary to spell out, as here, the address in full. The Latin word *ad*, followed by the name of a deity in the genitive (that is, the 'belonging-to') case, was a recognized elliptical usage for 'to (or at) the temple of . . .'. Cicero writes *ad Opis*, for 'to the temple of Ops'; Horace writes *ad Vestae* for 'to the temple of Vesta'.

To have chosen to write out the address so precisely, these early London taverners must have been persons of an orderly, meticulously painstaking type of mind.

Again, though the common words for 'temple' in Rome itself were rather *templum* or the less pretentious *aedes*, London, we see, chooses the correct but less common *fanum*.

In order as much to clarify the etymological derivations as to save space, I have not set the original Latin 'address' against each church-name, but merely given the name of the temple or other Roman London institution from which the name of the church has been derived.

To give an example, it is clear, from the -ph(-f) ending to Botolph, that this modern name is derived from a Latin word ending in -m; that is to say, the modern phrase 'St Botolph' must have been derived from a phrase of which the ending in Latin was . . . *ad mulctam*, 'alongside of the customs-post'.

What I have done in this list is to simplify matters by merely quoting as follows:

St Botolph   *mulcta*   Customs-post, *douane*

[1] To which it had 'strayed' from the tavern in Size Lane!

In no case yet known to me have I been able to find that the original *meaning* has persisted. Just as in Rome, the name of the Capitolium – the Capitol – has changed over the years to Campidoglio, 'the Fields of Oil', so have the names of Roman London, whilst still preserving the basic sounds, changed their meanings out of all likeness to their originals.

All Hallows Barking	*collegium Saliorum ad collem palatinum*	College of the Salii on the Palatine Mount (of Londinium).
All Hallows Lombard Street	*collegium Saliorum in via lambecta*	College of the Salii (priests of Mars Gradivus) in 'Tidal Street'.
All Hallows on the Wall	*collegium Saliorum juxta vallum muri*	College of the Salii by the (earth) inner fortification of the Wall.
All Hallows Staining	*collegium Saliorum Martis Statoris (*Martis Standinis)*	If this identification is correct, the title of Mars Stator ('the Up-holder') must have had a London form, *Mars Standens.
All Hallows the Great	*collegium Saliorum Martis Gradivi*	College of the Salii of Mars Gradivus. 'Grad-ivus', which has sup-plied the first part of 'Gracechurch', here has become the word 'Great'.
All Hallows Bread Street	*collegium Saliorum in via meridiana*	College of the Salii in South Street (for to 'Bread' has the Latin word *meridianus* here evolved).
All Hallows Honey Lane	*collegium Saliorum ad Senatum (Londiniensem)*	College of the Salii near the Senate. The change of initial S to H – *Senatum*–Honey–marks the name as a very early one.
All Hallows the Less	*collegium Saliorum*	Like All Hallows the Great, this stood in Upper Thames Street until burnt down by the Great Fire of 1666. As it was built over the entrance gate to 'Cold Harbour', it must

227

		originally have stood in close proximity to the *collybus*, the exchange by the Thames.
St Antholin Watling Street	*fanum Antinoöu*	Temple of Antinoüs.
St Alphage	(Meaning not yet determined) Possibly *Statio Alphitarii*	? Office of regulator of grain (*polenta*) supply.
St Andrew by the Wardrobe	*antrum*	Lock-up, military (small) prison.
St Andrew Holborn	*antrum*	Lock-up military (small) prison.
St Andrew Hubbard	*antrum super* (*fluminem*)	Lock-up above the River. I have taken 'Hubbard' to be the modern representative of *super*, 'above' (i.e. the River Thames), but 'Hubbard' may have another derivation.
St Andrew Undershaft	*antrum*	Lock-up. If 'Under' is an English word, and not merely a variant (as 'Andrew' itself is) of *antrum*, then this particular *antrum* may have been an underground cell. The original meaning of Latin *antrum* is 'cave'.
St Anne & St Agnes, Aldersgate	*horrea stanni stagnique*	Warehouse for tin. The Romans adopted the Celtic word for 'tin', that the Celts themselves pronounced both *stagnum* and *stannum*. The use of both words here may indicate a subtle difference of meaning between *stannum* and *stagnum* of which the record has been lost.
St Anne, Blackfriars	*statio annonae ad plagam fretensis*	'Branch-office, Ministry of National Welfare', on the shore

		of the Estuary (i.e. the Fleet River).
St Augustine, Watling Street	. . . *augustinus*	'London. . . .' Obviously some official institution, to which the title *augustinus*, 'of London', was attached. Further evidence may reveal which type of official institution occupied the site long ago. The use of *augustinus* rather than *londiniensis* marks the name as not earlier than the latter part of the fourth century.
St Bartholmew by the Exchange	*matronalia*	Feast of Mars for married women, held on March 1st.
St Bartholomew the Great, West Smithfield	*matronalia*	Feast of Mars for married women, held on March 1st
St Bartholomew the Less, West Smithfield	*matronalia*	Feast of Mars for married women, held on March 1st.
St Benet Fink	*vendita. . . .*	'Things on sale' (i.e. market, bazaar, etc.).
St Benet Gracechurch	*vendita in via Gradiva*	'Things on sale' (i.e. market, bazaar, etc.) in the Street of Mars Gradivus.
St Benet Sherehog (St B. Serog, temp. Henry III)	*vendita ad Serapaeum*	Bazaar by the Temple of Serapis (whose marble head was found in the Mithraeum, in nearby Walbrook, in 1954).

But this church was also dedicated to 'St Osyth' which in earlier times appears as 'Cite', 'Osyde' or 'Cidis'. 'Sancte Cidis' is, in fact, none other than 'Sanct' Isidis' or 'of Holy Isis'. And thus

229

we have found where
that famous jug originated:
at 'St Osyth's', in which
name we may *now*
recognize the Latin:

fanum Isidis

The Temple of Isis!
This is an identification
of the first importance.
It means that the
temples of the two
Egyptian gods,
Isis and Serapis,
either stood close
together or were
housed in the same
building. It really is
extraordinary that the
word 'Isidis' survived
– so little altered to
'Cidis' – until the
thirteenth century!

St Botolph Aldersgate

*mulcta ad portam
(aquilonicam) alteram*

Customs-house by
'The Other (Northern)
Gate'.

St Benet Paul's Wharf

*vendita ad (Senatum)
Populumque*

Bazaar by the
Municipal Senate.

St Botolph Aldgate

mulcta ad portam altam

Customs-house by the
'High Gate'.

St Botolph Billingsgate

*mulcta ad portam
fluminiam juxta
palatum Bellonarium*

Customs-house at the
River-Gate by the
'Bellona' embankment.

St Botolph Bishopsgate

*mulcta ad portam
bissulcam*

Customs-house by the
'Two-furrowed Gate'.

St Bride, Fleet Street

horrea Braduales

The 'Marcus Appius
Bradua' department-
store.

Christ Church, Newgate
Street

Chrysoaspides (?)
(Barracks of)

(Literally 'with
golden shields'.)
The imperial cohort of
the Divine Caesar,
Alexander Severus.

St Christopher-le-Stocks

*statio crustulariorum ad
porticum stoicam*

Shop(s) of the
pastrycooks and
confectioners in the
the Stoic plaza.

St Clement, Eastcheap

(Meaning not yet
determined)

St Dionis Backchurch

fanum Dionysii et Bacchi

Temple of Dionysus
Bacchus.

St Dunstan in the East	*ad danistam*	'At the banker's, moneylenders', etc.
St Dunstan in the West	*ad danistam*	'At the banker's, moneylenders', etc.
St Edmund King and Martyr	*ad administrationem*	At 'the Council offices'.
St Ethelburga	*aedilicius mercatus*	The Aedile Market.
St Faith under St Paul's	*collegium Fetialis* (or *Fetialum*)	College of the Fetiales – Roman priest-heralds. (N.B. that the College of Heralds today is still very near 'St Faith's'.)
St Gabriel Fenchurch	*fanum Cabirialis*	Temple of the Cabiri, Samothracian demon-gods.
St George, Botolph Lane	(Meaning not yet determined)	
St Giles Cripplegate	*fanum Dialis ad circlum*	Temple of Semo Sancus Dius Fidius by 'the Ring' (Gate).
St Giles-in-the-Fields	*fanum Dialis Fidialis*	Temple of (Semo Sancus) Dius Fidius.
St Gregory-by-St Paul's	*statio gregariorum*	Infantry (non-legionary) barracks.
St Helen Bishopsgate	*fanum Selenes ad portam bissulcam*	Temple of Selene (the Moon Goddess) towards the 'Two-furrowed Gate'.
St James Garlickhithe	*scalae gemoniae*	Staircase down which the bodies of executed criminals were dragged with hooks, to be thrown into the Thames.
St John the Baptist upon Walbrook	*Dianium*	Temple of Diana.
St John Zachary	*statio diurnae* (for *diurnorum*) *saccararii*	Record-office of the City Treasurer.
St Katherine Colman	*statio catenarii ad collybum*	'Chain-keeper's' post by the Exchange.
St Katherine Cree	*statio catenarii ad cratem*	'Chain-keeper's' post by revetment defence-work
St Lawrence Jewry	*lautumiae juridiciae*	(Remand) prison of Legate's judicial advisers.

231

St Laurence Pountney	*lautumiae poenitationis*	(Convict) prison.
St Leonard Eastcheap	*statio legionaria*	Legionary post.
St Leonard Foster Lane	*statio legionaria ad fastos*	Legionary post by the official notices.
St Leonard Milk	*statio legionaria militaria*	Legionary post
St Leonard Shoreditch	*statio legionaria*	Legionary post
St Magnus the Martyr	*fanum Magnae Matris*	Temple of the Great Mother (of the gods), i.e. Cybele.
St Margaret, Lothbury	*statio mercatorum ad litum*	Market 'by the river'.
St Margaret Moses	*statio mercatorum messis*	Office of the merchants of the year's produce (*messis*).
St Margaret, New Fish Street	*statio mercatorum ad fiscum*	Market by the Treasury.
St Margaret Pattens	*statio mercatorum ad patientem (ostium rivuli)*	Market by the navigable creek
St Martin-le-Grand	*fanum Martis Gradivi*	Temple of Mars Gradivus
St Martin Ludgate	*fanum Artemis juxta portam ad litorem*	Temple of Artemis by the (Fleet) rivergate.
St Martin Orgar	*statio Artemidis arcturi*	Headquarters of Artemis's Bear-keeper (or Bearward).
St Martin Outwich	*fanum Artemidis in udo vico*	Temple of Artemis in the Marsh, i.e. at the south-east corner of the *trinundinae*, the 'every third week' market – now Threadneedle Street.
St Martin Pomary	*fanum Artemidis ad pomoerium*	Temple of Artemis (or, possibly, in view the fact that it stood in or near the *vicus militaris* 'military compound' the Temple of Mars) by the *pomoerium*.
St Martin Vintry	*fanum Artemidis Venatricis*	Temple of Artemis the Huntress.
St Mary Abchurch	*statio sacomarii* . . .	Office of a Market Weights-and-Measures Inspector.

St Mary Aldermanbury	*statio sacomarii alteri manupretii*	The Deputy Inspector (or Controller) of Workmen's Wages.
St Mary Aldermary	*statio sacomarii altarium* (the last word metathesized to *altamariu'*)	Office of Supervisor of the Sacrificial Offerings.
St Mary-at-Hill	*statio sacomarii aedilicii*	Office of the Aediles' Sacomarius, probably the official who collected the *vectigal aediliciorum*, money paid to the Aediles for public exhibitions.
St Mary Bothaw	*statio sacomarii ad mulctam*	Weights-and-Measures Office by the Customs-post (i.e. the *douane* belonging to the *cancellarius vicus*).
St Mary Colechurch	*statio sacomarii ad collybum*	Office of the inspector by the banking exchange.
St Mary-le-Bow	*statio sacomarii* (or *sacomariorum*) *ad forum boarium* (or *in foro boario*)	Office of the Cattle Market inspectors.
St Mary Mounthaw	*statio sacomarii ad munimentum*	Weights-and-Measures Office by the (Thames) River Rampart.
St Mary Matfellon	*statio sacomarii in medio mille*	Rampart 'at half-mile'
St Mary Somerset	*statio sacomarii* . . .	It is tempting to connect the earliest recorded form, 'Sumersete', with Latin *summersus*, 'submerged', etc; but the meaning is not clear, and we must leave the derivation as not yet proved.
St Mary Staining	*statio sacomariorum stagni*	Office of the Inspectors of Tin. (Earliest recorded form of the name, 1189, is 'Staninge'.)

St Mary Woolchurch Haw	*statio sacomarii ad vallum . . .*	Weights-and-Measures Office by the embankment (i.e. of the Walbrook river). The latter part of the name is decidedly obscure. '. . . church Haw' could be from Latin *cerrusatum*, 'painted with white lead', but though the wooden palings of Roman embankments were so painted, would this very ordinary fact have been mentioned?
St Mary Woolnoth	*statio sacomariorum venalicii*	Office of the Inspectors of the Slave Market (*see* page 217).
St Mary Magdalene, Milk Street	*statio sacomarii medicinalis* (through a doubly metathetized form, **mec'dilanis*)	Office of Inspectors of Medical Practice. The name, 'Magdalen' or 'Magdalene' occurs early in London records, and must therefore be an original name.
St Mary Magdalen of the Guildhall	*statio sacomarii medicinalis*	Office of the Inspectors of Medical Practice attached to the Basilica of Justice.
St Mary Magdalen, Aldgate	*statio sacomarii medicinalis ad altam portam*	Office of the Inspectors of Medical Practice at the eastern gate of the City.
St Mary Magdalen, Old Fish Street	*statio sacomarii medicinalis ad fiscum occidentalem*	Office of the Inspectors of Medical Practice attached to the senior Imperial Treasury (*Fiscus*).
St Matthew, Friday Street	*fanum Matutae*	Temple of Matuta. Roman temple still a church.
St Michael Bassishaw	*macellum ad basilicam*	Market by the Basilica.
St Michael Cornhill	*macellum in cornula*	Market on the eastern 'Horn' of the City.

St Michael Crooked Lane	*macellum in via cruciale*	Market in 'Torture Street'.
St Michael-le-Querne	*macellum in cornu occidentale*	Market on the western 'Horn' of the City, i.e. by the Cattle Market.
St Michael Paternoster Royal	*macellum ad patientem ostium rivuli*	Market by the navigable mouth of the stream (i.e. a small tributary of the Walbrook). 'Royal'—earlier 'riole'—is derived from Latin *rivuli* or *rivalis*: either would have become 'royal'.
St Michael Queenhithe	*macellum vinarium*	Vintners' market. This, by the way, confirms that the district was, in Roman times, and for long after, a centre of the winetrade. The old forms of the name, e.g. 'St Michael de Quenheth' (1294), plainly indicate the derivation from the original Latin: *vinum*, 'wine', became *guin* in Old Welsh.
St Michael Wood Street	*macellum ad vadum*	Market. It is not easy to determine the original of 'Wood', which may be the same as the 'Huda' which is the earlier form of '-hithe'. And both *may* be from Latin *vadum*, which means either 'stream' or 'ford'.
St Mildred Bread Street	*castellum militum meritentum*	Barracks of the serving soldiers.
St Mildred Poultry	*militaria polluctura*	Military sacrificial banquet (i.e. the place where it was held).

235

St Nicholas Acon	(Meaning of 'Acon' not yet determined[1]) *fanum Jovis Nicaei*	Temple of Jupiter Nicaeus.
St Nicholas Cole Abbey	*statio nexilis ad collybum*	Registrar's office by the Banking Exchange.
St Nicholas Olave (or St Nicholas Bernard)	*statio nexilis ad aulam vernariam*	Registry of the household slaves.
St Olave, Hart Street	(Meaning not yet determined)	Hall of . . .
St Olave Jewry	*aula juridicia*	Court of the Law.
St Olave, Silver Street	(Meaning not yet determined)	Hall of . . .
St Pancras, Soper Lane	*pancratium superlatum*	'Super', 'mammoth' complete athletic exhibition. (The *pancratium*—pronounced 'pancratsium' throughout the Empire from the first century onwards—included both wrestling and boxing.)
St Peter-upon-Cornhill	*praetorium ad cornulam*	The Praetorium (Governor-general's H.Q.) on the 'Little Horn' i.e., the eastern of London's twin hills.
St Peter-le-Poer	*praetorium purpuratum*	Praetorium 'of the Imperial Dignity'.
St Peter, Paul's Wharf	*praetorium in palo . . . arma*	Praetorium 'in-the-Marsh' (i.e. by the then much more sedgy and muddy foreshore of the Thames). The last word, which almost certainly ends in -*arma*, escapes recognition as yet. The word 'Paul's' here has a different derivation from that of the seemingly identical word in the phrase 'St Paul's'. Here 'Paul' is derived from original

[1] But see St Thomas Acon.

		Latin *palus*, 'marsh, fen'—in Old Welsh, *pawl*.
St Peter Westcheap	*praetorium in vestibulo (viae) capidis*	Praetorium at the beginning of 'Sacrifice Street' (i.e. the modern 'Cheapside').
St Sepulchre	*vicus sepulcralis*	Burying-place. (In this case, the word has hardly changed, which seems unlikely. Yet that a word should change a little only, rather than a lot, is not impossible, and in support of the theory that modern 'Sepulchre' (as here) derives from some such word as Latin *sepulcralis* we may reflect that this was an ancient burying-place just outside the Wall.)
St Stephen Walbrook	*stipendiarium ad vallatum*	Office of the Tax-collector by the river-embankment (i.e. of the Walbrook tributary).
St Stephen, Coleman Street	*stipendiarium ad collybum*	Tax-collector's office by the Banking Exchange.
St Swithin London Stone	*sedes lanistanis*	School where gladiators are trained. (Latin *lanista* means 'a trainer of gladiators'.)
St Thomas the Apostle	*(castellum?) (flumini) Tamesae appositum*	(*Probably* Fort) close to the Thames. Whether or not the building referred to was a fort, the operative phrase means 'near the Thames'—*Tamesae appositum*: 'Thomas Apostle'.

St Thomas Acon (Acres)	Either *domus sacra* or (much more likely) *domus agraria*	Temple, shrine. Offices of the *Triumvir Agrarius*, one of the three commissioners who managed the division of public lands.
Holy Trinity the Less	(Meaning not yet determined)	
Holy Trinity, Minories	(Meaning not yet determined)	
St Ursula's Chapel	*sacellum ursularium*	Chapel of 'the Little She-bear' i.e. of Artemis. The form 'St Ursula' seems a reconstructed form, a 'back-formation' from Latin, *ursula*, through Kymric, *orswll*.
St Vedast, Foster Lane	*ad diem fastum* or *ad diebus fastis*	'By the publicly-displayed Court Kalendar.' London pronunciation was, originally *a'die'fast'*, which then became metathesized to *a'fie'dast*, and so developed to modern 'Vedast'.

Appendix II

The gods of Roman London and the sites of their temples

Divinity, etc.	Latin name	Modern derivation
Anna Perenna	sacellum Annae (or Annanis) Perennae	St Anne's Fraternity (in church of St Michael, Cornhill).
Anna Augusta	templum Annanis Augustae ad plagam fretensis	St Ann Blackfriars.
Apollo	templum Apollinis	Honour of Bononiae (in church of St Magnus the Martyr).
(Candens) Apollo	templum Candinis Apollinis	Cain-and-Abel's Alley (one in Bishopsgate Street Within, one in Angel Alley, Houndsditch).
Antinoüs	fanum Antinoöu	St Antholin, Watling Street. St Anthony's Hospital, Threadneedle Street.
Artemis	fanum Artemidis juxta portam ad litorem	St Martin Ludgate.
	fanum Artemidis in udo vico	St Martin Outwich.
	fanum Artemidis ad liminem statio Artemidis arcturi	'The Artirce' in Lime Street. Headquarters of the Bear-keeper of Artemis (St Martin Orgar).
	fanum Artemidis ad pomoerium fanum Artemidis Venatricis	St Martin Pomary. St Martin Vintry.
Bellona	fanum Bellonae ad palatum Bellonarium	Billingsgate.

Divinity, etc.	Latin name	Modern derivation
Bacchus (Dionysus/)	*fanum Dionysii Bacchique*	St Dionis Backchurch.
Belin-Sabazios	*templum Belinis Sabaziou*	'The Bell Savage' (*or* the Belle Sauvage). The word 'the' (remnant of *templum*) is always placed before the phrase 'Bell Savage'.
	Ad Sabaziou	Sabb's-quay.
Bona Dea	*sacellum Bonae Deae*	Bond Court.
Cabiri	*fanum Cabirialis juxta viam Gradivam*	St Gabriel Fenchurch (*or* Fanchurch).
Cybele	*fanum Magnae Matris*	St Magnus Martyr.
Diana (as distinct from *Artemis*)	*Dianium*	St John the Baptist-upon-Walbrook.
Dionysius (and Bacchus)	*fanum Dionysii Bacchique*	St Dionis Backchurch.
(Semo Sancus) Dius Fidius	*templum Dialis ad circulum* (or *circlum*)	St Giles Cripplegate.
	templum Dialis Fidialis	St Giles-in-the-Fields.
Fetiales (priests)	*collegium Fetialis* (or *Fetialum*)	St Faith-under-St Paul's.
Isis	*fanum Isidis*	St Osyth's *or* Siselane. ('Sancte Cidis', 1358).
Jupiter Dolichenus	*fanum Jovis Dolicheni*	Do Little Lane.
Jupiter Nicaeus	*templum Jovis Nicaei*	Nicholas Lane (via Nicaealis).
Mars (*College of Leaping Priests of*)	*collegium Saliorum ad collem palatinum*	All Hallows Barking.
	collegium Saliorum in via lambecta N.B. That these priests were attached to a temple of Mars Gradivus is proved by the name:	All Hallows, Lombard Street.
		Via Gradiva Gracechurch Street.
(Mars Stator *or* Standens)	*collegium Saliorum Martis Statoris* (or in all probability, a London form, *Standinis*)	All Hallows Staining.
	collegium Saliorum Martis Gradivi N.B. That this was a	All Hallows the Great.

Divinity, etc.	Latin name	Modern derivation
	most ancient temple of Mars, and that, accordingly, he was worshipped here under his old name of Semo ('Seed'), in his aspect of a god of the Crops, is proved by the survival, until late mediæval times, of the alternative name of the church: 'Parochia omnium sanctorum *Semanchirch*' (1285). Though the adjective 'Great' is derived from 'Gradivus', yet the fact of this church's (temple's) immense antiquity may have made it the chief of all the 'All Hallows' churches of London. Since the Arval Brothers worshipped Mars under his ancient aspect of Semo, this may well have been a sanctuary of this mysterious religious brotherhood.	
	collegium Saliorum in viam meridianum	All Hallows Bread Street.
	collegium Saliorum ad Senatum Londiniensem	All Hallow Honey Lane.
Mars Gradivus	*templum Martis Gradivi*	St Martin-le-Grand.
Matronalia (Feast of Mars for married women)	*vicus matronalicus*	St Bartholomew the Great.
	vicus matronalicus	St Bartholomew the Less.
	vicus matronalicus	St Bartholomew-by-the-Exchange.
Matuta	*fanum Matutæ*	St Matthew Friday Street
Mothers, The (The Three Mothers)	*templum Matrum*	La Maderhawe (in parish of St Olave, Hart Street, 1286).
Selene	*templum Selenes* 'It has been suggested,	St Helen, Bishopsgate.

Q

Divinity, etc.	Latin name	Modern derivation
	from the discovery of Roman remains, pavements, etc., in the neighbourhood, that the site . . . had been occupied by an extensive Roman building.' (Harben, quoting *Gent. Mag.* Lib. VX, pp. 42–5)	
Serapis	*Serapæum*	Soper's Lane *and* (St Benet) Sherehog ('Soper' and 'Sherehog' being both derived from 'Serap'). N.B. The head of a statue of Serapis was found in the Mithraeum, in nearby Walbrook, and that 'St Benet Sherehog' (burnt down in the Fire of 1666) was dedicated to both 'St Benet Shorog and Seinte Site' (1363); in other words, to two imported *Egyptian* deities: Serapis and Isis, whose temples always stood together.
Semo Sancus Dius Fidius	(See under Dius Fidius)	

Appendix III
Latin words and their Old Welsh derivatives

This selective list demonstrates the changes which overtook certain Latin words after their having been adopted by the speakers of British (or Old Welsh). This word list should be consulted by the reader to provide a check on the author's method of finding Latin originals in modern London names.

Latin	Old Welsh	Meaning
abecedarium	agwyðawr	hornbook, n.; alphabetical, adj.
admissus	emys (plural)	admitted to an audience (of an important person).
adorare	aðoli	to adore.
Aegyptus	Aipht	Egyptian.
Agricola	Aircol	husbandman. (But here a proper name: the well-known Governor of Britain.)
Alpinus	Elfin	Alpine.
altus	alt	high, lofty.
angelus	angel	messenger, holy man, angel.
antecenium	ancwyn	luncheon.
Antonius	Anhun	Anthony (proper name).
apostolus	abostol	apostle.
Aprilis	Ebrill	April.
argentum	aryant	silver.
arma	arff	arms, weapons.
ascendo	escynn	I ascend.
asinus	asyn	ass.
axilla	ascell	armpit.
baiula	baeol	female porter.
baptizare	bedyðio	to baptize.
barba	barf	beard.
beneficium	benfyc	benefit.
bilis	bustl	bile, anger.
bracc(h)ia	bre(a)ch	(human) arms.
bucca	boch	mouth.

243

Latin	Old Welsh	Meaning
caballus	ceffyl	nag, hack, pack-horse.
calamus	calaf	pen.
caldaria	callawr	'hot rooms'.
caldus	call	hot.
campus	camp	field.
cancellarius	canghellawr	enclosed, protected, 'out of bounds'.
cancellus	cagell	enclosure, barrier.
candela	cannuill, canvil, etc.	candle, torch.
capistrum	cepister	halter, muzzle.
carcarem	carchar	prison.
caritatem	cardawt	charity.
caseus	caws	cheese.
castellum	castell	fort, refuge.
catena	cadwyn	chain.
caucus	cawc	drinking-vessel.
cavilla	cabl	jest.
cavitatem	ciwawd, ceudod	hollow, opening.
cella	kell	store-room, hut.
centrum	cithremmet	centre.
cera	cwyr	wax.
cingulum	cingel	belt (also used figuratively. Cf. our 'Green Belt').
cippus	ciph	stake, grave-stone.
civitas	ciwed	city.
cloppus	clop	thief.
coag'lum	caul	rennet.
cocina	cegin	cook-shop.
cocus (*Late Latin*)	cog	a cook.
colonia	colun	Roman 'colony'.
col'pus	cwlf	a blow, buffet.
columna	colofn	column.
commendo	cymmyn	I entrust to.
communio	kymun	I fortify well.
comparo	cymharu, cymmaru	I arrange, match.
compello	cymhell, cymmell	I assemble.
co(n)denso conde(n)so	cynhwyso	I make dense, press together.
confessio	kyffes	confession, admission.
consecro	cysegr	I dedicate (to a god).
co(n)solor	cysuro	I console, comfort.
co(n)silium	cussyl	council, assembly.
Constantinus	Custennhin	Constantine (the Emperor).
construendum	cystrawen	a gathering together.
contendo	cynhen	I exert, etc.
contrarius	cythrawl	opposite, fronting.
contrudo	cythrud	I thrust together.
conventio	cynfaint	assembly.
corregia	corruui	shoe-tie, boot-lace,

Latin	*Old Welsh*	*Meaning*
coxa	coes	hip.
creatura	creadur	creature.
crotalia	cleteriou	rhythm of castanets.
cubiculum	cuðigl	bed-chamber.
cultellus	cultell	small knife.
cultrum	cwlltr	ploughshare.
Daniel	Deinioel	Daniel (*the Prophet*).
David	Dewi	David.
decantorum	deganwy	singers, choristers.
deficio	diffygio	I forsake, abandon.
descendo	dyscynn	I descend.
diabolus	Diawl, *plural*: diefil	devil, Satan.
Dies Martis	Diu Maurth	Tuesday ('Mars's Day').
diurnatum	diwarnawt	daily duty.
disco	dyscu	I learn, study.
donatus	dunaut	something given, a gift.
draco	draci (*later Welsh*)	dragon.
episcopus	escop	bishop.
eterni (*m. gen.* or *pl.*)	etern	eternal.
faba	ffa(f)	broad-bean, horse-bean.
fagus	ffawyd, fau	beech-tree.
fata	ffawt	fate, destiny.
Febr(u)arius	Chwefrawr	February.
firmamentum	ffurfafen	firmament, sky.
fontana	finnaun	spring, fountain.
forum	dor	market-place.
fossa	fos	ditch, trench.
fructus	fruid	fruit, crop, yield.
fuga	ffo	flight, escape.
gemma	gem, gemmou	bud, gem.
germanus	garmawn	blood relative, *n.*; related by blood, *adj.*
gladius	cledyf	sword.
Graeca, *f.* or *neuter pl.*	Groeg	Greek.
graphium	grephiou	writing style.
grex	grega, gre	flock, herd.
hapsus	heusawr	woollen bandage.
hora	hawr	hour.
humilis	ufyll	low, small, slight, etc.
imparem	amhar	odd, uneven, etc.
imperator	amheradwr	commander-in-chief, emperor.
imprægno (Late Latin)	ymrain	impregnate.

Latin	Old Welsh	Meaning
instruo	ystryw	I build, erect, etc.
intervenio	athrwyn	I intervene.
Iovem, *acc.*	Iof	(to) Jove.
Iovis, *gen.*	Yeu	(of) Jove.
Iuðas	Iuðas	Judas.
Iudeus	Idew	Jew, *n.*; Jewish, *adj.*
laicus	lleyg	lay, of the laity.
latro, *n.*	lleidyr	mercenary, bandit.
laxus	lais	wide, loose, open.
legenda	lleen	'prescribed reading'.
leo	lewo, lew	lion.
locus	loc	place, 'spot', locality.
maceria	magwyr	enclosure, garden-wall.
magister	meistr	master, lord.
maior	mere	greater, bigger, major.
manica	manec	sleeve.
Marcianus	Marchion	Marcianus (proper name).
Marianus	Meiriawn	Marianus (proper name).
Martellus	Morthwyll	
martyrum, *gen. pl.*	marthyr (mod. merthyr)	(of) the martyrs.
matutina	meitin, meittyn	the morning hours.
memoria	myfyr	memory.
mensis	mis	month.
me(n)sura	mesur	measure, measurement.
monachus	manach, mynach; *pl*: myneich	monk, monks.
monumentum	mynwent	memorial, monument, statue, tomb, etc.
Natalicia	Nadolic	Christmas feast.
nona	nawn	ninth, *f.*
nota	nod	mark, sign, note, etc.
nuptialia	neithiawr	nuptials.
occa	occed	harrow, *n.*
occasio	achaus	opportunity, happy chance.
organum	orian	implement, instrument.
pagus	pau	'the country', a village.
paperus	pabuir	papyrus, paper.
papillio	pebyll	butterfly.
paratus	parawt	ready, prepared.
patella	patel	pan, dish, plate.
peccatum, *acc.*	pecaud	sin, offence.
pensum	pwys	task, duty, day's work.
perfectus	perfeith, pirfeith	perfect, excellent.

Latin	Old Welsh	Meaning
permedius	perued	in the middle.
peto	pedi	I travel to, I attack.
piper	pubyr	pepper.
planta	plant	shoot, twig, sprig.
plagus (*for* plaga)	pla	flat surface, plain.
pletta (plecta)	pleth	twisted, plaited, etc.
pluma	plu(f)	feather.
Pondus	Pwnn	weight.
pop(u)lus	pobl, *pl*: pobloet	people, nation, citizen.
porta	porth	door, gate, etc.
portare	porth	to carry.
postis	post	post, door-post.
praedium, praedia	preið	mortgaged property.
preceptum	pregeth	precept.
presentem	presen	present, *adj*.
privatus	pried	state- or privately-owned.
probare	profi	to approve, to sanction.
prudens	pruð	skilled, prudent, etc.
psalterium	sallwyr	psalter.
pullicinium	pilgeint	chicken-run.
pulverem, *acc*.	pylor	dust.
punctum	pwyth	Point, small hole.
purus	pur	Clean, pure, etc.
puter, putris	podar	rotten, putrid, etc.
putrire	pydru	to decay, to corrupt.
Qua(d)ragesima	Carawys	Quadragesima Sunday.
quartarium	chwarthawr	fourth-part, quarter.
qu(i)esco	cyscu	I rest, stay quiet.
radius	reith, reid	stake, spoke of wheel.
rastrum	rascl	scraper, hoe, rake.
remus	rum, ruif	oar.
Romani, *n.pl*.	Rufein, Rumein	the Romans.
ruina	rhewin	collapse, overthrow.
Sabrina	Hafrenn	River Severn.
sagitta	saeth	arrow.
saliva	haliw	saliva.
Salomo	Salovi, Selim, Selyf	Solomon.
sanctus	seith, sant	holy, sacred.
Saturnus	Sadwrn, Sadurn	Saturn.
scala	yscawl	stair, staircase.
sc(h)ola	ysgol	school.
securus	segur	carefree, quiet, secure.
sedes	swyð	chair, abode, temple.
serpens	sarff	serpent, snake.
sextarius	hestaur	a sixth, a measure of weight.

Latin	Old Welsh	Meaning
signum	swyn	mark, token, sign.
sol'dus	swllt	dense, compact, solid.
spiritus	yspryd	spirit.
spolia	yspeil	booty, spoils of war.
spongos (*Late Latin*)	ysbwng	sponge, *n.*
stabellum	ystafell	room, chamber.
stabilis	sefyl	firm, steady, stable.
stella	istwyll	star.
stola	ystol	woman's gown, robe, 'stole'.
stupula (stipula)	sufl	cornstalk, reed pipe.
stratura	strotur	paving, pavement.
stumblus, stumilus	swml	goad, spur.
taberna	tafarn	shop, tavern.
Tacitus	tacit, Tegyd	silent; Tacitus, the Roman historian.
tempero	temperaff	divide, qualify, mix.
templum	temhyl	temple.
tempore	tymor, temmor	(by or with) time.
terminus	termin, terfyn	boundary, limit.
testis	test	witness.
torta, *f.* or *neuter pl.*	torth	twisted, crooked.
tostus	tost	roasted, baked, toasted.
tres	tri	three.
tri- (*in compounds*)	tri-	
tribus	tref	tribe, clan.
turma	torf	troop, throng, crowd.
Uriconium	Guiragon	Uriconium (now Wroxeter).
vagina	gwein	scabbard, sheath, etc.
vectis	gueith	pole, bar, lever.
verbum	berf	word.
versus	gwers	against, opposite to.
vesper(um)	gosper	day's end, evening.
vig'lia	gwyl	wakefulness, keeping watch, vigil.
vinum	guin	wine.
virgo	gwyry	virgin, maiden.
virtus	gwyrth	manliness, merit, etc.
vitalis	guithaul	vital, living.
vitrum	gwydr	glass, woad.
Vitalianus	Guit(h)olion	Vitalianus (proper name.)

REMARKS

It is impossible, with the limited space at my disposal, to undertake here even a moderately complete analysis of the changes undergone by Latin words on their adoption into Old Welsh. However, I shall note some of the more striking characteristics of those Old Welsh words of whose Latin origin there can be no doubt. It must be remembered that there are more than eight hundred of such words, a fact which seriously entitles us to regard Old Welsh as worthy of inclusion within the Romance group of languages.

A further point – this time of warning. Except for a few words, almost no written records survive from the period with which this book deals. What knowledge we have of Old Welsh of the period when London and the southern parts of her *territorium* constituted an enclave of Romania within an ever-encroaching ring of Saxondom is derived from manuscripts of much later date, where even faithfully-rendered writings of an earlier period necessarily underwent some inevitable modernizations. We may say that we can assert, with more or less of confidence, that it is possible to recover the forms of Old Welsh *as it probably was* in the sixth and seventh centuries.

What ought to be interesting to us modern British – especially now that 'Accepted English' has been rejected by the great communications monopolies in favour of Cockney and other regional dialects – is to observe that the speech idioms which converted Latin words into Welsh words are precisely those speech idioms which have survived, in common English speech, to this day: the substitution of the intervocalic dental by a glottal stop (Latin, *imperator*; Old Welsh, *amheradawr*; Modern Cockney, *em':rer*); the violent syncope, due to the elision of vowels in unstressed syllables (Latin, *episcopus*; Old Welsh, *escop*; Modern Cockney, *bishp*, *bisher* or even *bish*); and some other phonological peculiarities which link Modern English, in its most 'popular' form, with the speech of those people who were Londoners when Maxim was Wledig in Caer Lud.

Consonants

c The treatment of c, in Latin words imported into Old Welsh, supports Professor L. R. Palmer's statement (*The Latin Language*) that there is no unequivocal evidence of the palatalization of c until the sixth century. 'In Classical Latin', he says, 'this sound was pronounced as a plosive [k] in all positions.' The evidence is clear that it was so pronounced in the Province of Britain: Latin, *beneficium*; Old Welsh, *benfyc*; also *cella*, *kell*; *cera*, *cwyr*; etc. In certain medial positions, it softened to g.

d Invariably weakened, this dental was either completely suppressed (*admissus > emys*) or aspirated (*adorare > aðoli*) when it fell between two vowels or between a vowel and a nasal sonant. It retained its original sound initially (*David > Dewi*, etc.).

f Retained its sound initially, except for some curious exceptions, where initial f becomes either χ (*febr(u)arius > chwefrawr*) or d (*forum > dor*). Before a, i and u, initial f was pronounced long, an idiom represented by the duplication of the letter (*fata > ffawt*; *fuga > ffo*, etc.).

g Retained its sound initially, but suffered elision medially in some words (*aegyptus > aipht*) or became c before l (*gladius > cledyf*). As elsewhere in

Romania, G was palatalized before a front vowel, hence Old Welsh *aryant* < *argentum*.

H Initially, represents an original Latin s, but only in words imported early into Welsh. Thus Latin *Sabrina* becomes Old Welsh *hafrenn*, and Latin *saliva* becomes Old Welsh *haliw*, but later Latin *sanctus* (a word of strictly Christian context, by the time of its importation) becomes Old Welsh *seith* or *sant*. In Old Welsh, H, medially, represents a Latin dental or plosive, replaced in Old Welsh by a glottal stop (cf. *imparem* > *amhar*; *contendo* > *cynhen*).

Initial *Latin* H generally remains (*hora* > *hawr*), but is dropped before U (humilis > ufyll), perhaps evidence that the pronunciation of this vowel as the French or Germans (ü) now pronounce it was an Old Welsh idiosyncrasy. We know that the 'French U' sound was heard in Latin, for the Emperor Claudius proposed to add a letter to the alphabet to indicate this sound.

L Latin L retained initially in Old Welsh (*laxus* > *lais*), but sometimes replaced by surd L (*laicus* > *lleyg*). Medially, the L is often retained, but sometimes disappears (*nuptialia* > *neithiawr*).

M The phenomenon of the 'lenition' of intervocalic M is common to all the Celtic languages. This intervocalic M changed in Old Welsh to a bilabial fricative [β], represented in ancient manuscripts by either F (*memoria* > *myfyr*) or W (*monumentum* > *mynwent*). In modern Breton, the lenition of *intervocalic* M affects a preceding *initial* M (Modern Breton *merc'h*, 'girl, daughter', but 'my daughter' is *va verc'h*, not *ma merc'h*.) I mention this because, though Old Welsh *writing* does not indicate any infection of initial M, yet there is evidence that the 'Old Welsh' spoken in London lenited M both intervocalically and initially, if I have correctly derived *Fyfoot* (-lane) from Latin *monumentum* (Old Welsh *mynwent*, where only the intervocalic M is lenited).

N Latin N retained unchanged initially. Medially, Old Welsh tends to suppress (doubtless after an intervening stage of nasalization) N before a dental (*contrudo* > *cythrud*), but as this is also a Latin speech idiom (*conjunx/conjux*; *consul/cosol*) it may not be significant. Medially, however – especially in initial syllables – where the strong stress accent fell, the N was retained (*candela* > *canvil*; *angelus* > *angel*; *Antonius* > *Anhun*, etc.). In a final position, N tends to be retained (*alpinus* > *elfin*; *Constantinus* > *Custennhin*, etc.).

P Initially, Latin P is retained (*postis* > *post*; *praedium* > *preið*). Medially, Old Welsh tends to vocalize the plosive, so that P > B (*papillio* > *pebyll*; *paperus* > *pabuir*, etc.). It should be noted that the modern English habit of suppressing initial P in such words as *psalter*, etc., has an ancient precedent in Old Welsh, where Latin *psalterium* became *sallwyr*. As elsewhere in Europe, P disappeared before T: *baptizare* > *bedyðio*.

QU Latin initial QU became either C or χ in Old Welsh. (Cf. *quadragesima* > *carawys*; *quartarium* > *chwarthawr*.)

R Latin initial R is retained in Old Welsh. Medially, Latin R can change
to L (*rastrum* > *rascl*), disappear altogether (*probare* > *profi*) or – and this
in the majority of cases – remain (*paratus* > *parawt*). In a final position,
it usually remains (*piper* > *pubyr*).

S Latin initial S changes to H ('rough breathing' rather than the Germanic
aspirate) only in words imported *early* from Latin: *Sabrina* > *Hafrenn*;
saliva > *haliw*. Later imports from Latin retain the Latin S: *sagitta* >
saeth; *Saturnus* > *Sadwrn*. The British Celts resemble the Irish, in
learning, from a conquering people, to change an essential speech
idiom. In 'basic' Old British speech patterns, an initial Indo-European
sibilant became a 'rough breathing' (or aspirate) as it did in Greek.
In Gaelic, initial Indo-European P was dropped. Yet the Irish learnt
to use the initial P (*Patricius* > *Padraig*) through contact with Rome.
Initial Old Welsh S, like initial Old Irish P, is a good indication of the
antiquity of a word. Where initial S is followed by a voiceless plosive, a
prosthetic vowel often develops: *scala* > *yscawl*; *spiritus* > *yspryd*.

T Initially, Latin T remains, as it often does medially (*testis* > *test*;
matutina > *meitin*; *postis* > *post*, etc.). But usually, medial T becomes either
D (*peto* > *pedi*; *puter* > *podar*) or is aspirated (*portare* > *porth*; *sanctus* >
seith; *vitalis* > *guithaul*). Sometimes T > C (*rastrum* > *rascl*).

V Initially, Old Welsh did not distinguish between Latin vocalic and
consonantal V, treating them both alike (*Uriconium* > *Guiragon*; *vagina* >
gwein). The spelling GW, GU – occasionally GO (*vesperum* > *gosper*) seems
to indicate a bilabial fricative [β], but with a faint guttural overtone.
We know, from a London inscription, that Latin V (pronounced like
our initial, consonantal w) had already undergone considerable local
modification by the mid-third century, for on a marble group con-
taining Bacchus and Silenus, there is an inscription, HOMINIBVS BAGIS
BITAM ('Life to wandering men'), which, classically, should have been
written: HOMINIBVS VAGIS VITAM. Here, then, London speech usage
appears to differ from that of 'national' Old Welsh, or perhaps the
bilabial fricative of London usage – [β] – later acquired a guttural
overtone, represented by the Old Welsh spelling GW-, etc. By the way,
Old Welsh *berf* from Latin *verbum* is not an exception to the rule: *berf*
is merely the metathesized form of *verbum*.

Z A rare letter in Latin, and appearing only in words derived (always
rather self-consciously) from the Greek. The letter did not begin to
become at all common until Christianity stepped up the import of
Greek words into Latin. Old Welsh treats it, when it rarely occurs, as
the Spaniards do to-day: *baptizare* > *bedyðio*.

NOTE 1

Metathesis – the transposition of letters or syllables within a word – is a
phenomenon common to all languages, and is perhaps the most fruitful
source of language-change. Besides *verbum* > *berf*, noted above, the reader

should also notice such metathetical forms as (metathesis of consonants) *axilla* > *ascell* and (metathesis of vowels) *cavitatem* > *ciwawd*.

NOTE 2

In the body of the book, I have often mentioned my derivation of '(The) Cock Inn' from Latin *cocina*, 'cook-shop, eating-house'. Yet reference to the word-list above shows that Latin *cocina* became *cegin* (and not *cogin*) in Old Welsh. That there may be considerable uncertainty between short E and short O is plainly enough indicated by the very common American pronunciation of the words *telephone, telegraph, telegram*, etc.: '*toll*-pho,' '*toll*-grav,' '*toll*-Graham'. Doubtless the Londoners said 'coquin' and 'cogin'' – and the out-of-town Old Welsh said 'cegin', just as I pronounce the word clerk as 'clark', and an educated American pronounces it 'clurk'.

Vowels

An examination of the rules governing the changes of Latin vowels into Old Welsh vowels is impossible here; the subject is far too complex, and I can only refer the reader to my textual observations (cf. page 64, where, in talking of the change of Latin *monumentum* into Old Welsh *mynet*, I refer to the 'o-mutation').

The Old Welsh vowel-changes were greatly affected by the preceding consonant. After C (almost always hard) and T, the Latin vowels tended to remain curiously unaffected (*cancellus* > *cagell*; *caritatem* > *cardawt*; *catena* > *cadwyn*; *taberna* > *tafarn*; *Tacitus* > *Tacit*; *tempero* > *temperaff*; *terminus* > *terfyn*, etc.). After S, too, Latin vowels tend to remain fairly unchanged in Old Welsh (*saliva* > *haliw*; *Salomo* > *Salovi*; *scriplum* > *scribl*, etc.) but other consonants, notably D and P, effect profound changes in the quality of the following vowels (*donatus* > *dunaut*; *pullicinium* > *pilgeint*). And though Latin vowels remain unchanged after initial R (*rastrum* > *rascl*), they also change considerably: *radius* > *reith*; *remus* > *rum, ruif*; *ruina* > *rhewin*. For a complete examination of Old Welsh phonology, the interested reader is referred to the sources quoted in the Bibliography.

The pattern of the Latin-into-Welsh changes

If we note how Latin words altered on their adoption into Old Welsh, we shall observe the following influences as being principally responsible for the (often fundamental) changes:

1. In Old Welsh (as in Modern English) the very heavy *stress* accent fell on the first syllable. This had the effect of preserving the first syllable, often with the sounds transferred unchanged from Latin to Old Welsh. And it is this retention of Latin sounds in the first syllable, unchanged or only slightly modified (see above) which has made it possible to identify so many London names of the present with their Latin originals of fifteen hundred years ago; cf. Candlewick Street from *cancellarius vicus*, etc.

2. But the strong stress accent on the first syllable had the effect of leaving the rest of the word singularly vulnerable to erosion. The history, indeed,

of many Latin words adopted into Old Welsh is a history of a gradual dropping of endings (*asinus* > *asyn*; *angelus* > *angel*; *antecenium* > *ancwyn*, etc.). Bit-by-bit, literally, the word sheds each successive end, until nothing is left of the original but the 'hard core' of the original first syllable. If we are to believe Max Müller, Modern French *même* is original Latin *memetipsissimus*, and though Old Welsh will not show such a high degree of erosion, Modern Welsh will.

3. However, sound changes – particularly the lenition of intervocalic M – were brought about *before* the dropping of endings, with the result that the change remained even after the ending which had produced it had been dropped. An example is to be found in the history of the Latin *arma*, 'weapons of war, arms'. On its adoption by the speakers of Old Welsh, the intervocalic M – lying between A (the R being untrilled) and another A – was lenited into [β], represented by the spelling F (or FF). Latin *arma* then changed into Old Welsh *arffa*. Following normal Old Welsh practice, the ending -*a* of *arffa* was dropped, and the word now ended in -*ff*, this -*ff* having been produced by the ending that the word had dropped.

4. The common Modern English and Modern American pronunciation of, say, *motor* as *mo'er* has been inherited from Celtic, where Latin *pater*, 'father', was pronounced *pa'er*, yielding Modern French *père*.

At first, the dropped intervocalic dental is replaced by a glottal stop (represented in Old Welsh spelling by H – *imperator* > *amheradwr*), but soon the glottal stop itself grows shorter, lighter and less regarded, until it, too, is dropped and the original word is one syllable less. This is what has happened to, for example, the Latin *sedes*, 'abode, habitation, temple, etc.', which appears in Old Welsh *swyð*. Word-shortening owes a lot to this replacement of intervocalic dentals by glottal stops; but the knowledge of how a word has been shortened enables us to restore the original form. Knowing, for instance, what had happened to change Latin *sedes* into Old Welsh *swyð*, I was enabled to recover the Latin original behind the very English name 'St Swithin', and to discover *sinum*, 'wine bowl', in the common English tavern-name 'Swan' – originally *ad sinum*, 'at the Sign of the Flowing Bowl'.

Appendix IV
Some Notes on the Text

Page 19

A crescent-crowned female head in terra-cotta, together with the name, 'Half Moon', of a modern tavern surely indicate the former existence of a temple of Juno Lucina in or near Gracechurch Street.

Page 21

Mr Jack Lindsay writes: 'Is there an adjective "corbitensis"? I know only "corbita". But the formation is correct.' I think that we may assume 'corbitensis', but it is *possible* that 'Corbett's Court' derived from an original 'ad corbitis'—'where the sailing-barges lie up.'

Page 22

Mr Lindsay writes: ' "Vicus cancellarius'." "Cancellarius" means "door-keeper", later "secretary". I suppose that in latish times it did get a bigger meaning, as "chancellor" comes from it.' I suggest that my assumed semantic development was inherent in the (Late Latin) word 'cancella' (whence our modern 'chancel') with the meaning 'barrier, screen'.

Page 30

Mr Lindsay asks: ' "Nicaeus". Apart from the Livy passage quoted (which may mean the Latin "Triumphator" or the like), have you any evidence for its usage in Latin-speaking areas?' Yes, the word was very widespread, in Asia and Europe (even India!) as a name for persons and towns—*Nice*, Alpes Maritimes, is an European example. The word appears in many forms in Late Latin: Nicaeanus, Nicaeensis (*sic*), Nicaensis, Nicensis, Nicaenus, (Castellum) Nicense. As 'Nicaea,' it was a fairly popular woman's name, which—seeing that 'Nicaea' must have generated the 'Nicoles,' 'Nicolettes' of later ages—must have had a derived form 'Nicaela.' Though my assumed 'Nicaelis' remains unattested as yet, I feel that it is this form which lies behind '(St) Nicholas (Lane)'. Elsewhere in London, 'Nicholas' appears to be derived from 'nexilis'—'tied or bound together' (i.e. by legal contract).

Page 31

Mr Lindsay comments: ' "Pomoerium" is properly the limit of the city auspices (religious), but of course it got civic and defence significances.'

254

Page 31
If, as seems likely, the first part of the name 'Smithfield' (occurring in both east and west Londinium) is Latin 'semotus', 'cut off, separated'—that is, from the walled part of the city—it would mean that executions in East and West Smithfield were not taking place within the city limits proper. This was in accordance with Roman urban law.

Page 31
Aldersgate. 'Alter' here could well be translated 'second' or even better 'additional' (i.e. gate to the north). It was obviously a later gate, and its construction should be considered in relation to the facts that due north of it lay the 'succingulum'—'the belt' (Soukinge Lane)—and the 'vestibulum' ('approach')—Goswell Street. Both words are clearly related to (probably additional) outer defences of the now walled city.

Page 47
It is tempting to connect the well-known pub-name, 'Dog and Duck' with the alternative pronunciations of original Latin 'dux, ducem', 'military commander, general'. Pub-names seem to me to offer one of the richest sources of information concerning Roman Britain.

Page 54
'Falcon Square', in the area of the Cripplegate Fort may echo the name of Q. Pompeius *Falco*, Legate in Britain A.D. 118–19 at that highly critical period when Legio IX was destroyed by the Brigantes and Hadrian hurried to Britain. Falco was replaced by A. Platorius Nepos, in whose term of office the building of 'Hadrian's Wall' began.

Page 56
Mr Lindsay reminds me that the phrase 'elysii campi' occurs in Vergil, Tibullus and Ovid. It was evidently a phrase of great popularity throughout Romania. It is therefore not surprising to find it used in London.

Page 65
In any Roman fort (for which read 'city') of normal lay-out, the east–west street was called the 'Via Principalis'. It connected the 'Porta Principalis Dextra' (gate to the right: east) with the 'Porta Principalis Sinistra' (gate to the left: west). In most cases, the 'Via Principalis' ran immediately 'above'—that is, to the north of—the Praetorium, originally the tent of the camp-commandant, whatever his rank. The name survives in 'Prince's Street'—once an east–west street—to the west of the present Bank of England.

Page 73
Though the earliest mention of the present Old Jewry is in an Inquisition as to the Church of St Olave, 1181, and the street is there called 'The Jewry', later forms (1336) 'la Elde Jurie' and (1559) 'Jure' or 'Jurie Lane' are far less ambiguous, making the connection with the original Aula

Juridicia far more obvious. Its other early names, 'Colechurch Lane' and 'Sakfrere Lane' refer, respectively to the 'collybus' or exchange there situate and to the treasury ('thesaurus') of the Saccararius or City Treasurer.

Page 78
St Botolph of Icanhoh. I say that the site of Icanhoh 'has never been identified'. In honesty, I should point out that Grant Allen (*Anglo-Saxon Britain*, London: S.P.C.K., *n.d.*) identifies Icanhoh with Boston, Lincolnshire, but does not cite his authority.

Page 80
Mulcta. Mr Lindsay comments: 'You are quite right that mulcta (multa) was used for "fine". I don't know it as "customs barrier", but I suppose it could have been used for any place where summary fines and imposts were made.'

Page 81
It occurs to me that the 'Folgate' of Norton Folgate may simply be a variant of 'mul(c)ta', with the last syllable of the word metathesized and with the 'm' of 'Mul(c)ta' lenited to the sound now represented as 'f'.

Page 95
It is certainly not impossible—or even unlikely—that at least one of the 'All Hallows' churches that I identify with temples of Mars was a temple of 'Salus', the Goddess of Health (the Greek Hygeia). 'Salus' and 'Salii' (or, better, the singular 'Salius') would all yield a sound like 'Hallow' in Old Welsh. In this connection, Mr Lindsay comments: 'I fear I cannot imagine such a Latin cult and fraternity as that of the Salii or (page 108 *ff.*) that of the Arvales being transplanted, but I may be wrong.' But we know that cults just as exotic—that of Isis, for example—were transplanted.

Page 103
The evidence for a temple of Juno Moneta is admittedly slender, and is based on the fact that a tenement named 'Menterhous' ('monetarius') is mentioned in a deed of 10 Edward II. It is true that the Latin 'monetarius' means, from the fourth century on, 'relative to money', and thus 'coiner, minter'. But originally it meant 'connected with (the worship) of Juno Moneta', and this may be the origin of the name 'Menterhous'. I once believed that the temple of Juno Moneta had existed where the Royal Mint now stands, but I am less convinced today. However, traces of a Celtic goddess may be found in that ancient part of London. Royal Mint Street was once called Rosemary Lane, a name strikingly evocative of the Celtic divinity, Ro-Smerta, whose name may be perceived, perhaps, in the name, so far unexplained, of the medieval Manor of the Rose, in ancient Dowgate Ward.

Page 115
St Matthew Friday Street. So far, this is the only 'pagan' temple that I have traced which has become a Christian place of worship. Matuta was the goddess of the dawn; Roman equivalent of the Greek Leucothea ('The White Goddess'). As the Anglo-Saxon equivalent of at least some of Matuta's aspects was Frigga or Freya, it is indeed tempting to see the 'Friday' of 'Friday Street' as a gloss (Frigga or Freya) on the Latin Matuta. Is it possible that the Greeks worshipped Leucothea a mile or two out of London at 'St Luke's'? An interesting speculation! And 'Lucas' (now 'Love') Lane may echo the worship of Leucothea in central Londinium.

Page 125
Mr Lindsay comments: 'Antinoüs was hardly long enough lasting in his cult to beget so many Anthonys.' It is true that the cult of Antinoüs swept through the east, rather than the west; but so much was being imported, in men and ideas, from the east, that it is hard to say today what was 'eastern' and what 'western'. What, I think, was the appeal of Antinoüs in Britain was his intimate connection with the Saviour of the Province, the Emperor Hadrian. Gratitude towards Hadrian must have inclined many to take up the cult of Hadrian's deified lover.

Page 130
Latin 'vado', 'I go'. 'He goes', 'vadit', would be something like 'gweit' in Old Welsh (compare Old Welsh 'gwein' from Latin 'vagina', 'scabbard, sheath'.) It is easy to see how this would come to be the Anglo-Saxon 'gate'.

Page 131
Mr Lindsay doubts that the council of a civitas or municipium would be called a senate. 'It was a curia', he points out; 'the curiales were the local senators.' True, but echoes of the term, 'senate' – 'Sweeting's Alley' is but one – are so numerous that it is hard to resist the conclusion that, 'regular' or not, London's curia was dignified (or dignified itself) by the title, 'senate'. Could this, perhaps, have been associated with London's becoming 'Augusta'? (*See also* page 195.)

Page 136
Note how 'bear garden' has survived in the common idiom. 'You children! You've turned this room into a bear-garden!'

Page 181
The Romans were great fish-eaters. With them, it was not a case of 'chips with everything', but rather of 'fish with everything'. They liked their fish to be strong in flavour: the surviving recipe for their famous fish-sauce, garum (or garon) makes that obvious. The name of the so-far-unidentified fish greatly esteemed of the Romans – *tragus* – demonstrates their love of potent flavours, since 'tragus' also meant 'goat' and – by analogy – the

R

rank smell of unwashed armpits. I think that the origin of the name 'Green Dragon' (eleven Green Dragon Courts, two Green Dragon Inns and one Green Dragon tavern) is in the phrase 'Granaria tragica'—'where *tragus* fish is to be bought'.

Page 215

'Porticus', in classical Latin is a 4th declension noun of feminine gender. In Late Latin, the tendency was to treat all nouns ending in '-us' as of the 2nd declension and masculine gender. The ablative in '-o' quoted by Souter (SS. Ioh. 10. 22. ap. Hier. tract. in psalm. 95 p. 139. 5, 6) shows that 'porticus' became a 2nd declension masculine noun. The 'plaza' at the bottom of Cornhill would then have changed its name from 'Porticus Stoica' to 'Porticus Stoicus' – even, probably, 'Porticus Stoichus' – for this latter form would be more likely to yield the later 'Stocks' of the Stocks Market.

Bibliography

(Some of the more important books consulted)

Bailey, C. *Phases in the Religion of Ancient Rome*, Oxford University Press, 1932.

Baudiš, J. *A Grammar of Early Welsh*, Oxford University Press, 1924.

Buck, C. D. *A Grammar of Oscan and Umbrian*, 2nd edn, Boston, 1928.

A Comparative Grammar of Greek and Latin, Chicago University Press, 1933.

Burn, A. R. *Romans in Britain*, Oxford: Blackwell, 1932.

Carcopino, J. *Daily Life in Ancient Rome* (transl.), London: Penguin, 1956.

Cousin, J. *Evolution et structure de la langue latine*, 1944.

Devoto, G. *Storia della Lingua di Roma*, 2nd edn, 1944.

Ernout, A. *Les éléments dialectaux du vocabulaire latin*, Paris, 1909.

Morphologie historique du latin, 2nd edn, Paris, 1924.

Textes latins archaïques, Paris, 1947.

Ernout, A. and A. Meillet. *Dictionnaire étymologique de la langue latine*, 3rd edn, Paris, 1951.

Fraser, H. *History and Etymology of the Celtic Languages*, 1923.

Gomme, Sir L. *The Governance of London*, London: T. Fisher Unwin, 1907.

Glover, T. R. *The Ancient World*, Cambridge University Press, 1935.

Grandgent, C. H. *An Introduction to Vulgar Latin*, Boston, 1907.

Grant, M. *The World of Rome*, London: Weidenfeld & Nicolson, 1960.

Harben, H. *A Dictionary of London*, London: Herbert Jenkins, 1918.

Haverfield, F. J. *The Romanization of Roman Britain*, 4th edn, Oxford: Clarendon Press, 1923.

The Roman Occupation of Britain, Oxford, Clarendon Press, 1942

Home, G. C. *Roman London*, London: Eyre & Spottiswoode, 1926.

Jackson, K. H. *Language and History in Early Britain*, Edinburgh University Press, 1953.

Kent, R. G. *The Sounds of Latin*, 3rd edn, Baltimore, 1945.

The Forms of Latin, Baltimore, 1946.

Lethaby, W. R. *Londinium*, London: Duckworth, 1923.

Lewes, H. and H. Pederson. *Concise Comparative Celtic Grammar*, Oxford, 1938.

Lindsay, W. M. *The Latin Language*, Oxford: Clarendon Press, 1894.

A Short Historical Latin Grammar, 2nd edn, Oxford: Clarendon Press, 1915.

Meillet, A. and J. Vendryès. *Traité de grammaire comparée des langues classiques*, 2nd edn, Paris, 1948.

259

Merrifield, R. *The Roman City of London*, London: Benn, 1965.
　Roman London, London: Cassell, 1969.
Morris-Jones, J. *Welsh Grammar*, Oxford University Press, 1913.
Muller, H. F. and P. Taylor. *A Chrestomathy of Vulgar Latin*, Boston: D. C. Heath, 1932.
Niedermann, M. *Phonétique historique du latin*, 2nd edn, Paris, 1931.
Ogilvie, R. M. *The Romans and Their Gods in the Age of Augustus*, London: Chatto & Windus, 1969.
Palmer, L. R. *The Latin Language*, London: Faber, 1954.
Preller, L. *Les dieux de l'ancienne Rome*, 1884.
Quennell, M. and C. H. B. *Everyday Life in Roman Britain*, London: Batsford, 1924.
Rose, H. J. *Ancient Roman Religion*, London: Hutchinson, 1949.
Souter, A. *A Glossary of Later Latin to 600 A.D.*, Oxford University Press, 1949.
Stow, J. *A Survey of London*, London: Dent.
Strachan, J. *Introduction to Early Welsh* (Celtic Series No. 1), Manchester: Victoria University, 1909.
Thurneysen, R. *Keltische Sprachen*, 1916.
Wartburg, W. von. *Evolution et Structure de la Langue Française*, Berne: Francke, 1946.
Whatmough, J. *The Foundations of Roman Italy* (Methuen's Handbooks of Archaeology), London: Methuen, 1937. (Has full bibliography.)
Webster, Graham. *The Roman Army*, Chester: The Grosvenor Museum, 1956.
Windle, Sir R. C. A. *The Romans in Britain*, London: Methuen, 1923.

Index